Medieval Architecture, Medieval Learning

Titus Livius writing his history and the founding of
Rome, Paris, Bibliothèque Nationale, Ms. fr. 273, f. 7.

Yale University Press

New Haven and London

Medieval Architecture, Medieval Learning:

Builders and Masters in the

Age of Romanesque and Gothic

Charles M. Radding and William W. Clark

Published with the assistance of the F. B. Adams, Jr.
Publication Fund

Designed by Sally Harris/Summer Hill Books,
Weathersfield, Vermont.
Set in Trajanus type by Keystone Typesetting, Inc.,
Orwigsburg, Pennsylvania.
Printed in the United States of America by
Arcata/Halliday, West Hanover, Massachusetts.

Library of Congress Cataloging-in-Publication Data

Radding, Charles.
Medieval architecture, medieval learning : builders and
masters in the age of romanesque and gothic / Charles
M. Radding and William W. Clark.
    p.   cm.
Includes bibliographical references (p.   ) and index.
ISBN 0–300–04918–8 (alk. paper)
1. Architecture, Romanesque. 2. Architecture, Gothic.
3. Architecture—Philosophy. I. Clark, William W.,
1940–
II. Title.
NA390.R33 1991
723'.4—dc20   90–26065
                                          CIP

The paper in this book meets the guidelines for
permanence and durability of the Committee on
Production Guidelines for Book Longevity of the
Council on Library Resources.

10   9   8   7   6   5   4   3   2   1

For Jonah and Sarah;
For Vivian

Contents

Texts

Illustrations

Dream of the Magi. Photo: Hirmer Fotoarchiv, Munich.

80. Chartres, Notre-Dame, statue-columns of the right jamb of the central portal. Photo: Hirmer Fotoarchiv, Munich.

81. Paris, Notre-Dame, restored plan and current plan (after Clark/Bony and Clark/Leconte).

82. Paris, Notre-Dame, ambulatory. Photo: Hirmer Fotoarchiv, Munich.

83. Paris, Notre-Dame, nave aisles. Photo: Hirmer Fotoarchiv, Munich.

84. Paris, Notre-Dame, chevet wall. Photo: J. Herschman.

85. Paris, Notre-Dame, nave wall. Photo: J. Herschman.

86. Paris, Notre-Dame, restored and current nave sections (after Clark/Sanders and Chancel).

87. Paris, Notre-Dame, interior. Photo: G. Boullay.

88. Laon, Notre-Dame, restored plan and current plan (after Clark/Sanders and Sanders/Boeswillwald).

89. Laon, Notre-Dame, view across transept. Photo: W. Clark.

90. Laon, Notre-Dame, nave wall. Photo: J. Herschman.

91. Laon, Notre-Dame, interior. Photo: Hirmer Fotoarchiv, Munich.

92. Mantes, Notre-Dame, restored plan and current plan (after Bony and Chauliat).

93. Mantes, Notre-Dame, interior. Photo: Hirmer Fotoarchiv, Munich.

94. Mantes, Notre-Dame, chevet exterior. Photo: D. Vermand.

95. Mantes, Notre-Dame, restored and current nave sections (after Clark/T. H. King).

96. Reims, Saint-Remi, plan of the eleventh-century church and current plan (after Ravaux and Deneux).

97. Reims, Saint-Remi, exterior of the chevet. Photo: Hirmer Fotoarchiv, Munich.

98. Reims, Saint-Remi, ambulatory. Photo: Hirmer Fotoarchiv, Munich.

99. Reims, Saint-Remi, chevet interior. Photo: Hirmer Fotoarchiv, Munich.

100. Canterbury Cathedral, restored plan, ca. 1185, and current plan (after Clapham and Archaeological Journal).

101. Canterbury Cathedral, exterior of Trinity Chapel. Photo: W. Clark.

102. Canterbury Cathedral, interior. Photo: M. Thurlby.

103. Bourges, Saint-Etienne, plan (after Branner/Capron).

104. Bourges, Saint-Etienne, cross-section (after Branner/Capron).

105. Bourges, Saint-Etienne, chevet exterior. Photo: W. Clark.

106. Bourges, Saint-Etienne, outer ambulatory. Photo: W. Clark.

107. Bourges, Saint-Etienne, inner ambulatory. Photo: J. Austin.

108. Bourges, Saint-Etienne, chevet piers. Photo: J. Austin.

109. Bourges, Saint-Etienne, ambulatory piers seen from above. Photo: J. Boulas.

110. Bourges, Saint-Etienne, chevet interior. Photo: Hirmer Fotoarchiv, Munich.

111. Bourges, Saint-Etienne, nave from ambulatory. Photo: J. Austin.

112. Bourges, Saint-Etienne, full elevation. Photo: R. Branner.

113. Chartres, Notre-Dame, current plan and crypt plan (after Burckhardt and Merlet).

114. Chartres, Notre-Dame, section of chevet, interior and exterior nave elevations, and nave section (after Mayeux, Dehio, and Goubert).

115. Chartres, Notre-Dame, nave wall. Photo: Hirmer Fotoarchiv, Munich.

116. Chartres, Notre-Dame, nave interior. Photo: Hirmer Fotoarchiv, Munich.

117. Chartres, Notre-Dame, nave exterior. Photo: Hirmer Fotoarchiv, Munich.

118. Chartres, Notre-Dame, aerial view from the east. Photo: Collection Viollet.

119. Reims, Notre-Dame, plan (after Chauliat and Deneux).

120. Reims, Notre-Dame, nave section (after T. H. King).

121. Reims, Notre-Dame, chevet interior. Photo: Hirmer Fotoarchiv, Munich.

122. Reims, Notre-Dame, ambulatory and chapels. Photo: Hirmer Fotoarchiv, Munich.

123. Reims, Notre-Dame, chevet exterior. Photo: J. Austin.

124. Amiens, Notre-Dame, plan (after Addiss and Murray).

125. Amiens, Notre-Dame, north side-aisle. Photo: W. Clark.

126. Amiens, Notre-Dame, nave elevation. Photo: Hirmer Fotoarchiv, Munich.

Abbreviations

CCCM	*Corpus Christianorum, Continuation Mediaevalis*
CIMAGL	*Cahiers de l'Institut du Moyen-Age Grec et Latin*
Dronke, *Philosophy*	*A History of Twelfth-Century Philosophy*. Edited by Peter Dronke. Cambridge, 1988.
MGH	*Monumenta Germaniae Historica*
PL	*Patrologia cursus completus, series Latina*. Edited by J.-P. Migne. Paris, 1844–64.
RTAM	*Recherches de Théologie Ancienne et Médiévale*
Renaissance/Renewal	*Renaissance and Renewal in the Twelfth Century*. Edited by Robert L. Benson and Giles Constable. Cambridge, Mass., 1982

Acknowledgments

This book had its origins, appropriately enough, in Paris during the summer of 1980 when the authors first met. The acquaintance occurred at the insistence of Peggy Brown, who expressed the opinion that "we thought alike." What she meant by this is far from clear, but her intuition has proved correct. Within a year, not quite knowing what we were getting into, we began collaborating on a book. Lest this sound too simple, we should add that the book we have written is not exactly the one we thought we started. The overall structure of the argument emerged only gradually, resulting in our having to prepare more elaborate evidence with more careful attention to details of the unfolding of historical developments than we had originally expected.

The work on the book was divided as follows. Each of us took responsibility for research in his area of expertise, Radding for learning, Clark for architecture. Radding wrote the first complete draft, which was revised and corrected by both authors. Clark collected and selected the photographs and other visual materials.

The encouragement of many friends and colleagues has carried us through this process. Four in particular have read and commented on the entire manuscript: Maija Bismanis, Judith Calvert, Maureen Flanagan, and Charles Wood. Both authors share responsibility for any errors that remain. We benefited enormously from discussions and the exchange of ideas with Jean Bony, Peggy Brown, Vivian Cameron, John Casbarian, Stephen Jaeger, Danny Samuels, John O. Ward, and Ron Witt. John Cameron and Tom Lyman read the Romanesque sections, corrected our mistakes, and made many helpful suggestions. Some of the material was presented over several years at conferences in Kalamazoo and in Canada, which gave us the advantage of discussions and comments from, especially, Jeremy Adams, Madeline Caviness, Joel Herschman, Virginia Jansen, Allan McNairn, Richard Schneider, Malcolm Thurlby, and Bonnie Wheeler. Still other colleagues helped us to find or generously permitted the reproduction of photographs and drawings: Jim Addiss, James Austin, Pam Blum, Gerard Boullay, John Cameron, Eric Carlson, Anne Shaver Crandell, the late Sumner Crosby, Joel Herschman, George Jansen, Virginia Jansen, Danielle Johnson, Tom Lyman, Robert Mark, Stephen Murray, Dominique Vermand, and Jean Villette, who graciously allowed us to publish his reconstruction sketches of Fulbert's cathedral at Chartres. Radding's interactions with practicing architects at the American Academy in Rome contributed to refining the ideas underlying this book. Michigan State University and the City University of New York provided funds toward the purchase of some of the plates and payment for the rights of reproduction. Chuck Grench of Yale University Press has guided this work toward publication for several years. Jane Hedges edited the text into a clearer and more precise form, and Sally Harris carefully and sensitively designed the book. We express our gratitude to them all.

Introduction:
Art History as
Intellectual History

The great buildings of the period between the first quarter of the eleventh century and the first quarter of the thirteenth resulted from a cultural transformation that left no aspect of life unchanged. Equally important works, if less immediately accessible ones, in philosophy, law, and many other fields profoundly altered nearly every branch of higher learning. It has been easy to assume that these works, all created in the same historical moment and all breaking sharply with earlier traditions, are somehow related. But it has been harder to state with any precision just what the relationship is. In part this has been due to lack of sources, for there is little possibility of placing in a specific educational or social context masters and builders whose very names have not come down to us. But the broader difficulty has been one of conceptualization: How does one compare a vault to a syllogism, a building's elevation to a philosophical treatise?

Our solution to this problem will be to discuss eleventh- and twelfth-century architecture and scholarship as disciplines in formation. Specifically, we shall examine the communities of specialists—the builders and masters—and the way they approached the intellectual challenges of their professions. We shall not argue, as has been done before, that a web of mutual influences bound these men together; in fact, builders and masters probably had only minimal direct effect on each other's work. Nor shall we contend that the works produced by the builders and masters simply reflected the characteristics of the culture as a whole. To the contrary: much of our evidence shall show that during the eleventh and twelfth centuries builders and masters became more intellectually distinct, developing specialized knowledge and mental skills inaccessible even to their noble and clerical public. Rather than attempting to characterize medieval culture as a whole, we shall instead direct our attention to the processes that made it change. Thus, the focus on disciplines points to the essential role of specialization (or, looked at from a sociological viewpoint, of the division of labor) in the cultural transformations of the central Middle Ages.

1

Indeed, it is the organization of specialists into disciplines that makes the culture of 1200 so different from that of the early Middle Ages, both in what it produced and in its ability to sustain itself.

Moreover, by discussing these disciplines in parallel, we bring our evidence to bear on the question of how disciplines, as distinct from crafts or inert bodies of knowledge, come into existence. Architecture and philosophy are not the only disciplines whose formation took place during the medieval period. The history of law follows much the same pattern and with very similar dates.[1] And although it lies beyond the scope of this inquiry to consider whether similar patterns apply to the early history of other disciplines, including those in other periods, it is very likely that they do.[2]

Previous efforts to relate architecture to its historical context have usually taken one of two approaches. The first has been to consider buildings in their utilitarian aspect, as structures intended to house certain kinds of activities. Churches, for example, had to accommodate liturgical rituals that required certain interior furnishings (such as altars) and that involved space for sometimes sizable numbers of celebrants, clergy, and observers. Obviously the builder of a church was acquainted with those requirements although, because the interior fittings necessary for performing liturgical ritual were continually adapted to accord with changing liturgical practice, it is not always possible for us to be certain what precise instructions would have been given the builder of a specific church. It is an area of study about which we know too little and, alas, cannot learn much more.[3] One of the more remarkable aspects of Romanesque and Gothic churches is their adaptability to changing liturgical practice, an adaptability that absorbed changes without the need to transform the physical environment. Yet one must distinguish the study of buildings from the study of what we might term their "interior decoration." In looking at the buildings, we are looking at more than merely the skeleton or the shell around liturgical practice. Thus, we can still experience the architectural space, the container of liturgical practice, even though we cannot recover all of the specific details or furnishings central to that practice. In this book we shall analyze the attitudes of the builders as expressed in their results rather than attempting to recover the uses to which the spaces might have been put at a particular moment to satisfy the demands of even so knowing a patron as Abbot Suger.

The other approach to the study of architecture has involved seeing in art the embodiment of certain ideas, either specific or general. Otto von Simson's *The Gothic Cathedral*,[4] for example, uses the writings of Suger and the masters of the school at Chartres to argue that light and measure were the central objectives of the patrons of Gothic cathedrals. We shall have occasion below to discuss this interpreta-

1. C. Radding, *The Origins of Medieval Jurisprudence* (New Haven, 1988), treats the development of law from early medieval patterns roughly to the end of the first stage as defined here. For an overview of the longer period, see Radding "Legal Science 1000–1200: The Invention of a Discipline," *Rivista di storia del diritto Italiano* 63 (1990).

2. The obvious parallels are in the history of science, but studies have generally followed Kuhn by concentrating on changes within an existing discipline instead of the formation of disciplines. One possible example is thermodynamics. Cf. Thomas S. Kuhn, "Energy Conservation as an Example of Simultaneous Discovery," in *The Essential Tension* (Chicago, 1977), 66–105. Another is the history of analytical geometry. Both the algebraic and mechanical traditions that through Fermat and Descartes gave rise more or less independently to the principles of analytic geometry had a history of very slow and painful progress in the sixteenth century. In comparison, the advances made in the decades after Fermat's and Des-

cartes's work became known were very rapid, with but a very short time needed to arrive at calculus. See Carl B. Boyer, *History of Analytic Geometry* (New York, 1956), and Michael Sean Mahoney, *The Mathematical Career of Pierre de Fermat* (Princeton, 1973).

3. An excellent example of the information that ritual practice can provide about building use and altar location is C. Wright, *Music and Ceremony at Notre Dame of Paris, 500–1550*, Cambridge Studies in Music (Cambridge, 1989). Unfortunately, studies of this depth are all too rare for medieval buildings.

4. 2d ed. (Princeton, 1962). Conrad Rudolph, *Artistic Change at St.-Denis* (Princeton, 1990), rejects arguments relating Saint-Denis to a theology of light, placing Suger's aspirations instead in the context of the debate over monastic asceticism; but the objections to deriving architecture from theology apply to Rudolph as they do to Simson.

tion in some detail. But even if Simson could be proven correct in all he claims, he does not thereby explain Gothic style nor the education of Gothic builders. Light and measure were not only as much a part of Romanesque architecture as of Gothic, but there were many ways in which the Romanesque style (broadly defined) could have been adapted to increase interior light and otherwise changed without reorganizing the interior space as completely as Gothic builders did. The decisions to employ a particular set of constructional features were made by the builders seeking to fulfill the demands of their patrons, rather than by the patrons themselves.

A more ambitious attempt to relate medieval architecture to its cultural context was that of Erwin Panofsky in his *Gothic Architecture and Scholasticism*.[5] Panofsky described his purpose in these words (pp. 20–21):

In contrast to a mere parallelism, the connection which I have in mind is a genuine cause-and-effect relation; but in contrast to an individual influence, this cause-and-effect relation comes about by diffusion rather than by direct impact. It comes about by the spreading of what may be called, for want of a better term, a mental habit.

Panofsky was clearly pushing toward a more versatile conception of interactions between disciplines within cultures, but exploring the nature of these interactions was another matter. Panofsky's actual analysis has little to do with the mental processes of either masters or builders. What he did instead was to view both the scholastic *summa* and the Gothic cathedral from the outside, noting what seemed to him, the twentieth-century observer, to be the most salient features of the finished works. His remarks are often interesting and provocative, but they do nothing to recreate the mental worlds of builders or masters, nor do they explain the actual historical processes through which either architectural or intellectual styles developed.

In this book we shall establish a basis of comparison between learning and architecture by redirecting our attention from the monuments or treatises themselves to the individuals who created them. There are, indeed, not one but two levels at which parallels exist between builders and masters. One is at the level of the disciplines themselves. Indeed, when allowance is made for the break in traditions that occurred under the later Roman empire, both disciplines had their origins in this period. This simultaneity accounts for the coincidences Panofsky noted between philosophical and architectural development. The other basis of comparison exists at the level of the cognitive processes of the individual architects and philosophers. The ability to impose order on materials, to shape several variables into a whole, and to take account of potential differences in viewpoint: these skills matter whether it is space, sound, or doctrine that is being manipulated. A brief discussion of these lines of interpretation will make clear the principles on which this book is constructed.

DISCIPLINES

Thomas Kuhn once observed that historians' neglect of the history of science is only one aspect of their neglect of the history of disciplines in general.[6] Whatever interest historians may have in works of art or learned theories, they rarely concern themselves with the processes by which those artifacts or ideas came into being, leaving those questions to specialists who are often practitioners. Without approving of this indifference to disciplinary history in other periods, however, one can assert that the omission is more serious for historians of the Middle Ages. Historians of most periods can take for granted the existence of intellectual and artistic disciplines. Isaac Newton and Bernini, for example, were great innovators, but they were innovators within a context defined by other specialists and preexisting methods of solving problems. But in the eleventh or the twelfth century, the innovations are to be found as much in the methods by which specialists approached their work as in the production of finished masterpieces. From practitioners of a craft, or

5. (Latrobe, Pa., 1951).

6. "The Relations between History and the History of Science," in *The Essential Tension*, 150–56 [reprinted from *Daedalus* 100 (1971): 271–304].

custodians of specialized knowledge, builders and masters were transformed into members of disciplines.

What is a discipline? The obvious definitions equate a discipline either with a body of knowledge or with the specialists who possess that knowledge, and indeed those are the aspects of intellectual life that historians generally study. But such definitions fail to capture the qualities that make philosophy different from bookkeeping, or architecture different from carpentry. Carpenters and masons do have skills the rest of us lack, but one would not refer to carpentry as a discipline because the skills are confined to a comparatively narrow, repetitive range. Thus, for example, although carpenters are expected to be able to introduce minor variations into familiar forms such as the shape of a molding or the dimensions of a window, only the exceptional craftsman invents an entirely new form. In the early Middle Ages, similarly, there were specialists in theology and there were also theological doctrines. Yet the attitude of theological specialists toward doctrine was not one of systematic inquiry or, except for rare exceptions, one of debate. What changed in the eleventh and twelfth centuries was that philosophers and builders developed methods for solving new problems.[7] Instead of seeing their role as one of preserving ancient knowledge, they both expected to solve new problems and to create new forms, and they had the intellectual means to attain this objective.

In developing this comparison of architecture and philosophy as disciplines, we shall be using two kinds of criteria. The first concerns professional behavior—the extent to which their expertise formed builders and masters into socially and intellectually distinct groups. We will show, for example, that the geographical mobility of both masters and builders, which is often remarked upon for the early twelfth century, has its origins in the first half of the eleventh century. This is significant

evidence that their expertise was recognized by their contemporaries as something rare and valuable. No less important, however, is evidence about specialists' dealing with each other. Evidence on this point is relatively easy to come by for masters, because they often named their rivals and called attention to differences in doctrine. But the speed with which technical innovations spread through Europe provides evidence that builders also communicated with one another. In the early thirteenth century, for example, builders as far away as Spain altered their designs within a year or two after Parisian builders discovered problems with the flying buttresses of Notre-Dame.

The other basis on which builders and masters will be compared involves exploring the methods or mental processes by which they conceived of and attempted to solve problems: simply stated, we shall shift attention from *what* was created to *how* it was thought out. These mental processes cannot, of course, be observed directly, but they are none the less real for that. The analytical methods of a discipline are teachable—indeed, the continuity and survival of disciplines depended on such methods being taught to students. Yet these methods are not to be confused with a specific philosophical or architectural production any more than one would confuse the reasoning of a mathematical proof with the theorem demonstrated: although the theorem is fixed forever, the processes by which the theorem was proved can fruitfully be turned to other, new problems. We shall see below that the importance of innovators such as Abelard and the builder of the east end of Saint-Denis lay more in the problems they posed and the methods they used than in the specific ideas or forms they created—a point easily missed when we study the treatises or buildings instead of the processes by which they were produced. Despite the differences in media, the cognitive processes involved in holding individual details mentally suspended until they could be reconciled with several others are directly comparable.

Using these criteria makes it possible to compare the history of architecture and phi-

7. On this transformation as illustrated by the history of philosophy and theology, see M.-D. Chenu, *La Théologie au douzième siècle*, 3d ed. (Paris, 1976), and Jean Leclerc, "The Renewal of Theology," in *Renaissance/Renewal*, 68–87.

losophy (broadly defined) during the period from 1000 to 1200 in terms of discipline formation without necessarily arguing that these disciplines influenced each other directly. In what follows, we describe a three-stage process of discipline formation. These three stages are distinguished from each other, as from the predisciplinary period of the early Middle Ages, by the way in which specialists conceived of and attempted to solve problems. The principal achievement of the first stage, which began in the eleventh century and continued into the first decades of the twelfth, was the growing mastery both of a body of relevant expertise and of the analytical methods by which that expertise could be brought to bear on different problems. The second stage occurred when certain specialists ceased applying their methods to specific issues and began instead to construct coherent systems of ideas or, in the case of architecture, of designs. The work of Abelard and the master of Saint-Denis fall into this stage. The last stage, and the one in which it finally becomes possible to speak of established disciplines, occurs when the ability and desire to deal with systems of ideas and designs becomes the standard by which all practitioners of a discipline are measured. This stage, in which builders and masters explored the limits of the possibilities open to them, looking back to the past and updating the ideas they found to current uses, consumed the last half of the twelfth century and continued into the second decade of the thirteenth. The results of this exploration, moreover, formed the context in which thirteenth-century architecture and learning would develop.

COGNITION

The advantages of studying architecture and philosophy as disciplines, however, go beyond the making of comparisons or periodizations. Understanding how artists or scholars worked with their materials is an essential part of understanding why they produced what they did. It brings us as close as we can be to the creative process, a subject of enduring interest and fascination. But studying cognition is particularly important for historians of the eleventh and twelfth centuries because cognitive processes appeared then that were significantly different from those that had existed in the early Middle Ages. The manifestations of these changes naturally varied according to the area of endeavor. In the schools the effects of the new cognitive processes are to be seen most directly in changing standards of discourse and in the desire to explore the implications of the concepts of intention and nature for understanding the human and physical world. In architecture they are to be seen in the heightened concern, characteristic of both Romanesque and Gothic, with articulating three-dimensional volume. One of us has argued elsewhere that these concerns with volume and discourse, intention and nature—all issues to which the people of the early Middle Ages were largely indifferent—clearly indicate a cognitive shift away from the mentality of the early Middle Ages, one that caused people to look at their culture and their society in new ways.[8] Our present interest in the novelty of these concerns, however, is chiefly that they posed a complex set of problems for which no preexisting solutions were available. The efforts of builders and masters to solve them thus gave direction to the history of architecture and learning in the central Middle Ages.

Revealing the mental categories in terms of which scholars and builders both understood the central issues of their disciplines and endeavored to define solutions is, therefore, central to our purposes. But moving from the surviving works of learning and architecture to the cognitive processes by which they were created requires methods that vary according to the evidence involved: not only must buildings be handled differently from treatises, but within each medium there are some works about which we are better informed than others. Before beginning, therefore, we need to say a word about the analytical methods we will use.

The problems of studying cognitive processes through written sources have been dis-

8. See Charles M. Radding, *A World Made by Men* (Chapel Hill, 1985).

cussed at length elsewhere,[9] but the main point may be simply stated. Cognition, by its nature, is active. People not only *have* ideas; they make them—out of facts and out of other ideas. What we have in written sources, therefore, are not mental processes themselves but the end products of mental processes. Books present conclusions and supporting arguments in an order designed to appeal to the intelligence of the reader, not in the order in which they occurred to the author. Omitted are not only the many explorations and hypotheses that, by the time the mental work was done, had proved to be irrelevant, but often the particular point of inquiry that gave rise to the whole investigation. Using these end products to reconstruct the intellectual processes that created them means one must pay attention not to static formulations but to the flow of argument and the play of the authors' minds as they struggle to impose order on their material.

Studying cognitive processes in this fashion is not to be confused with studying the ideas produced. One common approach to the twelfth century, for example, is to group thinkers into schools according to their position on certain issues. The school of Chartres is the most famous of these twelfth-century schools, formed by grouping together thinkers with certain views of nature regardless of whether they actually studied at Chartres or with each other; but there are many others.[10] Yet the fallacy of these methods is patent, because what students learn from teachers is often less a *position* on a given issue than a *method* of arriving at and defending positions that can be applied to many issues. To measure Abelard's influence, or that of Bernard of Chartres, solely in terms of their positions on certain issues thus risks grouping them with students they never taught. But it also overlooks the influence those masters may have exercised at the level of intellectual method, an influence that could be important even for students who eventually held ideas at variance with those of their teachers. One purpose of this book is to emphasize the role of intellectual method in intellectual history. We shall see below that innovations in method often predate the ideas they produce by a generation or more.

Analyzing concepts dynamically, by studying how our subjects reasoned through issues, is a valuable approach to any work, from any period. In this book we shall take three additional steps: we shall explore how concepts change over time; we shall examine how thinkers tried to link concepts together to form intellectual systems; and we shall observe how changes in both these other areas gradually, over the eleventh and twelfth centuries, led to a reconceptualization of the scholar's task. Our attention, in short, will be on the dialectical interplay between individual thinkers and their intellectual environment, each responding to and shaped by the other.

When we turn from writers to builders, our methods will necessarily change because our evidence will be not texts but buildings. Of the builders themselves we know few personal details, usually not even their names, and they practically never speak to us in their own voices. The one exception is Gervaise of Canterbury, who presumably knew the builder's wishes firsthand, having perhaps served as the intermediary between the builder, William of Sens, and the construction crews. But because Gervaise's account, really a year-by-year chronicle of the construction, confines itself to conventional phrases, in fact it contributes little to our knowledge of the builder. Nor is it possible to fill the builders' silence by quoting the words of their patrons where these have come down to us. This approach has often been applied to twelfth-century architecture, most notably with Panofsky's suggestion that Abbot Suger wanted his new east end of Saint-Denis to be filled with light. Yet the deficiencies of this method were recently noted by Peter Kidson:

It ought to be obvious to art historians, if to no one

9. Radding, *A World Made by Men*, chap. 1.
10. On Chartres, see R. W. Southern, "The Schools of Paris and the School of Chartres," in *Renaissance/Renewal* and references given there. See also Valerie I. Flint, "The 'School of Laon': A Reconsideration," *Recherches de théologie ancienne et médiévale* 43 (1976): 89–110. For an example of the method discussed, with its strengths and weaknesses, see D. E. Luscombe, *The School of Peter Abelard* (Cambridge, 1969).

else, that patrons, even the most enlightened and exigent among them, do not normally invent styles. In the last resort, however meticulous or exceptional the brief, an artistic imagination is always required to translate the patrons' verbal specifications into visual forms. . . . So while it may be granted that any symbolism present in Gothic architecture was the contribution of the clergy rather than the craftsmen, at best it can have been no more than a partial and superficial factor in the design procedure.[11]

Thus, for example, although Suger mentions in general terms that the builder used geometric and arithmetic tools in laying out the nave of the new addition, he does not understand either precisely what those tools were or how they were employed.[12]

Despite this silence, it is possible by careful attention to chronology, building techniques, and historical context to infer from the buildings the mental processes by which the builder worked. Thus when we place Saint-Denis against the background of then existing buildings that the builder would have known, we can determine which architectural details he preserved, which he adapted, and which he abandoned in favor of new approaches. We shall see that he was concerned not only or even especially with light, but with devising means to integrate chapel, aisle, and central space—all of which in the Romanesque style had been formed of distinct and separate modules—into a space whose unity an observer would readily perceive. We shall also see that this objective required him to employ cognitive processes that differed from those of earlier builders. Instead of designing architectural elements such as windows, moldings, capitals, and columns sequentially as they were needed, the builder of Saint-Denis designed all of these elements in advance of the actual building so that they would interact to produce the effect he desired. Saint-Denis thus represented a departure not only in the effects it produced but, more importantly, in the demands it placed upon the cognitive ability of builders to keep in mind a variety of

11. P. Kidson, "Panofsky, Suger and St. Denis," *Journal of the Warburg and Courtauld Institutes* 50 (1987): 1–2.
12. Erwin Panofsky, ed., *Abbot Suger on the Abbey Church of St.-Denis and Its Art Treasures*, 2d ed. (Princeton, 1979), 99–100.

aesthetic objectives while planning every detail of the building.

Employing historical context for this purpose requires us to work with the buildings differently from what is sometimes done. To begin with, we must endeavor to consider both the buildings a builder knew, and that which he built, as they existed at the time. This means allowing not only for modern alterations in the name of restoration but also for medieval changes. Thirteenth-century additions may be important for understanding thirteenth-century architecture, but they tell us nothing about what the eleventh- or twelfth-century builder had in mind. We must always be careful to read history forward, not backward, keeping in mind only what the builders could see and know, not what was to come later. This is not as obvious as it seems. In *Gothic Architecture and Scholasticism*, for example, Panofsky works back to twelfth-century buildings using a model derived from thirteenth-century buildings and then cannot explain why the earlier buildings differ from his prototype. His confusion results from his setting for himself the task of explaining not actual buildings but the scholarly abstractions embodied by the terms *Gothic* and *scholasticism*. Whereas the builders of Laon and Paris had Saint-Denis before their eyes, Panofsky saw Laon and Paris in terms of Reims. We shall see below that strict attention to historical context permits us to disentangle the processes that guided the development of both philosophy and architecture in the later twelfth century.

For both architecture and learning, our focus on cognition means that we are studying actual (though sometimes anonymous) individuals. This does not mean that we believe generalizations about medieval culture are impossible. Indeed, one important justification for this approach is that it permits us to understand both architecture and learning as part of a common cultural transformation. If the architecture and learning of 1200 surpass that of 1000 in complexity and in intellectual and aesthetic coherence, that is not because both partook in a common zeitgeist but because practitioners in a variety of fields applied to their respective disciplines reasoning

qualitatively different from that of the early
Middle Ages. Focusing on cognition enables
us to understand how a builder chose one
particular element of design, or how a phi-
losopher came to defend one particular doctrine, instead of another. It thus also permits
us to share in the intellectual excitement of
this period, one of the most original and important in the history of our civilization.

PART I

THE ELEVENTH CENTURY

1 · Beginnings

I t is no simple task to define the moment at which builders and masters began to transform their areas of expertise into disciplines, but the decades on either side of the year 1000 seem most likely. This transformation is not marked by any major new achievements. Indeed, it is not until the last half of the century, after 1050, that architectural or philosophical works notably more complex than those of the Carolingian period become common. Yet those first, striking accomplishments, which have caused scholars to speak of a revival of architecture and learning around 1050, were themselves the result of shifts in builders' and masters' attitudes that go back at least fifty years earlier.

Given the importance of the early eleventh century, it is unfortunate that constructing a coherent narrative for either the architectural or intellectual history of the period is so difficult. Few early buildings or treatises survive intact; those that do often cannot be dated with any certainty; and none have been carefully studied. Such limitations to our knowledge make it impossible now, and probably ever, to say that a particular design or line of inquiry appeared first at a given place and time. Yet if we set aside the objective of discovering first appearances and tracing influences, it remains possible to discern the emergence of the methods that over the course of the eleventh century were to lead to increasingly sophisticated achievements. To do so, we must look not ahead but back, to the ninth- and tenth-century works that form the background to the early eleventh century. It is by their departures from the traditions they knew that the builders and masters of that crucial, formative period reveal their own interests and aspirations.

To begin with architecture, it is important to notice first that the innovations of the eleventh century had less to do with technical skill in masonry than with design. Although expensive, the art of working with stone had never entirely disappeared in the early Middle Ages. Lombardy in particular appears to have been famous for its masons. The Lombard laws make occasional reference to the "stonecutters of Como," and in the eleventh century

Lombard masons were often recruited for work north of the Alps. In addition to their mastery of the basics of stonework—cutting blocks and using them to build walls and vaults—these masters were particularly noteworthy for their ability to incorporate decorative schemes including elements such as pilaster strips and arched corbel tables into the masonry itself. But although their handling of surface decoration was often imaginative and original, the spatial design of buildings in the early Lombard style was generally imitative. For the most part, the masons copied buildings with which they were already familiar, perhaps modifying those forms to allow for the limits of their skill or resources or for some particular need of their patron, but introducing no major architectural innovations.

This kind of craft-based architecture, in which construction proceeds by copying, with little or no modification, structures known to the workers, is not unique to the early Middle Ages. It exists in most societies, and even in the twentieth century is responsible for most domestic architecture. A more planned and consciously innovative style of construction that produced the buildings now known as Romanesque originated from and existed alongside this craft-based construction in the eleventh century. The emergence of this style in the eleventh century may have something to do with the growing prosperity of European society at that time, for the major monuments of the eleventh and twelfth centuries were larger than comparable buildings of the ninth and tenth centuries. But equally important was the changing role of the master masons, whom we will call builders to emphasize their dual role in the design and construction of buildings. Throughout the Middle Ages, the principal responsibility for designing stone buildings rested with the master masons, and the practice of their discipline was virtually inseparable from the supervision of the actual construction: as late as the fifteenth century, Brunelleschi's earnings for his design of the *duomo* of Florence consisted primarily of the fees he received for overseeing the work site.[1]

Because every construction work site employing more than a handful of workers needs someone to organize the work, the existence of builders or master masons certainly dates back well before the eleventh century.[2] What was new in the eleventh century, however, was the ambition and originality of the designs that these builders conceived and executed. Simply stated, the shift is away from thinking of design in terms of flat, undifferentiated planes of walls and ceilings toward discovering means of delineating the spatial units and volumes contained within buildings; indeed, it hardly overstates things to say that the articulation of spatial volumes was central to the architecture of the late eleventh and early twelfth centuries. But this new direction in architecture involved more than a shift in taste or interest. Designing volumes posed problems that were cognitively more complex than designing flat surfaces and, by widening the boundary between what the builders did and what their patrons could readily understand, the new style served increasingly to separate builders into a distinct discipline.

The church of San Vincente at Cardona provides an example (Figures 1, 2, 3).[3] It is not a large building by the standards that would prevail within a few decades—San Vincente itself was built (as we know from surviving documents) between 1020 and 1040. Nor is it an elaborate structure by the standards of its own time. The nearby and contemporary Santa Maria of Ripoll was larger, having double side-aisles as compared to the nave with single side-aisles of San Vincente, a broadly projecting transept, and more apsidal chapels, being modeled after old St. Peter's in Rome (Figure 4). Cardona is devoid of carved sculptural decoration; Ripoll was more expensively produced, originally having sculpted capitals.

1. Richard A. Goldthwaite, *The Building of Renaissance Florence* (Baltimore, 1980), 351–96.
2. Spiro Kostof, "The Architect in the Middle Ages, East and West," in *The Architect*, ed. S. Kostof (New York, 1977), 59–95, with good bibliography.
3. For a general description of this building and the evidence concerning it, see Walter Muir Whitehill, *Spanish Romanesque Architecture of the Eleventh Century* (Oxford, 1941; repr. 1968), 45–51; and James Morton Addiss, "Spatial Organization in Romanesque Church Architecture," (Ph.D. diss., State University of New York at Binghamton, 1983).

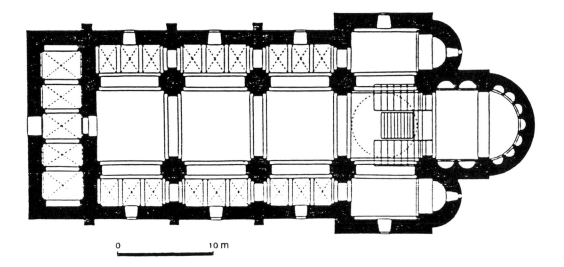

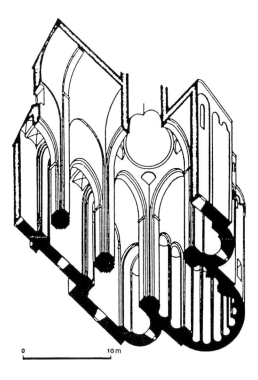

1. Cardona, San Vincente, plan.

2. Cardona, San Vincente, isometric section.

3. Cardona, San Vincente, interior view. The pilaster strips that produce the steplike profile of the piers visually link the piers to the transverse arches and articulate the wall from floor to vault.

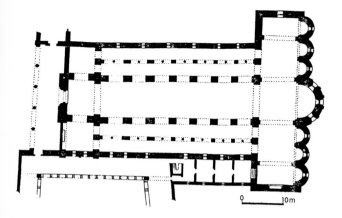

4. Ripoll, Santa Maria, plan.

What makes San Vincente worthy of our attention, however, is the articulation of the building's internal space. The means used were quite simple. The nave is divided into three identical bays by double pilaster strips that begin at the base of the piers, run up the wall, and finally join the transverse arches that mark the bay divisions in the barrel vault. The logic of the nave is echoed in the side-aisles, where three little groin-vaults appear between each pier. Instead of a vault, a low dome covers the intersection of the nave and transept. Up the steps lies the altar area, an extended apsidal chapel, whose shallow niches are marked off from the wall by rounded moldings. Although the pilaster strips, moldings, and other devices were ones that had been used in the Lombard tradition to articulate wall surfaces, the builder at Cardona employed them to make the building's internal space intelligible at a glance as a series of repetitive modules.

We can grasp the originality and significance of the design of San Vincente by placing it against the background of the architecture of the previous several centuries. The typical space of an early medieval building followed the lines of the early Christian basilica, with flat walls and often a flat ceiling as well except where decoration may have added visual articulation. This was not a matter of technical limitations. Crypts were usually vaulted, and architectural decoration was used elsewhere

in some structures, especially on apses and facades. But the relatively flat interior surfaces were suitable for decoration by mural painting, mosaics, or other ornaments, and it was in providing surfaces suitable for decoration that, following the early Christian examples, the builders were primarily interested. Departing from this aesthetic in favor of dramatizing the spatial units contained within the building, however, meant that the builder of San Vincente set himself a complex problem of planning and design. Architectural ornament could not simply be added at the end, like a painting on the wall; thus, it is not possible that the combination of piers, pilaster strips, and transverse arches that articulate the space was achieved haphazardly or by trial and error. This effect had to be planned at the beginning. The new style of building thus implied a different kind of mental work for the builder, with new cognitive skills that he had to master.

The thoroughness of the planning, moreover, is lent additional significance because Cardona does not appear to have been patterned after preexisting models. No similar buildings existed in Catalonia, and the only example of a church built using a bay system that is contemporary with San Vincente is the cathedral at Speyer in the Rhineland.[4] The distances do not, perhaps, entirely rule out any contact between Cardona and Speyer, or the possibility that the builders of Cardona and Speyer were both recruited from a third region, such as northern Italy. The distances involved were sizable, but not impossible: schoolmasters of the early eleventh century often traveled comparable distances,[5] and they would have been well placed to inform a bishop or abbot planning an ambitious building project of a skilled builder in another region. One might, for example, also hypothesize influences between both Speyer and Catalonia and Orléans, whose cathedral from

4. W. Horn, "On the Origins of the Mediaeval Bay System," *Journal of the Society of Architectural Historians* 17 (1958): 2–23.

5. For example, Adelman of Liège, a student at Chartres in the 1010s or 1020s, became master at Speyer and eventually bishop of Brescia. For more on the travels of masters, see below chap. 2.

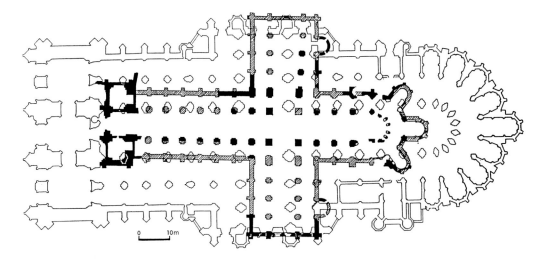

5. Orléans, Sainte-Croix, reconstructed plan of early church.

6. Orléans, Sainte-Croix, Martellange drawing of the ruins of the north transept in 1623.

7. Orléans, Sainte-Croix, Martellange drawings of the ruins of the north transept in 1623. The exterior of the east wall (left) and the interior (right). The remains of the pilasters that articulated both the interior and exterior wall surfaces are clearly visible in these drawings made before the north transept of the old cathedral was destroyed.

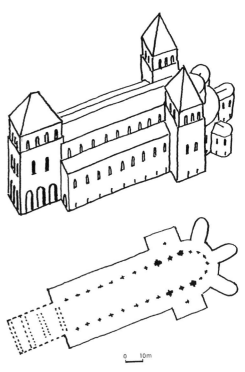

8. Miniature of Fulbert preaching in Chartres Cathedral. André de Mici's manuscript painting of Bishop Fulbert preaching in the eleventh-century cathedral. Clearly visible are the western tower, the roof of the nave and of the south side-aisle, the north tower, apse, and radiating chapels.

9. Chartres, isometric reconstruction and plan of Fulbert's cathedral. Jean Villette's reconstruction is based on careful study of the archeological evidence that confirms the features shown in the miniature.

the 990s also used pilaster strips (Figures 5, 6, and 7).[6] Yet the real point is not lines of influence, assuming that these could even be traced, given the faulty state of our knowl-

edge, nor is it a particular feature or combination of features such as pilaster strips and transverse arches. Indeed, Orléans and Speyer, neither of which was vaulted, differed from Cardona in that significant way. The important thing about all these examples, and such others as Fulbert's cathedral at Chartres, is that they reveal to us that builders of the early eleventh century were thinking of large spaces as consisting of multiple, smaller units and trying to find designs that conveyed that impression to viewers and patrons (Figures 8 and 9).[7]

6. Unfortunately, the surviving evidence for Orléans—principally the archeological excavations of the foundations and lower courses and the Martelange drawings made before the building's final destruction in the eighteenth century—is insufficient to allow definite conclusions on how the pilaster strips related to the builder's purposes. On the early church at Orléans, see Pierre-Marie Bun, "Les Fouilles du chanoine Chenesseau sous le choeur de la cathédrale Sainte-Croix d'Orléans," *Etudes ligériennes d'histoire et d'archéologie médiévales*, ed. R. Louis (Auxerre, 1975), 443–49; G. Chenesseau, *Sainte-Croix d'Orléans: Histoire d'une cathédrale gothique réédifiée par les Bourbons (1599–1829)*, 3 vols. (Paris, 1921); and Jean Nivet, *Sainte-Croix d'Orléans* (Orléans, 1984), esp. 28–39.

7. For Fulbert's church, see Harry H. Hilberry, "The Cathedral at Chartres in 1030," *Speculum* 34 (1959): 561–

The long period of experimentation suggests how difficult this mastery was to achieve, and we can appreciate some of the steps involved by considering the simple example of two dimensional spaces. Modern Western adults are accustomed to thinking of all flat surfaces, including those of our physical environment, in terms of two dimensions, but in fact the two-dimensional grid is a concept that is not perceived but constructed. Usually, of course, in familiar terrain we are unaware of the process by which the buildings, streets, rivers, and other objects of our perception are fitted into that construct; the mental work is done unconsciously. Complicated mental operations are involved, however, and we become conscious of them when we enter an unfamiliar city—particularly one like Rome or Boston, built on hills and lacking a grid street plan. The objects of perception are still there, and would indeed suffice for a person accustomed to reasoning concretely, but we do not know how to interpret them, how to integrate them into our mental grid. Then it is easy to get not only lost but hopelessly turned around, to believe we are headed north when we are going west or toward a river when we are headed away. We feel lost and become lost, in short, precisely because the grid in terms of which we are used to thinking is a product not of the environment but of our own minds.[8]

If two-dimensional spaces exist at such a remove from perception, it can come as no surprise that performing mental manipulations on volumes is cognitively more demanding yet. Not only are there three dimensions instead of two, but whereas surfaces are the same regardless of the angle from which they are viewed, volumes look different depending on where one stands. Keeping all of this in mind is not easy to do. Architectural students, for example, are commonly required to draw the sides of a stone or other three-dimensional objects that they cannot see. And designing in terms of volumes is even more difficult, because it requires performing mental operations on objects and spaces that as yet have no concrete existence. But it was precisely this ability that the builders of the early eleventh century both acquired themselves, as evidenced by their buildings, and passed on to succeeding generations of builders.

The cognitive skills of the builders who experimented with articulating volumes have their parallel in the learned culture of the early eleventh century. Scholars were not, of course, concerned with space or volume. The mental decentering they had to do involved placing themselves in another person's religious, social, or political position, not his or her position in physical space. But such role taking is comparable in cognitive complexity to the manipulations of space and volume performed by the builder of Cardona, and the effects of such reasoning on the world of learning were as marked as those in architecture.

The character of the changes can be illustrated by two early eleventh-century treatises against the Jews (Text 1). The first, dating from around 1010, was written at the command of emperor Henry II of Germany by a cleric of his court to answer a Christian who had converted to Judaism.[9] Neither side dis-

72; René Merlet and A. Clerval, *Un manuscrit chartrain du XIe siècle* (Chartres, 1893); Jan van der Meulen, *Notre-Dame de Chartres: Die vorromanische Ostanlage* (Berlin, 1975); and Hans Reinhardt, "Les Eglises romanes de la Champagne après l'an mil," *Cahiers de civilisation médiévale* 4 (1961): 149–58. As part of his larger study of Fulbert's church, Charles Stegeman is currently completing a thorough survey of the remains to produce an accurate plan.
8. Kevin Lynch, *The Image of a City* (Cambridge, 1960), defines the five aspects of what he calls imaging or cognitive mapping—the quest for logic and order in an environment. These can be compared to specific features of complex buildings such as cathedrals: *paths*—suggested directions of movement; *edges*—walls or other limiting surfaces; *distincts*—large configurations (nave, crossing point, aisle); *nodes*—chapels, towers, etc.; *landmarks*—generally eye-level indicators such as sculpted details, altars, and choir screens. In effect, the builders of the eleventh century were learning how to design structures that would take advantage of these different aspects of the way spaces are perceived.

9. Anna Sapir Abulafia, "An Eleventh-Century Exchange of Letters between a Christian and a Jew," *Journal of Medieval History* 7 (1981): 153–74; the text is printed in Alpert of Metz, *De diversitate temporum*, ed. Abulafia and H. van Rij, (1980). See also, in general, B. Blumenkranz, *Les Auteurs chrétiens latins du moyen âge sur les juifs et le judaisme* (Paris, 1963).

Henry II against the Jews

You say, Jew: "Why do you contradict the truth, fool?" First I should like you to answer the following question: whom do you consider to represent the truth, you or the prophet? If you say the prophet, I agree, for by showing you that I do not contradict him, I shall with justice prove that you have lied. . . .

Let us proceed to the following. You say: "Read Habakkuk, the prophet," not in whose book, as you say, but through whom God says: "I am God and do not change" (Mal. 3:6). I have already told you, Jew, that I shall nowise contradict the testimony of Habakkuk, and not only that of Habakkuk, but neither that of any of the prophets and I declare that I take my proofs from the law, for I worship him who has not come to destroy the law but to fulfill it (Matt. 5:17) [trans. Abulafia, "Eleventh-Century Exchange," 166–67].

Fulbert against the Jews.

"First we do not believe Christ has come," say the Jews, "because we do not believe that the sceptre of Juda has been taken away. For there are in many regions wealthy and educated Jews who rule their families strongly. And since we still see such rulers, we say that the sceptre has not been taken from Judah, nor has the Christ come." Anyone can mock them with humorous urbanity, and at the same time confute them by reason in this manner: O Jews, what happy misfortune! For if it is true what you say, must not he have made you exceedingly happy who completely ruined and destroyed you if, since you lose one king in a country, now in exile you find some many thousands of kings? But none of them is legally and spiritually anointed, no people follows them, nor is there even a people, on which account none of them is nor can be called either king or priest nor prophet nor leader of the tribe of Judah [PL 141: 316; trans. Radding].

Text 1. Tracts against the Jews by emperor Henry II and Fulbert of Chartres. Although both excerpts discuss texts of the Bible, Fulbert confines himself to the Old Testament, whose authority Jews accept, and addresses interpretations other than his own by showing the Christian view is the best possible.

tinguished itself for its courtesy. The convert's letter begins, "Why do you contradict the truth, fool?", while Henry's spokesman answered in still more violent language. ("To reply to the calumny, unbelieving Jew, that you just now have vomited forth from your blasphemous mouth against Christ and His saints, would be easy for anyone instructed in Christian combat . . .") More significant, however, is the fact that although both sides acknowledged the authority of the Old Testament and discussed principally texts drawn from it, neither side really engaged the arguments of the other or attempted to refute them. Assertion was answered by assertion, leavened only with a healthy portion of abuse.

This style of argument was not confined to disputes between Christians and Jews. Most early medieval intellectual controversies were similarly violent in tone, with argument consisting principally, as Philippe Wolff has described it, "of the two sides bombarding each other with a mass of quotations from the Scriptures and the Fathers of the Church."[10]

10. *The Cultural Awakening*, trans. Anne Carter (New York, 1968), 99.

In the mid-ninth century, for example, when double predestination was a hotly contested issue, although nearly all participants cited Augustine in support of their views, no one was moved by the others' quotations from Augustine to inquire what Augustine's views actually were, or how those quotations ought to be interpreted.[11] It was enough that the words of Augustine's texts were susceptible to the interpretation that they wished to defend.

It is therefore all the more remarkable to turn from the letter written on behalf of Henry II to the virtually contemporary sermons against the Jews written by Fulbert of Chartres around 1009.[12] There are three of these sermons, none longer than a few pages, and nothing in them would strike a historian of ideas as new. But while Fulbert's ideas were quite conventional (the main point, after all, was the superiority of the Christian faith), the means by which Fulbert argued his position was as new in its sphere as Cardona was in architecture. Not only did Fulbert realize that the meaning of texts, far from being self-evident, could be determined only through a careful process of interpretation, but he was able to set aside his own traditions sufficiently to be able to formulate arguments that did not depend upon the hearer already being a Christian.

The third sermon will serve as an example of Fulbert's method (Text 1). Here, as in the other sermons, Fulbert took as his point of departure Gen. 49:10: "the scepter will not depart from Judah . . . until he comes to whom it belongs, and to him shall be the obedience of the peoples." Because Christ was born shortly after the Romans had ended Jewish self-government, it had been a traditional item of Christian faith that this text was a prophesy of Christ, but it was Fulbert's innovation actually to attempt to refute the Jewish counterinterpretations. To the claim that

each Jewish father was like a king, Fulbert replied with irony, first observing that far from being a disaster, the diaspora meant that there were now many Jewish kings instead of one, and then asking whether the Jews were suggesting that the messiah would come only when all Jewish fathers were dead. To the contention that there might somewhere be a Jewish kingdom, Fulbert answered that as a house needs a foundation, walls, and a roof so a kingdom needs a king, country, and a people. "The kingdom of Judah, however, has lost its land, which has come into foreign hands; and it lacks a people, since the people are dispersed into all nations; and there has long been lacking a truly legitimate king [because there is no one left with the authority to anoint him.]"[13] Instead of denouncing the Jews' errors as resulting from evilness and stupidity, as Henry II's spokesman was to do, Fulbert treated his adversaries with respect, offering arguments that reasonable people could accept regardless of their background and relying upon the Jews' own intelligence to bring them to the Christian position.

More could be said about Fulbert because his letters, which survive in some abundance, permit a glimpse of how his ability to enter the mental world of his correspondents made him an effective participant in the turbulent politics of his time.[14] But for our present purposes it is enough to observe that Fulbert's place in the history of scholarship is comparable to that of the early eleventh-century builders in the history of architecture in that for both the innovations consisted less of the discovery of definitive solutions than in the formulation of problems that would continue to absorb the attention of specialists for the rest of the eleventh century. In what follows we shall consider how the masters and builders of the later eleventh and early twelfth century dealt with these problems and in the process transformed the very nature of their respective disciplines.

11. On this controversy, see M. L. W. Laistner, *Thought and Letters in Western Europe* A.D. *500 to 900*, 2d ed. (Ithaca, 1966); Jean Devisse, *Hincmar Archeveque de Reims* (Geneva, 1975), 1:118–280; J. H. Wallace-Hadrill, *The Frankish Church* (Oxford, 1983), 362–71; and Charles M. Radding, *A World Made by Men*, (Chapel Hill, 1985), 128–31.
12. *PL* 141: 305–18.

13. *PL* 141: 316B.
14. For more on Fulbert, see Frederick Behrends, ed. and trans., *The Letters and Poems of Fulbert of Chartres* (Oxford, 1976); L. C. MacKinney, *Bishop Fulbert and Education at the School of Chartres* (Notre Dame, Ind., 1957); and Radding, *World Made by Men*, 160–66.

2 · Masters

he schoolmasters of eleventh-century France inherited an academic tradition that originated in the Carolingian efforts to assure a literate clergy. Even then, teachers had gone beyond the bare essentials. Ninth- and tenth-century schoolmasters were responsible for bringing back into circulation many classical textbooks and for recovering from those books the essential terminology of grammar, rhetoric, and logic. They were also men with some literary ambitions. Most poets and historians of the tenth and eleventh century were schoolmasters, and they reached for an audience beyond their fellow canons or monks by circulating their works to schoolmasters elsewhere in Europe. But these early schoolmasters did not, for the most part, constitute a group clearly distinct from other educated clerics. Invariably members of ecclesiastical communities, their path of advancement lay within their cathedral chapter or monastery, and if their literary fame won them notice elsewhere, they moved not to remain schoolmasters but to become an abbot or bishop.

An eleventh-century version of this traditional kind of schoolmaster was Godfrey of Reims.[1] Godfrey was born in Reims and he made his entire career at Reims cathedral, receiving his education there and later serving as schoolmaster and chancellor from 1076 or 1077 until his death around 1095. His principal claim to fame was as a poet. Four of his letters in verse survive, three of them addressed to other poets of the time and the fourth addressed to his (presumably imaginary) ladylove. His themes and language were not particularly original—for example, he liked images about the Trojan war—and to modern readers, his poems seem highly imitative and pedantic. The best one scholar could do was to admire Godfrey's "dexterity in sifting from the ancient sources words and

---

1. This account is based on J. R. Williams, "Godfrey of Rheims, A Humanist of the Eleventh Century," *Speculum* 22 (1947): 22–45. A poem addressed to Godfrey by Baudri of Bourgeuil is printed in the collection of Baudri's works, *Les Oeuvres poétiques de Baudri*, ed. P. Abrahams (Paris, 1926), 151–58.

phrases needed in his own composition."[2] But the value his contemporaries placed on this kind of literary learning is suggested by the status of the poets to whom Godfrey addressed himself: all were, or became, bishops, and Godfrey himself was the object of an admiring poem by the noted poet Baudri of Bourgeuil.

Men such as Godfrey did not see their task as one of advancing learning beyond what they had received from their masters or the ancients. They won fame for what they knew, for their teaching, or for their literary artistry, not for the originality of their ideas. Yet in the eleventh century there also appeared, alongside these litterateurs, scholars of a very different stamp, with expertise in forbiddingly technical subjects and with the ambition to push frontiers of learning beyond where the ancients had left them. Such men often found a forum for teaching in ecclesiastical communities, and they were certainly willing to accept ecclesiastical advancement if their fame could win it for them. But the demand for their expertise meant that they could also easily move, as teachers, from one place to another and the most celebrated among them took advantage of this opportunity. This itinerancy of masters continued throughout the eleventh century, a period to which Haskins's remark, that schools followed masters, applies with as much justice as to the early twelfth century.[3]

The origins of this new career pattern can be seen quite early in the eleventh century, in the generation of Fulbert's students. Fulbert's prominence meant that there were many of these, several of whom had come from as far away as Liège and Cologne to study with him. That was not particularly new. From at least the eighth century, students had traveled to obtain learning they could not find at home, and monasteries had permitted them periods of leave for this purpose; then, after studying with perhaps more than one master, students typically returned to their original communities, where they often became teachers. Most of Fulbert's students from outside Chartres still belonged to this tradition: Bernard of Angers, for example, was recalled to teach at Angers after studying with Fulbert; Angelran returned to his monastery of St.-Riquier after ten years of study abroad, eventually becoming its abbot; and Olbert of Gembloux, after studying at Paris, Troyes, and Chartres, returned to his home monastery of Laubach and later became abbot at Liège. But for a few of Fulbert's students, teaching itself became a career. The most notable of these was Berengar of Tours, a student of Fulbert's in the 1020s who became archdeacon of Angers and then, in the 1040s, schoolmaster at Tours. It was clearly Berengar's teaching that was in demand, for he was not required to give up his position at Angers to take the new one at Tours, and he was not alone in this. Adelman of Liège, one of Berengar's fellow students at Chartres, taught at Liège and then at Speyer, before becoming bishop of Brescia. Even Lanfranc, Berengar's great antagonist in the eucharistic controversy, followed the career of a professional scholar, teaching at Avranches and then, after answering the call to a monastic life, opening a school at Bec.[4]

Although most of these masters continued to be based in cathedrals for teaching, their activities fundamentally altered the place of cathedral schools in intellectual life. In the ninth and tenth centuries, one can occasionally find monasteries or cathedrals such as Auxerre or Laon where a distinctive educational tradition is passed on from master to student through a succession of generations. In the eleventh century, however, no school succeeded in retaining a position of eminence for even two generations of masters. Chartres after Fulbert, Tours after Berengar, or Bec after Lanfranc have little to distinguish them from schools elsewhere in France—although in the last case the missing ingredient was not

2. Williams, "Godfrey of Rheims," 44.
3. Charles Homer Haskins, *The Renaissance of the Twelfth Century* (Cambridge, Mass., 1927), 368.

4. Fulbert's students are discussed by A. Clerval, *Les Ecoles de Chartres au moyen âge* (Paris, 1895), 58–93, although allowance must be made for his tendency to extend the claims of the school of Chartres, and by L. C. MacKinney, *Bishop Fulbert and Education at the School of Chartres* (Notre Dame, Ind., 1957), 12–24. The evidence on Berengar's career is given by Clerval, 77–78, and on Lanfranc by Margaret Gibson, *Lanfranc of Bec* (Oxford, 1978), 11–22.

talent but desire to teach on the part of Anselm. The abundance of opportunities open to masters is only part of the explanation for this change. Equally important was the growing distance between the cathedral chapters' needs for basic education and the masters' often abstruse intellectual concerns. Having a famous master in residence was a circumstance of which a community could be proud. But it was not a necessity.

The most important consequence of the masters' independence, however, lay in the development of scholarly inquiry: as the masters increasingly answered only to the opinions of their peers, the spirit of competition led them continually to reach for truths that had not been achieved before. In tracing this development, which constituted nothing less than the creation of scholarly disciplines out of previously stagnant areas of knowledge, we shall proceed in roughly chronological order from the eucharistic controversy in which so many of Fulbert's students were prominent, to the efflorescence of technical analysis of the liberal arts in the 1060s to 1090s, and finally to the generation of Anselm of Laon and William of Champeaux who dominated intellectual life around 1100.

THE DEBATE OVER THE EUCHARIST

The principal theological controversy of the eleventh century centered on Berengar of Tours and his contention that Christ's body was figuratively rather than physically present in the consecrated bread of the eucharist. The question itself was not a new one. In the ninth century it had been the subject of opposing treatises by two monks of Corbie and, the two sides having failed to engage one another's arguments, as was quite typical of the period, the issue had continued unresolved into the eleventh century. Yet although the eleventh-century debate began from positions laid down in earlier centuries, the argument was both more detailed and sustained than it had been before, and nearly thirty years elapsed from the first mention of Berengar's doctrines around 1050 until his final condemnation in 1079.

Many historians have seen the new character and scale of the eucharistic debate as a consequence of, in David Knowles's phrase, "the growing self-confidence of the schools," a self-confidence that itself resulted from the increasingly intense study of logic during the previous fifty years.[5] It is, indeed, to this view of the early eleventh century that we owe the usual genealogy of medieval philosophy that begins with Gerbert (who first taught the whole available corpus of logic at Reims), continues through Berengar, and culminates in the early twelfth century with Abelard and the early Parisian schools. Southern, for example, in an influential article on the eucharistic controversy, places it in the context of the development of learning, writing that "by the third quarter of the eleventh century, the bearing of the philosophic ideas contained in the *Logica Vetus* on long-established theological doctrines began to be a pressing problem."[6] It was not that the application of the liberal arts to theology was necessarily controversial. Although Heriger of Lobbes had discussed the eucharist using both logic and mathematics in his treatise from around the year 1000,[7] his efforts, as Margaret Gibson noted, "encountered no criticism, scarcely indeed any response."[8] But applying logical criteria to theological issues made it harder to overlook or reach a compromise on differences of opinion, forcing theologians to decide matters more clearly.

5. *The Evolution of Medieval Thought* (Baltimore, 1962), 94. For more detailed accounts of the debate, see J. de Montclos, *Lanfranc et Bérenger* (Louvain, 1971); Brian Stock, *The Implications of Literacy* (Princeton, 1983), 272–325; and Charles M. Radding, *A World Made by Men* (Chapel Hill, 1985), 165–72.
6. R. W. Southern, "Lanfranc of Bec and Berengar of Tours," *Studies in Medieval History Presented to Frederick Maurice Powicke*, ed. R. W. Hunt et al. (Oxford, 1948), 34.
7. *De corpore et sanguine Domini*, printed with incorrect attribution to Gerbert in *Oeuvres de Gerbert*, ed. A. Olleris (Paris, 1867), 279–88.
8. "The Continuity of Learning circa 850–circa 1050," *Viator*, 6 (1975): 13. This surprising result led Gibson to speculate that "such indifference to the effect of secular learning on true religion is explicable only when those concerned are few and academic: when there is no question of shaking the faith of simple men," but this suggestion overlooks the fact that it was the scholarly controversy about Berengar that won publicity for his opinions.
9. Southern, "Lanfranc of Bec and Berengar of Tours," 29–30.

This traditional account is wrong on a number of counts. To begin with, there is reason to doubt the sophistication of French dialectic in the decades before the eucharistic controversy. The career of Lanfranc is the key: although his contemporaries hailed him as a master of dialectic,[9] there is nothing in Lanfranc's learning that he is unlikely to have encountered during his school days in Italy.[10] The work he cites most commonly is Cicero's *Topics*, which provided him with categories of arguments that could be used to analyze the structure of biblical texts, while the more difficult works of Boethius and Aristotle that make up the *logica vetus*—the "old logic" available before the twelfth century—he employed rarely if at all.[11] That Lanfranc could succeed in France as a master of logic with such minimal preparation tells us that standards of learning in the arts before 1050 were far short of what they would be a few years later.

Berengar's own contributions to the eucharistic controversy also work against explaining the debate as an effect of new learning. To judge from the earliest sources—the letter to Ascelin written in 1050, which is probably Berengar's earliest surviving statement of his position, and from the arguments that reached Berengar's old schoolmate Adelman at about the same time[12]—Berengar at first based his case on two entirely different questions: how one distinguished a miracle from a natural event, and how one interpreted the relevant works of the Church Fathers. Both points, for example, are argued in the letter to Ascelin, and it was to Berengar's views of nature and his readings of specific patristic texts that Adelman made his reply. The technical arguments based on grammar appear considerably later, when the controversy was already well advanced, and they occupy only a few paragraphs in Berengar's long treatise *Rescriptum contra Lanfrannum* written at the end of the 1060s.[13] The new edition of the *Rescriptum* makes this point especially clear: Berengar does not cite Aristotle at all and makes only a handful of references to other works in the liberal arts.

At first glance, it might appear that there was little novel in Berengar's earliest statements on the eucharist—certainly nothing that would precipitate a controversy lasting thirty years and ending only with definitive judgments from Roman councils of 1078 and 1079 and the death of Berengar himself. Yet this impression would be mistaken. The idea of nature had, to be sure, never altogether disappeared, and books "On the Nature of Things" had occasionally been written in the early Middle Ages. But although the language of nature was familiar, it was simply without medieval precedent to use it as Berengar did in discussing phenomena. When Moses' staff turned into a serpent, he observed, it did so "manifeste" by a transformation of the matter of the staff, "while the bread and wine on the altar patently experience" no such transformation.[14] In effect, Berengar was arguing that in interpreting phenomena one must assume the operation of natural forces unless there is

10. For example, Lanfranc's manner of analyzing the premises of Paul's arguments—"This is an argument *a simili . . . a causa . . . a contrario.*" (See Southern, "Lanfranc of Bec and Berengar of Tours," 36–37)—was probably acquired as a young man in school in Pavia, for later eleventh-century Pavese jurists employed the same kind of analysis when discussing the Lombard laws. See, for example, the *Expositio* to the *Liber Papiensis*, MGH Leges, vol. 4, at Rothar 204, 221, 249, Liutprand 70, and Grimoald 1. Still closer to Lanfranc's style of analysis are passages from Anselm of Besate, *Rhetorimachia*, ed. by Karl Manihus, MGH, Quellen zur Geistesgeschichte des Mittelalters, vol. 2 (Weimar, 1958), esp. p. 102 and the marginal apparatus. Full evidence on this point will be presented in another place.

11. Gibson, *Lanfranc of Bec*, 49 concludes that "it is almost impossible to see [Lanfranc] as a pioneer in the study of the *logica vetus*." See also her comments, "Lanfranc's Commentary on the Pauline Epistles," *Journal of Theological Studies* 22 (1971): 104–5. Finally, Gibson shows (*Lanfranc of Bec*, 89–91) that Lanfranc in fact avoided Aristotelian terminology by referring to "qualities" and "essence" instead of "accidents" and "substance."

12. Berengar's letter to Ascelin, *PL* 150.66AD, was re-edited by R. B. C. Huygens, in *Texts and Manuscripts: Essays Presented to G. I. Lieftinck*, vol. (Amsterdam, 1972), 18–19; for Adelman's letter, see Huygens, "Textes latins du XIe au XIIIe siècle," *Studi medievali*, 3d ser. 8 (1967): 451–503.

13. *Rescriptum contra Lanfrannum*, ed. R. B. C. Huygens, CCCM 84 (Turnholt, 1988); two earlier editions of this work bore the title *De sacra Coena adversus Lanfrancum*.

14. *De Sacra Coena*, 126–27.

Ber: The Burgundian [Humbert of Romans] perishes by his own sword, like Goliath.

Lan: You call yourself David and Humbert Goliath. You would do well to call yourself Goliath, for you are the most arrogant of men, and you will perish by what you think, write and say, as though by your own sword. It is Humbert who is David . . . fighting for the Church with the shield of faith and the sword of the spirit which is the word of God (Eph. 6:16–17) [*PL* 150.412; trans. Margaret Gibson].

Ber: Whence the blessed Augustine in his epistle to Boniface: As, he said, the sacrament of the body of Christ is the body of Christ according to a certain mode, and the sacrament of the blood of Christ is the blood of Christ according to a certain mode: so the sacrament of faith, is faith.

Lan: The sacrament of the body of Christ is his flesh as much as is that Lord Christ himself which was immolated on the cross, clothed though it is by the shape of bread (*forma panis*) that we receive in sacrament, and his blood which we drink under the appearance (*species*) and flavor of wine. That is to say that flesh is the sacrament of flesh, and blood of blood. By flesh and blood, both invisible, intelligible, and spiritual, are signified the visible, palpable, manifest body of the Redeemer full of all grace, virtues, and divine majesty . . . [*PL* 150: 424; trans. Radding].

Ber: For who says, "Christ is the cornerstone," does not mean Christ to be entirely made of stone; so who says: "bread of the altar is only sacrament," or "bread of the altar is only the true body of Christ," does not deny but confirms that bread and wine are in the Lord's meal.

Lan: [After listing other figurative statements, which he concedes are not to be taken literally.] Nevertheless, as I said, no Catholic receives these sentences [as true], and the Christian religion does not admit them. For your former sentence is such that no one is confused. The latter however you do not accept, who are a denier of flesh and blood, nor do we who admit both propositions in the least deny that there are figures and sacraments of many celestial things. Besides, the likeness which you posit between Lord Jesus Christ and the cornerstone, ensnares you and aids us. For as one says "Christ is a cornerstone," not because Christ really is made of stone but on account of a certain similarity . . . ; in the same manner when the Bible calls bread the body of Christ, it is a matter of a sacred and mystical locution . . . [*PL* 150: 416; trans. Radding].

Text 2. Excerpts from Lanfranc's *Liber de corpore et sanguine Domini*. Even when he is not being bombastic, Lanfranc integrates the texts he quotes into an almost homiletic discourse instead of analyzing them to verify their meaning.

physical evidence to the contrary. But although such views would become common in the twelfth century, many of Berengar's contemporaries understood him to be denying God's omnipotence. As Ascelin wrote Berengar, "Nature is nothing other than the will of God. Anyone in sane mind who calls nature the cause of things . . . admits the will of God to be the origin of nature of every kind."[15]

Scarcely less radical was Berengar's approach to patristic discussions of the eucha-

15. *PL* 150: 67D.

rist, a subject for which Heriger's treatise can provide a useful comparison. Heriger had quoted extensively from the Fathers on both sides of the question, but he had done so without comment or analysis, making no attempt to resolve the contradictions apparent in their views; in a real sense, it was because he saw no means of reconciling those contradictions that he had to seek out analogies in logic and arithmetic by which they could be explained away. Lanfranc, in opposing Berengar, did much the same. Although his book, the *Liber de Corpore et Sanguine Domini*, follows the order of a now-lost book of Berengar's, quoting Berengar's arguments and giving a reply, Lanfranc often fails to engage Berengar's basic ideas, instead dealing only with the literal meaning of particular phrases or simply heaping denunciations upon Berengar for daring to venture original ideas. (See Text 2.) Moreover, when quoting patristic authority to support his own case, Lanfranc generally omits any careful analysis, thus overlooking any possibility that the text could mean anything other than what he thinks it does. (Gibson notes that "over half of his treatise is patristic quotation . . . rather tentatively elaborated.")[16]

Berengar, in contrast, explicitly and systematically weighed literal against spiritual interpretations, assessing the value of each reading for given texts. "It is obvious to your erudition," he wrote addressing Lanfranc, "that it is said no less as a tropological expression: 'bread, which is placed on the altar, after consecration becomes the body of Christ and wine becomes his blood,' than it is said: 'Christ is a lion, Christ is a lamb, Christ is the cornerstone.'"[17] (See Text 3.) This assertion is then followed by a demonstration that many passages in the Bible are meant to be read figuratively and that the Church fathers treated them as figures of speech. It is, indeed, in this context that Berengar's arguments about nature become important: since the language of the eucharist is inconclusive, the absence of any physical evidence for a change of bread into flesh must be decisive and the

physical evidence points unmistakably to the continued existence of the bread. Anyone can see, Berengar wrote early in the controversy, "that the words of the consecration do not cause the matter of the bread to withdraw. . . . That is so plain that to experience this suffices to convince even a schoolboy."[18]

Arguing that "the primacy of textual analysis based on logical principles is the basis for Berengar's attack on the unreasonable abuse of authority and on all forms of oral, popular, or crudely realist thinking," Brian Stock explained the difference between Berengar and his adversaries as between literate and oral approaches to texts.[19] But Stock's use of the terms *literate* and *oral* in this manner may reasonably be questioned, because the taxonomy is not one that directs our attention to an underlying process: whatever the differences between Berengar and Lanfranc in their attitudes toward texts (and Stock is certainly correct to insist upon them), they are not explained by the ability to read and write.[20] Berengar's methods, moreover, were not without precedent. Despite the difference in subject matter, Berengar's direct assault on the arguments of his opponents by considering alternate possible meanings of key texts bears obvious resemblances to his teacher Fulbert's approach in the treatises against the Jews. When Berengar's adversaries responded in kind—and it is hard not to notice that Fulbert's students were more skilled than Berengar's other opponents in attempting to engage rather than dismiss his arguments—the dispute became self-perpetuating in a manner quite unlike debates of the ninth and tenth centuries. Although neither side could dislodge the other, it was also impossible simply to let the matter drop.

It was in this context, when earlier arguments offered no resolution of the dispute, that Berengar looked to a grammatical analysis of language for support. Simply stated,

16. Gibson, *Lanfranc of Bec*, 91 incl. n. 1.
17. *Rescriptum*, 73.

18. *PL* 150: 65C.
19. B. Stock, *The Implications of Literacy* (Princeton, 1983), 280.
20. For evidence that literacy, as the term is commonly understood, was widespread before 1000, see Rosamund McKitterick, *The Carolingians and the Written Word* (Cambridge, 1989).

It is obvious to your erudition that it is said no less as a tropological expression: "Bread, which is placed on the altar, after consecration is the body of Christ and wine is his blood," than it is said: "Christ is a lion, Christ is a lamb, Christ is the cornerstone;" and that one conclusion (not more) is obvious from all those kinds of figurative expressions, that wherever something non-predicable is predicated, because a tropical locution is of non-susceptibles, one term of the proposition is taken tropically and the other in its proper sense. For example, the apostle said "The rock was Christ (*petra Christus erat*)" and it is obvious that the subject "rock"—that which gave forth water in the desert—is not entirely a susceptible of that predicate, that is "Christ" or the man/god; and that that apostolic proposition has a subject term that is "rock" properly speaking and a predicate that is "Christ" tropically speaking; whence the blessed Augustine says, "the stone is Christ in sign (*in signo*), and the true Christ—that is, considered according to the properties of things—is in flesh and the Word." Also when the Lord says of that bread which he originally advanced to such a privileged position that it was his flesh, "This" (*hoc*), that is this thing, this bread "is my body" (*est meum corpus*) he did not speak regarding properties (*proprie*), since the individual bread, which he had advanced to such a dignity that, when worthily taken, it availed to the salvation of the soul, was not susceptible of that individual predicated body which the wisdom of God made for himself in the virgin's womb; and thus the subject term, that is "bread," is to be considered in its proper sense and the predicate term, which is in the proposition "my body," is to be considered in its tropical sense, and that utterance which says, Christ is the highest cornerstone, accomplishes nothing for you but tells against you altogether.

[Berengar continues at length to discuss examples of this principle of interpretation, for example:] The blessed Cyprian says, "When the Lord calls his body bread made one from many grains, he indicates the people made one from [different] tribes, and when he calls his blood wine pressed from clusters and grapes and brought together, he indicates our flock," which statement I have inserted for this reason, because no one would doubt that the blessed Cyprian in this place used the term bread in its proper sense, although he wrote this not of the body of Christ born of the virgin, which is a proper locution, but of the people of Christ which is itself the body of Christ but tropically said. And the blessed Augustine in his commentary on the Gospel according to John speaking of the body born of the virgin which is not tropically but properly said to be a body . . . [pp. 73–74, 76; trans. Radding and Francis Newton].

Text 3. Excerpts from Berengar's *Rescriptum*. As with his master Fulbert, Berengar recognizes that other views are possible and develops arguments that his views are the best. Notice also how Berengar's use of liberal learning is subordinated to the question of interpretation.

Berengar's argument was that since every sentence required two parts, a subject and a predicate, a statement in which the existence of the subject was denied by the predicate was self-contradictory. He had in mind the sentence "Hic panis est corpus meum," a proposition that would be meaningless if the substance of the bread were entirely absent.[21] If he was beaten here, Berengar declared, nothing would be left to him—an excessive claim, since even in the 1060s this argument formed only a tiny part of his defense. But his shift to grammatical analysis, and his confidence in its ability to persuade, were well judged. The last decades of the eleventh century were to see many masters following the same path.

1070–1100

In the end, the resolution of the eucharistic controversy had less to do with scholarly arguments than with the judgments rendered against Berengar at papal councils in 1078 and 1079. Yet for the masters who had closely followed the debate, the lessons of the controversy went well beyond the immediate doctrinal issues. The frailty of reasoning based entirely on authoritative texts—as most learned works before the mid-eleventh century had done—was now exposed to all who considered the matter. The search was on to find a way out of this trap, and that effort spurred new and more intensive analysis of the old textbooks of both grammar and logic.

One of those who felt the urgency of this problem was Anselm of Bec—a fact that is particularly noteworthy because in many other ways he stood apart from his contemporaries. At a time when the importance of independent masters was growing, Anselm taught with reluctance and then only members of his own monastery.[22] And as other philosophers were turning their attention to the glossing of basic texts and the systematic exploration of technical issues, Anselm's own philosophical work generally took the form of meditations on central issues of the Christian faith. But although these characteristics of his vocation served to limit his influence both on contemporary masters and on succeeding generations, Anselm was very much a member of the philosophical generation that flourished between 1060 and 1090 in both the issues he chose to address and the means by which he attempted to solve them. (See Text 4.)

We may take as a point of departure Anselm's first work—the *Monologion*, written around 1077. It begins:

Some of my brethren have persistently asked me to write down some of the things which I have proposed to them in talk for meditation on the divine essence and certain associated topics . . . with this condition that I should persuade them of nothing on the authority of scripture, but plainly and simply put down whatever the argument might require, without overlooking any objections however fatuous.[23]

The formula was not always identical. In the *Proslogion*, Anselm addressed the Psalmist's Fool who "has said in his heart: there is no God." *Cur Deus Homo* he wrote in response to unspecified "unbelievers." But the effect was always the same: Anselm supposed situations in which reason alone had to defend the faith, without quotation from or analysis of authorities of any kind.

21. *Rescriptum*, 90–91, 92–93; the first statement of this doctrine was made in a lost work dating after 1059; it is noted by Lanfranc, *Liber de corpore et sanguine Christi*, PL 150: 418C. For Berengar's grammatical arguments, see also Southern, "Lanfranc of Bec and Berengar of Tours," 44–46.

22. The most important study of Anselm, and one that is in many ways a model of what the biography of a medieval intellectual figure should be, is R. W. Southern, *Saint Anselm and His Biographer*. (Cambridge, 1963). For Anselm's works, see F. S. Schmitt, ed., *Sancti Anselmi opera omnia* (Edinburgh, 1946); a recent English translation is that of Jasper Hopkins and Herbert Richardson (Toronto and New York, 1974–76).

23. The translation is Southern's, *Saint Anselm and His Biographer*, 51; Lanfranc's reaction to the project is discussed in the same place. Much the same idea, moreover, is repeated in chapter 1: "There may be someone who, as a result of not hearing or not believing, is ignorant of the one Nature. . . . If so, then I think that in great part he can persuade himself of these matters merely by reason alone if he is of even average intelligence."

For when we say "A man is" or "A man is not," what is signified by "man" is conceived before it is said to be or not to be. And so, what is conceived is a cause of the fact that "to be" is predicated of it. Also, if we say, "A man is an animal," *man* is a cause of there being, and being said to be, an animal. I do not mean that *man* is a cause of man's being, and being said to be, an animal. For by the name "man" we signify and conceive of man in his totality; and in this totality *animal* is contained as a part. . . . In this way, then, of whatever thing "to be" is predicated . . . the conception of this thing precedes and is a cause of this thing's being said to be (or not to be), and is a cause of the intelligibility of what is being said [facere 1, b; trans. Hopkins and Richardson].

Text 4. An excerpt from Anselm's *Philosophical Fragments*, illustrating his participation in the technical school discussions of his time. Anselm's more famous works applied the expertise developed through this kind of linguistic analysis to theological issues.

Thirty years earlier, such a project would have seemed pointless. Lanfranc, when Anselm sent him the *Monologion*, so little grasped its purpose that he suggested that some references to Augustine be added. But to Anselm's generation, the very difficulty that Lanfranc and Berengar had in agreeing about the meaning of authorities must have dramatized the necessity of finding other paths to certainty. Anselm's avoidance of authorities was not, therefore, simply an intellectual exercise, nor was it a literary device meant to create the impression of a meditation. It constituted a deliberate response to the condition of scholarship in the late eleventh century, when the old means of reaching agreement had shattered and scholars had to invent new ones.

It was also in every way typical of this period that Anselm believed that the way out of this dilemma lay through careful consideration of words and their meaning. Southern has noted how certain of Anselm's own arguments clearly tie him to the environment of the eucharistic controversy. "In form," he observed, Anselm's famous argument for the existence of God in the *Proslogion* is closely similar to that of Berengar. Berengar had asserted the continued existence of the substance of the consecrated Bread as a consequence of the grammatical structure of the sentence Hoc est corpus meum. In a similar way Anselm tried to show that in the sentence "God does not exist," the necessary implication of the subject is destroyed by the predicate, and therefore this sentence must be invalid and strictly meaningless. Whether he or Berengar succeeded in making good their claim is another question, but formally at least what they are doing is exactly the same.[24]

At first sight it seems that both Berengar and Anselm were confusing reality with language; forty years later, indeed, Abelard was to cut the connection altogether by insisting that logic has nothing to do with reality, although in his hands that position only opened the way for a consideration of what, given the limits of language, could be *said* about certain theological issues. But what was at stake in the last third of the eleventh century was not so much the definition of reality, or even of theological truths, for apart from the eucharist there were not really that many questions in need of settling. Rather, the need was to find a way for scholars, as scholars, to conduct a discussion with one another. In that sense, their purpose bears comparison with the rather similar concerns that resulted in a revival of linguistic logic around the beginning of this century.

Anselm, as has been said, occupies an unusual position with respect to the scholarship

24. Southern, *Saint Anselm and His Biographer*, 25.

of his time. Less marked by genius, but more typical of the masters of the late eleventh century, are two works by Anselm's contemporaries which suggest the intense research that appears to have been precipitated by the eucharistic controversy. One is Garlandus's *Dialectica*, the first general treatment of logic from the central Middle Ages. The other is a systematic gloss to Priscian's *Institutes* known today as the *Glosule*.

Although the details of Garlandus's life are obscure, the outlines have been reconstructed by L. M. de Rijk in the preface to his edition of the *Dialectica*. Garlandus seems to have been a native of the Lorraine who studied at Liege and taught for a while in England before 1066, some time later becoming master of St. Paul's cathedral at Besançon; de Rijk places his death in the late eleventh century, no earlier than 1084 (when he was still master at Besançon) and no later than 1100. In addition to the *Dialectica*, Garlandus wrote a *compotus* or book for calculating the ecclesiastical calendar; a book on the abacus; two books on music; possibly a book on grammar; a handbook known as the *Candela* on church doctrine, liturgy, and law; and commentaries on the Psalms and the Gospels. There is some need for caution in accepting all of these ascriptions, since Garlandus the Computist is easily confused with a twelfth-century Garlandus also of Besançon; but the dating of the *Dialectica* to the period between 1060 and 1075 seems reasonably certain.[25] In any case, apart from the strong interest in mathematics, both this range of activities as well as the geographical mobility suggested by Garlandus's movements from job to job are consistent with what is known about other masters of the period.

Garlandus's *Dialectica* is designed to provide an overview of the field, moving from genera, species, and accidents (book 1) to propositions (book 3) to syllogisms (books 5 and 6)—a structure entirely consistent with its purpose as an introduction to logic from which the reader would progress to Aristotle and Boethius. (He himself claimed only to be "excerpting from the rules of Aristotle and Boethius and where possible adding briefly to them according to our and our masters' views.")[26] Yet the modesty of purpose, simplicity of presentation, and the absence of explicit disagreements with classical logic should not deceive us into thinking that Garlandus worked as a compiler or arranger. Even where his discussion is based on the *logica vetus*, Garlandus did not so much summarize the presentation given in his sources as recast it into a new form appropriate for his own purposes. Book 1, for example, begins with a discussion of genera, loosely following the model of Porphyry's *Isagoge*. But the examples Garlandus used to illustrate genus are not Porphyry's but Boethius's, drawn from his commentary on the *Isagoge*, reworked, and simplified to fit Garlandus's scheme. In other places, moreover, Garlandus evidently substituted contemporary scholarly opinions for the views given in his authorities, as in his definition of dialectic as the science of speech or disputation (*sermocinabilis vel disputabilis scientia*).[27] The precise nature of Garlandus's relationship to his contemporaries unfortunately remains to be measured, because late eleventh-century glosses have neither been studied nor published. But his work leaves no doubt that these masters had moved beyond the mastery of classical learning to original investigations of their own.[28]

Involving as it did the study of words and propositions, the logic of the late eleventh century was intimately involved with semantics, touching at many points on the territory of grammar. The inverse of this approach,

25. Garlandus Compotista, *Dialectica*, ed. L. M. de Rijk (Assen, 1959).

26. ". . . excerpsimus aliqua ex eorum [i.e., Aristotle et Boethius] regulis non tenentes ordinem, sed inquirentes utilitatem et, insuper, si quid potuimus, secundum nos et magistros nostros compendiose addidimus" (Garlandus Compotista, *Dialectica*, 1).

27. Garlandus, *Dialectica*, 86. A similar definition is given in the introduction to the Glosule: "Nec dubitandum quin Logice supponatur, cuius ipsa grammatica tercia pars. Logice alia pars est sermocinalis, alia disertiua. . ." (See Margaret Gibson, "The Early Scholastic 'Glosule' to Priscian, 'Institutiones Grammaticae': The Text and Its Influence," *Studi Medievali* 20, no. 1 [1979]: 249).

28. See, for example, the discussion of Garlandus's treatment of universals in Martin M. Tweedale, *Abailard on Universals* (Amsterdam, 1976), 135–40. On Abelard's handling of universals, see chapter 4 below.

moreover, is to be found in the *Glosule* where, greatly embellishing Priscian's example, grammar was approached from the point of view of logic.[29] As important as its content, however, is what can be inferred from the *Glosule* about the audience for which it was written. Unlike Garlandus's work, which was ostensibly intended for relative beginners, the *Glosule* was written for advanced students and masters. It comes equipped with its own formal preface; its text is several times longer than the work it glossed, Priscian's *Institutes*, and it often raises complexities not apparent in Priscian. For example, the discussion of pronouns in book 12 leads to the following *quaestio*:

It is asked (queritur): when I say "I do not know what man came and he took my hat," what certain and finite person the pronoun "he" signifies, since it refers to an unknown man. To which we say that in this statement (oratio) "he" signifies a certain person, that is an unknown man, and I do not say certain because "he" informs us of his qualities, but because "he" used can be directed there to no other signifying thing . . .[30]

With such *quaestiones* we catch an echo of the working of the schools and of the increasing complexities of the masters' expositions. As in other areas of the liberal arts, ancient texts were being treated less as definitive summations than as springboards to further inquiries.

The last point to be noticed about the *Glosule* is its inclusion of the opinions of contemporary masters (see Text 5). The author of the *Glosule* was not, to be sure, always very good about making his references clear. Other grammar glosses of the period or a little later often give more attributions; indeed, it was by comparing passages in the *Glosule* with attributions made elsewhere that R. W. Hunt was able to show that it included the opinions of Lanfranc, Anselm, and Manegold (possibly, though not certainly, Manegold of Lautenbach), as well as some of the otherwise unknown masters of the late eleventh century.[31] But even if the *Glosule's* execution was sometimes poor, the attention to contemporary opinions, and sometimes even to conflicting views on the same subject, nonetheless marks a significant moment in the development of scholastic disciplines. Whereas earlier scholars had seen their task as preserving and expounding the learning contained in ancient texts, eleventh-century masters—deliberately and consciously—were addressing questions that had not previously been issues. Rather than the ancients, their point of reference had become their own peers.

ANSELM OF LAON AND WILLIAM OF CHAMPEAUX

Eleventh-century masters were not specialists. The opinions of Lanfranc, Anselm, and Manegold were recorded on rhetoric as they were on grammar, logic, and biblical studies, and a master doubtlessly lectured on all those subjects. But whereas the scholarly personalities of individual eleventh-century masters are difficult to perceive because so many of the sources come down to us in fragments or anonymously, in the decades around 1100 two masters appear of whom it is possible to say something more. Anselm of Laon and William of Champeaux are, unfortunately, best known through the characterizations of their one-time student Peter Abelard, a man never inclined to overestimate the abilities of others. But enough of Anselm's and William's work survives for us to construct independently of Abelard a far clearer picture of what

---

29. On the 'Glosule,' see R. W. Hunt, "Studies on Priscian in the Eleventh and Twelfth Centuries," *Medieval and Renaissance Studies* 1 (1941–43): 194–231; and Gibson, "The Early Scholastic 'Glosule.'"

30. "Queritur cum dico 'Nescio quem hominem inveni et is abstulit michi cappam,' an certam et finitam personam hoc pronomen 'is' in hac oratione significet, cum ad ignotum hominem referatur. Ad quod dicimus quia in hac oratione 'is' certam personam significet, scilicet ignotum hominem, nec dico certam quod 'is' eius qualitatem nobis notificet, sed certam quia 'is' ad nullam aliam rem significandam ibi potest dirigi" (quoted by Hunt, "Studies on Priscian," 201).

31. Hunt, "Studies on Priscian," 205–11. On Manegold, see F. Chatillon, "Recherches critiques sur les différents personnages nommés Manegold," *Revue du Moyen Age latin* 9 (1953): 153–70; and Wilfried Hartmann, "Manegold von Lautenbach und die Anfänge der Frühscholastik," *Deutsches Archiv für Erforschung des Mittelalters* 26 (1970): 47–149.

Guy of Langres used to say this verb signifies action in God alone, as when we say "God is," and passivity in all created things, as when we say "Man is," "Ass is," and so forth. And this opinion seems to be drawn from Macrobius, who says "stand" (*stare*) signifies action and passivity.

Archbishop Lanfranc said this verb that is "I am" (*sum*) signifies action in substances, as when we say "Man is," "Ass is" and the like; but passivity in all accidental things that exist not through themselves but through substances, as when we say "White is," etc. And thus that which to Master Guy is between God and creatures, to Lanfranc is between substance and accident.

Master Robert said that this verb does not have any substance, but rather signifies substantial differences (*differentias*) in something of which the subject is predicated, . . . as when we say "Man is," this "is" signifies rationality and mortality and so forth.

Master Garmundus said that the action of this verb is both substances and accidents. When we say "Man is an animal," there "animal" is the action of that verb that serves as a copula; when we say "This color is white," this "white" is the action of that verb, and so forth.

Master Durandus of England used to say that this verb signified action proper and passivity proper . . . [from Hunt, "Studies on Priscian," 224–25; trans. Radding].

Text 5. The *Glosule*'s discussion of the substantive verb, giving the views of several masters. These opinions could then be the subject of further discussion at the hands of other masters.

and how they taught than is possible for any earlier masters.

The older of the two was Anselm, who taught at Laon from before 1100 until 1110 (when he became dean) or 1115 (when he became archdeacon).[32] He died in 1117. Some of Anselm's comments on grammar, rhetoric, and logic survive in twelfth-century glosses, confirming that he taught the usual curriculum of studies, but now, as in his own time, he is chiefly known for his exposition of the Bible. This was not a new subject in the late eleventh century. Berengar and Lanfranc had also lectured on the Bible—it may be significant that Lanfranc took up the subject only in 1055, after the beginning of the eucharistic controversy.[33] Masters of the subsequent gen-

eration built extensively on this base, with the result that by Anselm's time there existed an extensive body of commentary focused especially on the Psalms and Pauline epistles.

Anselm of Laon's accomplishment was to gather glosses selected from this material together with his own comments into a running commentary on the Psalms and Epistles. The impulse is clearly the same as motivated the author of the *Glosule* or, in another field, the compiler of the *Expositio* of the Liber Legis Langobardorum.[34] Anselm's work met even greater success than theirs, eventually becoming the basis of the ordinary gloss (*glossa ordinaria*) to the Bible, but here the most important thing to notice is the way in which glossing the Bible tended to open up questions

32. On Anselm, see Odon Lottin, *Psychologie et morale aux XIIe et XIIIe siècles* (Louvain and Gembloux, 1959), vol. 6; Valerie I. Flint, "The 'School of Laon': A Reconsideration," *RTAM* 43 (1976): 89–110.
33. Beryl Smalley, "La Glossa ordinaria. Quelques prédécesseurs d'Anselme de Laon," *RTAM* 9 (1937): 365–

400; Gibson, "Lanfranc's Commentary on the Pauline Epistles," and "Lanfranc's Notes on Patristic Texts," *Journal of Theological Studies*, n.s. 22 (1971): 435–50.
34. On this see Charles M. Radding, *Origins of Medieval Jurisprudence* (New Haven and London, 1988), 125–39.

for systematic scholarly discussion that otherwise lacked a place in the basic curriculum. Marcia Colish has recently called attention to the fact that many of Anselm's own glosses, apparently originally Biblical glosses, addressed questions of morality,[35] and the same tendency can be seen in some discussions of theological issues. In each case, moreover, subsequent generations were to spin such discussions off to form distinct academic subjects in their own right.

If Anselm is now known chiefly for his work on the Bible, William of Champeaux is known principally for his work in the *artes*. Again, the

contrast must not be drawn too sharply. William himself was a student of Anselm's for a while and continued to quote his opinions. But William was famous, as we are told by Abelard, for his teaching in grammar and logic, and in addition to his opinions in those areas we possess works in rhetoric that may be his and that in any case reflect his teachings on the subject.[36] What survives is little more than fragments, but it is enough to permit us

35. Marcia Colish, "Another Look at the School of Laon," *Archives d'Hist. doctrinale et litt.* (1986): 7–22.

36. Karin Margareta Fredborg, "The Commentaries on Cicero's *De Inventione* and *Rhetorica ad Herennium* by William of Champeaux," *Cahiers de l'Institut du moyen âge grec et latin* 17 (1976): 1–39; N. J. Green-Pedersen, "William of Champeaux on Boethius' Topics According to Orleans Bibl. Mun. 266," *CIMAGL* 13 (1974): 13–30. For William's relationship to Anselm of Laon, see Fredborg, 14–15, citing Abelard, *Historia Calamitatum*, ed. Monfrin, 67.

Commentary to De Inv. 1.7.9:

It is also to be noted that since invention in dialectic is different from judgment, this invention is taken in a broad sense to contain judgment. We see, therefore, what is invention in dialectic and what is judgment, so that afterward we can better understand in what manner each includes the other.

Invention teaches to reason out which points (*loci*) have some affinity with the term placed in the question and to choose one argument derived from them through which one tries to prove the case. Judgment indeed is a polishing of the argument since it renders the invented argument effective by constituting proofs and reasons so that the invented point might exert its force—that is, syllogisms or other modes of proof and argumentation—and so that the reasoned out argument is unfolded.

Commentary to De Inv. 1.31.51:

All argumentation, i.e., argument is treated and explained, *either by induction or reasoning*. This refers to the division of argumentation that it is induction or reasoning. This reasoning contains the syllogism. For orators do not use enthymeme as dialecticians do, nor do dialecticians need ornate and varied words that orators do to move their audiences. Induction contains that which is known in dialectic as the use of example and induction [from Fredborg, "Commentaries on Cicero's *De Inventione*," 22, 25; trans. Radding].

Text 6. Excerpts from William of Champeaux's commentary on Cicero's *De Inventione*. Note how the gloss procedes phrase by phrase, classifying the divisions of the material, giving definitions and examples, and resolving difficulties.

to follow the same master as he moves from subject to subject in his curriculum of studies.

For the most part, William's opinions confirm what has already been said about the state of learning around 1100. He notes the opinions of other masters, especially Anselm and Manegold, and the level of commentary in general is high, often dealing with issues not explicitly raised in the texts he glosses. Even if we did not know of his later rivalry with Abelard, there would be no mistaking that his work emerged from the circle of professional masters. Especially noteworthy, moreover, is the focus on language and argument that shows itself regardless of the subject being discussed. (See Text 6.) Karin Fredborg has observed, for example, that William's rhetorical commentaries focus on problems of argument at the expense of issues such as memory and style relevant for public speaking; it is a rhetoric close to dialectic, and indeed William even classed rhetoric with dialectic as a branch of logic.[37] His work thus illustrates how the work of the schools continued along the lines that had been laid out during the eucharistic controversy, well after that particular issue had been settled.

The eleventh is one of the few medieval centuries never to have had a renaissance claimed for it, and, indeed, the events traced in this chapter had little to do with the recovery of lost classical texts: the titles in monastic libraries in 1100 were little different than they had been in 1000. Yet the intellectual world of 1100 was very different from that of a century earlier. Masters were becoming professionals, with careers less and less tied to a particular monastery or cathedral school, and with reputations to earn and defend. As part of this professionalization, moreover, they ceased to be content to repeat, or refine, what they had learned in books. They asked new questions, and even in dealing with old ones felt free to discard traditional answers and venture solutions of their own. The point is not simply novelty, however. Such changed circumstances and self-conception meant that masters set ever more exacting standards of technical competence for each other and for their students, preparing the way for more dramatic accomplishments in the future. In the next chapter we shall see how a similar process transformed the practice of eleventh-century architecture.

37. Fredborg, "The Commentaries on Cicero's *De Inventione*," 21–22. Fredborg also noted that William's are the only rhetoric commentaries in which the issues of universals were discussed.

3 · Builders

In exploring the development of the discipline of architecture between 1050 and 1150, the first problem we encounter is the attitude of the monastic chroniclers who provide the principal narrative sources for this period.[1] As far as the monks were concerned, the men responsible for their new buildings were either the abbots who initiated the project (and raised the money to pay for it), the brothers who represented their wishes to the actual workers, or—more rarely—the lay patron who provided the resources for the completion of the project: these are the people who are described as *architectus* or are credited with having built of a church.[2] The men who actually directed the placement of bricks and stone were of less interest. One chronicler, for example, described Queen Emma of England as having "built" (*construxit*) Saint-Hilaire-le-Grand at Poitiers "by the hand of Walter Coorland."[3] The master mason-builder Walter was important enough to the project for the monks to view Emma's aid in sending him

1. There exist a number of works that discuss master masons in the Middle Ages. Pierre du Colombier, *Les Chantiers des cathédrales*, rev. ed. (Paris, 1973); Y.-M. Froidevaux, *Techniques de l'architecture ancienne, construction et restauration* (Liège, 1985); Jean Gimpel, *The Cathedral Builders*, new ed., trans. Teresa Waugh (New York, 1985); John Harvey, *The Medieval Architect* (London, 1972); and Lon R. Shelby, "The Education of Medieval Master Masons," *Medieval Studies* 32 (1970): 1–26, and "The Role of the Master Mason in Medieval English Building," *Speculum* 39 (1964): 387–403. These works, however, do not generally distinguish the eleventh- and early twelfth-century evidence from the much more abundant material concerning the later Middle Ages, and therefore must be used with great care when discussing the earlier period. A good collection of sources is Victor Mortet, *Recueil de textes relatifs à l'histoire de l'architecture et à la condition des architectes en France au Moyen Age. Tome I: XIe-XIIe siècles* (Paris, 1911).
2. N. Pevsner, "The Term 'Architect' in the Middle Ages," *Speculum* 17 (1942): 549–62.
3. "[Anno] MXLIX, . . . Istud monasterium [sancti Hilarii Pictavensis] ex parte construxerat regina Anglorum per manus Guaterii Coorlandi" (*Chronicon Sancti Maxenti Pictavensis* in the *Chroniques des églises d'Anjou*, ed. Marchgay and Mabille [Soc. hist. de France] [1869], quoted in Mortet, *Recueil*, 140–41). Coorland witnessed charters at Saint-Hilaire between 1077 and 1090, (Mortet, *Recueil*, 141, n. 4), which both dates his tenure and suggests that he enjoyed a relatively high social status. See also the language used to describe the roles of Gunzo and Hézelon in the building of Cluny III. Kenneth John Conant, *Cluny: Les Eglises et la maison du chef d'ordre* (Mâcon, 1968), 76–77; Carolyn M. Carty, "The Role of Gunzo's Dream

to Poitiers as a major act of patronage, but he was not personally significant enough to be seen as the builder. As artisans, builders moved in a different social world from monks and often escaped their notice.

Doubtless there were some monks who were skilled enough at building to have taken an active hand in design, but the more usual course must have been for the builders' employers to lay out general guidelines within which the builders had to work.[4] Some sense of what those guidelines may have been is provided by one of the rare descriptions of buildings from before 1150, that of the *Consuetudines Farfenses*. Based on the customs of Cluny, of which Farfa was a daughter house, this document is very precise in specifying certain details: the exact dimensions of different monastic buildings, the number of windows and balconies, the size of the monks' cells, the placement of the refectory table are all given with great care.[5] Because these were the matters of greatest practical concern to patrons, it is probably correct to imagine an architectural commission of the eleventh or twelfth century as consisting of similar details, with perhaps additional, general remarks about buildings the patron liked or disliked. Certainly, later medieval architectural contracts took this form. But such contracts would have left most practical and aesthetic decisions to the builder who, employing his knowledge, experience, and talent, would have had to determine such questions as the size and placement of windows and vaults and to issue instructions concerning moldings and sculptural decorations.

The other main obstacle to understanding medieval builders has been the tendency to assimilate the position of master masons to that of ordinary masons or stonecutters. Some

historians, indeed, have gone so far as to treat the builders' contribution to design as a craft secret or skill analogous to that of shaping actual stones,[6] and this bafflement concerning the builders' role was perhaps shared by some of their contemporaries. One thirteenth-century preacher, for instance, wrote disapprovingly of master masons "who carried measuring rods about the worksite telling others where to cut stones, who received the greatest wages, and yet who never cut stones themselves."[7] As Pierre du Colombier observed, the scandal resulted from the fact that the preacher saw the masons as workers, yet they did not work with their hands.[8]

No comparable description of master builders at work survives from the period before 1150, but other evidence makes it plain that their contemporaries recognized their distinctive contribution. In the first place, they were paid higher wages than other masons and the contract often ran for several years. For example, the 1129 contract between builder Raymond of Montfort and the archbishop of Lugo provided that in addition to his yearly salary of six silver marks Raymond should receive annually thirty-six meters of cloth, seventeen loads of wood, as well as shoes and clothes as needed and a monthly allowance of food, salt, and candles.[9] These

in the Building of Cluny III," *Gesta* 27 (1988): 113–24. On Saint-Hilaire, see the articles of Marie-Thérèse Camus, "La Reconstruction de Saint-Hilaire-le-Grand de Poitiers à l'époque romane: La Marche des travaux," *Cahiers de civil. méd.* 25 (1982): 101–20, 238–71; "Les Voûtes de la nef de Saint-Hilaire-le-Grand de Poitiers du XIe au XIXe siècle," *Bulletin archéologique*, n.s. 16 (1980): 57–94.

4. A. Dimier, *Les Moines Bâtisseurs* (Paris, 1964).

5. Conant, *Cluny*, 42–45; Charles B. McClendon, *The Imperial Abbey of Farfa* (New Haven and London, 1987).

6. See, for example, Shelby's remarks: "Closer attention to the education of the masons would reveal the indissoluble bond between the medieval architect and the living traditions of the mason's craft.... For instance, much ado has been made about the great skill which Gothic architects displayed in the molding of space and volume, and in the modulation of light and shade upon, in, and through the architectural forms they used. But is not this skill merely an extension, on a monumental scale, of the basic requirement of the stonecutters' art?" ("The Education of Medieval Master Masons," 26). In fact, of course, there is an enormous distance between the motor skills needed to shape stones and the cognitive skills used in designing buildings and supervising other workers.

7. See the sermon by the dominican Nicolas de Biard, ca. 1261: "Magistri cementariorum, virgam et cyrothecas in manibus habentes, aliis dicunt: *Par ci me le taille*, et nihil laborant; et tamen majorem mercedem accipiunt, quod faciunt multi moderni prelati" quoted in Victor Mortet and Paul Deschamps, *Recueil de textes relatifs à l'histoire de l'architecture et à la condition des architectes en France, au Moyen Age. Tome II: XIIe-XIIIe siècles* (Paris, 1929), 290–91.

8. Colombier, *Chantiers des cathédrales*, 58.

9. Gimpel, *Cathedral Builders*, 57; Colombier, *Chantiers des cathédrales*, 76.

terms are not to be confused with the daily wage of an ordinary artisan. The relative prosperity of builders is also attested by evidence that several eleventh-century English master masons owned land; one mason, though perhaps more in charge of maintenance than building, even held property valued at a knight's fee.[10]

Perhaps the most significant indication of the builders' special position, however, is given by the efforts ambitious patrons expended in recruiting a master mason. Ordinary stonecutters also had to be sought abroad, but the reason had to do with the need for a sizable numbers of workers and the recruitment seems to have been conducted on a wholesale basis. Efforts made to hire a builder, in contrast, were directed toward specific individuals. Queen Emma's help in recruiting Walter Coorland from England to Poitiers has already been noticed, and Walter was kept on the job even after the expenses of construction were assumed by Countess Agnes of Burgundy. Similarly, Raymond, the well-paid builder of Lugo, was French, and the monastery of La Trinité at Vendôme loaned one of its monks, John the Mason (*cementarius*), to the bishop of le Mans for the construction of the cathedral there. John proved a disappointment to both the bishop and his abbot, because he left both in the lurch to travel to Jerusalem.[11]

Since they were not laborers, clerics, or gentlemen, master masons fit uneasily into the medieval conceptions of social hierarchy, yet their distinct abilities were recognized and rewarded in practice even before 1150. But although documents can tell us something about the careers and status of builders, they have nothing to say about how those men went about designing a building in this period when architecture was changing from a craft to a discipline. For that purpose, the only clues are provided by the buildings themselves, and it is to that subject we now turn.

UNITY AND DIVERSITY IN ROMANESQUE ARCHITECTURE

When one considers the architecture of the century beginning in 1050, the sheer abundance of the evidence stands at first as a barrier to understanding. Because this period saw an unprecedented boom in construction built on a scale that proved largely adequate to the needs of subsequent generations, literally thousands of buildings survive ranging in size from small parish churches to massive cathedrals. This numerical abundance, moreover, is matched by an extraordinary diversity of styles. Although each region has its own characteristics, as do some monastic orders, even the buildings within an given style often reveal substantial variations of floor plan, elevation, and ornament. Efforts to construct a classification system for the architecture of this period have therefore largely failed, with the result that even accounts of regional "Romanesque schools" often devote more space to listing varieties than common features.[12]

Cutting across this enormous diversity of forms, however, is the modular conception of space developed in the first half of the eleventh century. Because transepts, side chapels, aisles, and naves could all be treated modularly, this conception provided builders with a means for designing buildings to meet a variety of commissions. And because a variety of architectural elements such as pilaster strips, half-columns, moldings, and columns could be used to define the modules, this approach was also adaptable to the particular skills of the builder's work force. This very adaptabil-

11. Mortet, *Recueil*, 292–94.

12. See, for example, the treatments in Kenneth John Conant, *Carolingian and Romanesque Architecture 800–1200*, 2d ed. (Pelican History of Art) (Baltimore, 1966); P. Lasko, "The Concept of Regionalism in French Romanesque," in *Akten des XXV. Internationalen Kongresses für Kunstgeschichte, Wien, 1983*. Vol. 3, *Probleme und Methoden des Klassifizierung*, ed J. White (Vienna, 1983), 17–25; A. Mussat, "L'Etude régionale: Identité culturelle et expressions artistiques, mythes et réalitiés," in *Akten des XXV Internationalen Kongresses für Kunstgeschichte*, 37–44; and Neil Stratford, "Romanesque Sculpture in Burgundy: Reflections on Its Geography, on Patronage, on the Status of Sculpture and on the Working Methods of Sculptors," in *Artistes, artisans et production artistique au moyen âge* (Paris, 1990), 3:235–63.

10. See, for example, the entries under Blithere, Hugh the Mason I, Robert the Mason I, and Wimund in John Harvey, *English Mediaeval Architects*, 2d ed. (Gloucester, 1984). Harvey suggests that the engineer Wimund may have designed the great hall of William II at Westminster.

ity of application, indeed, largely accounts for the diversity of Romanesque architecture, as minor variations in either the patrons' needs or the craftsmen's abilities could inspire a builder to develop a variation on the styles in which he had been trained.

AN EXAMPLE: SAINT-SERNIN OF TOULOUSE

Positioned on one of the main pilgrimage roads leading to the shrine of Santiago of Compostela, Saint-Sernin was begun before 1080 with the clear intention of attracting those pilgrims, whose numbers were then steadily increasing, to the relics of St. Saturninus, apostle of Languedoc. This meant, in the first place, that the new church would sit atop the burial site of St. Saturninus, where a much smaller structure then stood. Moreover, to emphasize the importance of St. Saturninus, the building was to be both large and modeled after old St. Peter's in Rome, with its five-aisled nave and broadly projecting transept. Finally, because substantial support for the building was to come from the count of Toulouse, the count's entrance portal in the transept was to be accorded particular importance.[13]

Construction began with the peripheral

wall of the chevet, laid out around the existing fifth-century apse, which was left intact as long as possible. Analysis of the archeological evidence suggests that the first builder not only laid out and built the east end but built the lower courses of the walls and piers in the transept and eastern bays of the nave. Another campaign, lasting until the death of the second builder Raymond Gairard in 1118, continued building the upper parts of the east end, while laying out and erecting the enclosing wall of the nave and facade up to the level of the windows. Although the upper levels of the nave were not completed until the end of the thirteenth century, there was, by then, little possibility of confusion: subsequent builders had only to follow the pattern already laid out in the lower wall (Figure 10).

To see how the modular conception of space guided the design of Saint-Sernin, let us look first at the east end where construction began (Figures 11 and 12). This area had to contain radiating chapels, an ambulatory, and a high altar area raised over the *confessio* containing the relics of St. Sernin. Thus, it was architecturally the most complex part of the church, and designing it involved a series of decisions, some of which had to be made immediately whereas others could be deferred. Throughout the process of working out the design, however, the builder kept two principles in mind. He emphasized the limits of his spatial units, that is, he accentuated the edges between the chapels, ambulatory, and central space. And he subdivided the ambulatory and central space into repeating units, which he organized into sequences according to the area involved.

The first problem the builder faced was how to make the five radiating chapels that shared this exterior wall distinct entities. He probably began by laying out the peripheral wall and marking the position of the ambulatory bays around the existing apse, leaving it intact until the first chapels were completed. Once the bays were marked out, the builder knew where articulating ornament would have to be placed, leaving open the question of what that ornament would be. That decision, however, could not have been delayed long, because the ornament that marked the

13. On the question of pilgrimage churches, the chapter in Conant, *Carolingian and Romanesque Architecture*, 91–106 has been replaced by the article by Thomas Lyman, "The Politics of Selective Eclecticism," *Gesta* 27 (1988): 83–92. On Saint-Sernin in particular, see Marcel Durliat, "La Construction de Saint-Sernin de Toulouse au XIe siècle," *Bulletin monumental* 121 (1963): 151–170; Durliat, "La Construction de Saint-Sernin de Toulouse. Etude historique et archéologique," in *La Construction au moyen âge.* (Paris, 1973), 201–211; O. Foucaud, "La Restauration de Saint-Sernin de Toulouse de 1860 à 1862," *Bulletin monumental* 147 (1989): 333–44; and the studies of Thomas Lyman, "Notes on the Porte Miègeville Capitals, and the Construction of Saint-Sernin in Toulouse," *Art Bulletin* 49 (1967): 25–36; "The Sculpture Programme of the Porte des Comtes Master at Saint-Sernin in Toulouse," *Journal of the Warburg and Courtauld Institutes* 34 (1971): 12–39; "Terminology, Typology, Taxonomy," *Gazette des Beaux Arts*, 6th ser. 88 (1976): 223–27; "Le Style comme symbole chez les sculpteurs romans," *Cahiers de Saint-Michel de Cuxa* 12 (1981): 161–79; and "Format and Style: The Adaptation of Cartoons to Reused Marble at Saint-Sernin," in *Artistes, artisans et production artistique au moyen âge* (Paris, 1990), 3:223–63.

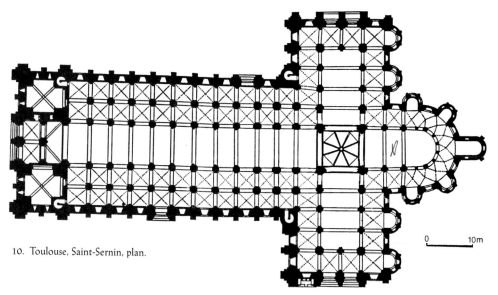

10. Toulouse, Saint-Sernin, plan.

0 |_____| 10m

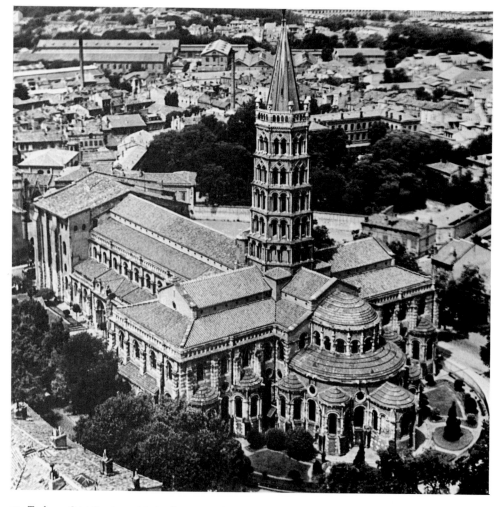

11. Toulouse, Saint-Sernin, aerial view from east. The distinct differences in height clarify the visual articulation of the exterior ornamental scheme and make each unit clear.

12. Toulouse, Saint-Sernin, eastern end.

13. Toulouse, Saint-Sernin, interior of ambulatory. At the lower level of the outer wall the large half-columns constituted the only articulation. Ornamental details were introduced at the base of the windows.

bay divisions on the inside and outside of the peripheral wall had to be incorporated into the foundation and lower courses of this peripheral wall—in this case, half-columns with large bases on the interior and pilaster strips on the exterior (Figure 13). As the peripheral wall went up, the builder had further decisions to make about the size, positioning, and articulation of windows. For example, he reduced the size of the exterior pilaster strips to accommodate the windows, in fact replacing the pilaster strips with narrower half-columns. Finally, in the higher courses of the chevet wall, the builder made the ambulatory taller than the chapels, a decision that is immediately apparent in the external massing.

As the peripheral wall was going up, the builder was also making decisions about the internal supports of the east end. Placement of those supports was already implicit in the original layout of the bay divisions. The choice of half-columns for the bay divisions of the peripheral wall set the limits upon the alternatives for inner supports, although more than one option remained: in practice the builder chose columns to match the half-columns, but piers faced with half-columns would have done as well (Figure 14). By the time the exterior wall was completed, the inner columns and some of the upper wall would also have been built in order to permit a roof to be constructed before vaulting began.

Once one or more of the radiating chapels and ambulatory access bays were usable for services, the builder could remove the old apse and begin work in the central area. Here, he found that some of the decisions already made could not be implemented without making some adjustments. The width of the bays, adequately proportioned in the ambulatory, proved less appropriate for the central area, and the builder used columns in the hemicycle instead of the larger compound piers he devised for the straight bays of the chevet, transept, and nave. In moving to the straight bays, moreover, he found the rectangular bays of the chevet too shallow and deepened them into squares. His general approach to the space, however, remained the same, with the bays as the key conceptual

14. Toulouse, Saint-Sernin, ambulatory and hemicycle from east. The columns that carry the ambulatory vaults and upper wall are positioned in relation to the peripheral wall but are carried on top of the outer wall of the crypt. The height of the crypt wall accounts for the difference in floor level between the ambulatory and the main altar space.

unit and divisions within the chevet clearly marked off from one another. The floor of the altar area was elevated over the *confessio* and therefore higher than the ambulatory, providing the viewer with a clear boundary between the two; in addition, the vaults of the main vessel were substantially higher than those of the ambulatory (Figures 15 and 16). The builder also employed different types of architectural ornament to mark off divisions both vertically and longitudinally within each area. For example, he placed a horizontal molding at the base of the ambulatory and chapel windows and another at the level of the chapel vault, making clear not only the difference between the chapels and the ambulatory, but the height changes as well. The result is that the viewer perceives the whole east end as formed by the combination of smaller, distinct units, organized in sequences.

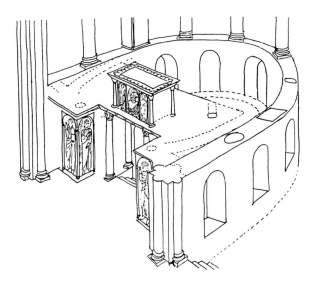

15. Toulouse, Saint-Sernin, reconstruction of the high altar.

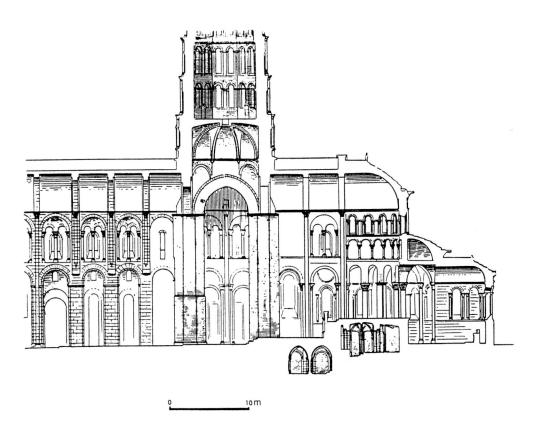

0   10 m

16. Toulouse, Saint-Sernin, section of chevet.

17. Toulouse, Saint-Sernin, interior of nave, looking east.

18. Toulouse, Saint-Sernin, inner side-aisle. The piers have pilaster strips around a square core, as at Cardona, but here they are part of a grander and more complex structure.

19. Toulouse, Saint-Sernin, outer side-aisle.

In the transept and western extension of Saint-Sernin, where the spatial problems were less complex, the builders again took special care to delineate the boundaries between modules and to organize them as sequences of units (Figures 17, 18, and 19). Some of the means by which they achieved this effect had precedent in the east end. For example, the use of half-columns, now mounted on pilaster strips, supporting the transverse arches against the peripheral wall continued the pattern established in the ambulatory and altar area, and, as in the east end, the edges of modules are accented by the shape of the piers: to someone looking down the nave or aisles, the flat surfaces of the piers set at right angles to the flow of space stop the eye at the beginning of each module before allowing one to see the sequence. The use of these elements leaves no doubt that the builders intended for the viewer to read the aisles, nave, and transept as sequences of identical additive units, a purpose that guided many of the specific aesthetic decisions made in the course of construction. Indeed, the spatial majesty of these sections lies not only in their enormous scale but in the clarity of the units moving longitudinally to form the nave space and aisles, and both laterally and vertically to form the stacked sequence that achieves the height.

This analysis of the details that articulate and organize the spaces of Saint-Sernin should not cause us to forget that this combination of particular elements was meaningful only within the context of the design strategy of the builders of Saint-Sernin. Other architectural elements or ground plans could have been used within the context of the strategy with equal effect, and, in fact, the handling of details did change as construction proceeded. The articulation of the exterior, for example, was accomplished on the chapels by half-columns and on the transept and nave by a return to heavy pilaster strips. Yet because later builders worked within the modular conceptions laid down by the first, these variations in detail did not affect the unity of the whole building. What mattered at Saint-Sernin was not the details the builders chose; it was the way they used them.

VARIATIONS

This conception of space as composed of discrete, repetitive units defined by carefully delineated boundaries and organized into additive sequences is central to late eleventh- and early twelfth-century architecture, at least north of the Alps. The situation was somewhat different in Italy, where the early Christian basilica continued to dominate church design. But the interaction between builder, craftsmen, and patrons in the process of construction meant the conception could be expressed in a variety of ways. Each builder would have his own traditions within which he was trained or with which he was familiar, and he would naturally approach any new project from the perspective of this experience. Yet a builder, if he traveled any distance, would probably have traveled alone or with a very small crew. Many, probably most, of the craftsmen on a site would have been local artisans, familiar with regional styles of sculpture and masonry, as well as locally available materials. Faced with the choice of retraining their workers or finding ways to incorporate into their designs the techniques and regional practices that the workers knew, most builders probably chose the latter course. As a result, building and artisanal styles of two regions are frequently revealed in the same building.

To the interaction between modular building strategies and regional building practices one must also add variations in earlier local traditions and the needs or ambitions of patrons. In effect, we can usually distinguish three or four levels of thinking operating simultaneously in any Romanesque building. There will be the old—the preceding buildings on the site—together with the new; the changes in building techniques and constructional sources—stone vaulting, for example—that were not available to earlier builders; and, finally, the programmatic requirements of the patrons. These requirements certainly encompass architecture, for the building creates the spatial framework around the liturgy, but also specific iconographic references. In the case of Toulouse, the choice of the ground plan was meant to connect the Apostle of Languedoc to the best-known Apostle's shrine, Old St. Peter's in Rome.

The church of Saint-Etienne of Caen, built in the late eleventh century for William the Conqueror, can serve as another example of the interplay between all these different factors (Figure 20).[14] To begin with, the enormity of the scale at Caen must be understood as a reflection of the royal, indeed imperial aspirations of an important secular patron. The most obvious regional characteristic at Saint-Etienne is the degree of structural articulation and visual logic expressed so clearly in the architectural elements: the units are larger, for example, and the decoration stands more prominently away from the wall. Other, more specific details, are also based on regional techniques, although even where regional precedents existed the builder did not so much copy his exemplars as rework the details into an original design. The double

14. Allowance, of course, must be made for alterations to the eleventh-century design, including the addition of rib-vaults to the main vessel in the twelfth century, reconstruction of the chevet in the thirteenth, and replacement of the aisle groin-vaults in the sixteenth century. See E. G. Carlson, "A Charter for Saint-Etienne, Caen," *Gesta* 25 (1986): 61–68; Carlson, "The Abbey Church of Saint-Etienne at Caen in the Eleventh and Early Twelfth Centuries" (Ph.D. diss., Yale University, 1968); and E. Lambert, "Caen romane et gothique," *Bulletin de la Société des Antiquaires de Normandie* 43 (1935): 5–70.

20. Caen, Saint-Etienne, interior of the nave. The space was conceived in terms of modules defined by single bays. The double bays result from the later addition of vaults.

1070

bays are almost square, with identical compound piers, but we find expression of these big square bays only in the alteration of simple half-columns and half-columns set in front of pilaster strips on the upper wall.[15] The Norman elevation of three nearly equal stories consisted of groin-vaulted aisles, galleries at the second story covered with half-barrel vaults and, at the third story, clerestory windows behind a wall-passage with later rib-vaults. Although the impression given to a viewer in the nave is similar to other, earlier Norman churches, the upper nave wall is structurally very different, being in fact two separate walls with a tall slot of passage space

between them.[16] Still, the additive quality of the series of units that make up each major part of Saint-Etienne, aisles, galleries, and so forth, and the bold rhythmic cadence created by the architectural ornament are generally characteristic of Romanesque architecture.

Another example of "regional" Romanesque is provided by the nave of la Madeleine at Vézelay.[17] Vézelay is usually said to be Burgundian, and indeed many of the basic elements employed at Vézelay are found in other local churches. For example, the nave of Vézelay has details similar to those at Avallon, Saulieu, Autun, and even Cluny III. The nave of Vézelay is a broad, low, and long structure that is characterized by a two-story elevation, consisting of compound piers with elaborate historiated capitals and, above them, single clerestory windows (Figure 21). The proportions of the square aisle bays, plus their relatively low height, contribute to the feeling of lateral expansion. The rich decorative vocabulary that articulates the piers, the windows, and the walls is found in a series of nearby buildings, none of them quite as richly ornamented as the mountaintop pilgrimage sanctuary. To categorize Vézelay as "Burgundian" Romanesque, as if the builder had simply worked a few variations on an existing type or scheme, seriously misstates the relationship between the buildings and prevents us from asking questions that illuminate the process by which these buildings were constructed. The presence of "Burgundian" elements do not make Vézelay a specific copy of any other building.

The last example takes us to Perigueux, to the unusual domed church of Saint-Front, now the cathedral.[18] The use of domes is not entirely anomalous (Figures 22, 23). San Marco in Venice is domed, obviously under

15. These general ideas can be seen at, for example, Jumièges. However, there the effect of double bays was achieved by alternating columns and compound piers and by powerful diaphragm arches that created a rhythm in the space while carrying the roof.

16. J. Bony, "La Technique normande du 'mur épais' à l'époque romane," *Bulletin monumental* 98 (1939): 153–88.

17. F. Salet, *La Madeleine de Vézelay* (Melun, 1948).

18. Marcel Aubert, "Eglise Saint-Front," *Congrès archéologique (Périgueux)* 90 (1927): 45–65; Musée d'Angoulême, *Paul Abadie, architecte, 1812–1884*, ed. Claude Laroche et al. (Angoulême, 1984), 87–101; Canon J. Roux, *La Basilique Saint-Front de Périgueux* (Périgueux, 1920); Jean Secret, *Saint-Front* (La Pierre-qui-Vire, 1970).

21. Vézelay, la Madeleine, interior of the nave. The prominent moldings and contrasting colors articulate the wall and the spatial units of the nave.

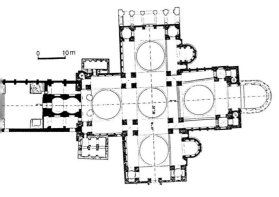

22. Perigueux, Saint-Front, plan.

23. Perigueux, Saint-Front, interior of the nave. The giant spatial modules of Perigueux's domes are delineated by the wall surfaces and the four great supporting piers.

the influence of Middle Byzantine churches in Constantinople, although the immediate inspiration of Saint-Front was not San Marco but the earlier domed cathedral of Saint-Etienne in Perigueux itself. But the point worth noticing about Perigueux is that even though domes were aesthetically and structurally quite different from vaults, the builder's underlying conception was nonetheless as modular as at Saint-Sernin, Vézelay, and countless other Romanesque examples. As in other buildings, the builder at Perigueux took great care to delineate the edges of the spatial modules with decorative elements, and although the actual domed modules differ in appearance from the smaller vaulted modules that were more common, the overall impression is that the internal volume consists of identical additive units, now on the giant scale necessary to accommodate the domes.

In general, the concept of "regional" Romanesque architecture has been the creation, not of the builders, but of art and architectural historians seeking to organize an unwieldy body of information through the cataloguing of details. But whatever the particular details, the key to understanding Romanesque architecture is the basic organizing scheme that transcends regional variation and was in general use among all the master builders of the late eleventh and early twelfth centuries. Although the builders of Saint-Sernin, Saint-Etienne, Vézelay, and Perigueux freely borrowed and combined features they encountered elsewhere, they did so in the service of their own designs. Their shared organizing principle was based on repeating spatial modules assembled in additive sequences. The emphasis on the regional nature of Romanesque architecture, therefore, has obscured rather than illuminated our understanding of the common conceptual basis used by the builders during this crucial period in the history of medieval architecture.

ROMANESQUE SCULPTURE

Growing directly out of the modular approach to building is the development of Romanesque sculpture. Sculptors did not have an entirely free hand. The builders decided how many capitals were needed, for example, and what size they would be. But within those rather general requirements, almost any subject or style of sculpture would serve the general purpose of marking edges of spatial modules, giving the sculptors considerable freedom. They responded by producing the sculpture that in its variety and imagination is one of the glories of late eleventh- and early twelfth-century art.

Romanesque sculpture is usually divided into two categories: the figure sculpture in tympana and other prominent areas associated with entrances, and the interior architectural sculpture including both capitals and the carvings that embellished liturgical areas. But the differences between the types of sculpture do not necessarily coincide with a division of labor among sculptors, and many carving techniques were common to both. Perhaps the most striking way of demonstrating these parallels is to examine one building in which the same artist was responsible for both: Saint-Lazare in Autun.[19] The inscription at the feet of Christ in the tympanum gives us the name of the sculptor: Gislebertus. In his work, moreover, we can see a stylistic unity reflected not only in his figures but in the sense of abstract composition that emphasized architectural limits both by following and by straining against them.

The figure sculpture in the tympanum and other prominent areas of display around the west facade entrance provides an example of this interaction with the architectural limits (Figure 24). In the tympanum of the Last Judgment, the figures surrounding Christ—the crowding, teeming demons on one side

and the Apostles and saved souls on the other—define the semicircle by filling nearly all of the available space, even to the extent of touching the edges. In contrast to these dramatic events, the ethereal and serene figure of Christ dominates the composition by its relative openness and size. This contrast creates a sense of tension between the sculptures, with their agitated, linear surfaces, and the strict geometrical limits imposed by the architectural context. The same tension, moreover, appears in the individual roundels of the arches framing the Last Judgment. In the representation of the labors for April, for example, (Figure 25) the head of the human figure, his feet, the feet of the animals, and a branch overlap the frame, as do the feet of Taurus (Figure 26) in the adjoining roundel. Similarly, in the representation of September, the head of the figure crushing grapes, the vat in which he appears to be squatting, and the vines themselves all touch or overlap the edge. In addition, all of these scenes are positioned so that the viewer can easily read them and still see their relationship to the tympanum. All of these scenes fit within a general abstract framework that dictates that every possible area be used and that the sculpture always reflect a sense of dynamic tension reacting to the precisely defined architectural limits.

An attentive analysis of the capitals Gislebertus carved for the interior (Figure 27) reveals how the same concerns governed his solutions to the problem of accomplishing the visual transition that is the primary function of any capital—in this case from the lower pilaster strips on which the capitals rest to the wider abacus blocks they support. The variety of individual decorative and figural or historiated capitals is, in fact, directly attributable to the quest for a solution or series of solutions to this problem. Like the majority of his contemporaries, Gislebertus conceived the capital in two, sometime three, horizontal zones with primary accents in the center along the vertical axis and at the two upper corners. Secondary accents occur at the sides near or at the bottom of the capital and at the center of the top of the capital, occasionally spilling onto the abacus block (Figure 28). The strong

19. Denis Grivot and George Zarnecki, *Gislebertus, Sculptor of Autun*, 2d ed. (New York, 1961); Willibald Sauerländer, "Gislebertus von Autun," *Festschrift Theodor Müller: Studien zur Geschichte der europäischen Plastik* (Munich, 1965), 17–29; and Otto Karl Werckmeister, "Die Auferstehung der Toten am Westportal von St. Lazare in Autun," *Frühmittelalterliche Studien* 4 (1982): 208–36.

24. Autun, Saint-Lazare, tympanum of the west portal.

25. Autun, Saint-Lazare, west portal archivolt roundel, April.

26. Autun, Saint-Lazare, west portal archivolt roundel, Taurus.

27. Autun, Saint-Lazare, nave.

central vetical axis underscores the symmetry of the compositions, while the arrangement of the decoration around the lower edges emphasizes the transition to the main face and, hence, to the central axis. This basic organizational schema was derived from classical Corinthian capitals through the intermediary of late Roman examples, such as those still visible on the gates of Autun. The schema was abstracted to emphasize the flattened format of pilaster capitals, although the transition from the edges to the front of the capital is a reminder of the older, rounder format. The center of the main face can be viewed as a positive area with the most prominent elements of decoration or as an area approached and framed by ornament leaving the central axis in shadow for dramatic visual appeal.

The five foliate capitals reproduced in Figures 29 to 33 illustrate some of the diversity of which this general scheme was capable. At first glance, the capitals depicted in Figure 29 and 30 seem quite different in design, one with leaves on the edges and sides and the other with a coiled, vinelike foliage on the face of the capital. But compositionally, they follow the same basic pattern, with emphasis arrayed in zones from bottom to top, with the upper, lower, and side edges of the capital clearly delineated. Part of this effect, too, results from deep undercarving to highlight contrasts between light and shadow, especially in the capitals where the basic design is farthest from the classical Corinthian. Variations in the same basic design can be seen on capitals in which empty spaces replace foliage as important elements of visual emphasis.

A similar conception governed the layout of the figural capitals. For example, on the capital identified by Grivot and Zarnecki as the Dream of Nebuchadnezzar (Figure 34), a superbly asymmetrical tree and two human figures serve to mark out the zones, whereas in the hieratically arranged capital showing the Suicide of Judas (Figure 35), the paired demons of the lower zone match the curving foliage buds in the upper corners and the suspended body of Judas lies along the center axis. Even the historiated, narrative capitals have compositions adjusted to conform to this abstract formula. The Flight into Egypt (Figure 36) has a clear horizontal directionality provided by Joseph along the right edge. Mary holding the Christ Child forms the central vertical axis, which is further emphasized by the frontality of Christ. Crisply carved foliage buds accent the upper left corner, and the bottom edge is marked by a series of circular designs. A final, interesting example is provided by the capital of the Stoning of Stephen (Figure 39), in which the sheer number of participants renders unnecessary more than a few spiraling foliage tendrils that suggest setting and emphasize the figure of the protomartyr. The judge and executioners spill around the narrow sides of the capitals and form a series of parentheses that frame the figure of Stephen. The heads and raised arms accent the upper corners just as the seated figure of Stephen forms the center axis in the middle and lower zones.

Most sculptors were not as inventive as Gislebertus. Indeed, it was part of his genius that he was able to create such a range and variety of designs for the capitals, all the while carefully emphasizing the role of the capital in its architectural context, that of transition, and compositionally marking the edges or limits of the form. But that does not alter the main point that it was the emphasis of Romanesque on establishing the boundaries between modules that provided the opportunity for sculptors to experiment. The abstract sense of how the design should accomplish the transition is limited to a few possibilities; yet the actual working out of the solution within the framework produces the myriad of variations that, perhaps better than any other single feature, distinguishes Romanesque sculpture and architecture.

Some have suggested that, in addition to being the principal sculptor of Autun, Gislebertus was also the builder in charge of the whole project. Support for this view can be found in the significant alterations to the architectural design that coincided with his arrival on the site and in his presence at the worksite for nearly the entire remaining period of construction. This was a far longer time than would have been needed to complete the carving of the capitals—which

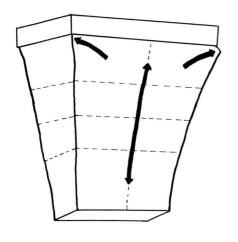

28 to 33. Autun, Saint-Lazare, schematic diagram of the capital structure and five foliage capitals. Whether they have two or three zones, the foliate capitals all reveal the abstract schema of organization.

34 to 39. Autun, Saint-Lazare. Six historiated capitals. The historiated capitals all make visual reference to the schema of organization but alter it to suit the scene and the subject.

34. Dream of Nebuchadnezzar.　　35. Suicide of Judas.

36. Flight into Egypt.　　37. Dream of the Magi.

38. Fall of Simon Magus.　　39. Stoning of Stephen.

might have required as little as a few days each—and he could easily have devoted a substantial portion of his time to supervising the masons' work. Yet no less significant is Gislebertus's ability, as witnessed by his capitals, to conceptualize three-dimensional forms prior to executing them. Not only was his ability in this regard significantly superior to other early twelfth-century sculptors, but the same mental capacity, applied to architectural space rather than sculpture, was to make the builder of Saint-Denis the most original architect of the twelfth. In this sense, Gislebertus stands in the same relationship to the builder of Saint-Denis as the masters of the early twelfth century do to Abelard.

Compared with the attention that has been directed to Romanesque architecture, the work of eleventh-century schoolmasters has been given relatively little notice. This is not surprising. Under the best of circumstances, architecture can be more immediately appreciated than philosophy or grammar, and the brief eleventh-century glosses that survive provide even historians of ideas little to work with. Yet viewed from the perspective of the history of disciplines, the development in eleventh-century architecture and learning are surprisingly similar. In both cases, one can trace the growing professional distinctiveness of a group of specialists sharing certain approaches to their work—a distinctiveness, moreover, that also found expression in the steadily increasing technical competence displayed in their productions. About the importance of the achievements of eleventh-century builders and masters, it is enough to observe that no one would mistake a building or treatise from 1120 with one even forty years before. Even greater achievements of the Middle Ages lay ahead, but the decisive break with the past had already been made.

PART II

FOUR CRUCIAL DECADES

St. Denis, Abbey Church started 1140

4 · Transformations: Abelard and Saint-Denis

From being craftsmen who took the learning and styles of the past and adapted them to contemporary use, builders and masters had by 1100 transformed themselves into self-aware and consciously innovating members of disciplines. But the 1130s saw a quantum leap in the level of intellectual sophistication required of masters and builders as they shifted their attention from solving individual issues to constructing whole systems of solutions to intellectual and aesthetic problems. Masters moved from dealing with isolated texts that could be glossed or *quaestiones* for which definite answers could be proposed to constructing systems of thought in which the effects of an answer to one issue impinged upon the answer to other equally complex issues. The cognitive processes required for this kind of work had their counterpart in those employed by builders who, now endeavoring to devise increasingly complex and integrated spaces, found themselves having to design small details with an eye to the effects each decision would have on the whole. The results, in each case, were works that departed from previous standards while setting challenges that would engage the attention of successive generations until the end of the twelfth century.

We will examine the changes in learning through Peter Abelard's works on logic and ethics, though other works of his or of his contemporaries such as Gilbert of Poitiers could have served equally well. But there is nothing arbitrary about our choice of an example for architecture. The new east end of Saint-Denis, executed on the commission of Abbot Suger, has no equals in the 1130s and was not (as we shall see in the next chapter) rivaled until the 1150s.

ABELARD AND THE EARLY PARISIAN SCHOOLS

In the early 1130s, when Abelard returned to Paris from his self-imposed exile in Brittany, he joined an intellectual community unlike any that had previously existed in medieval

Europe. Until the rise of Paris as an educational center, the typical form of schooling had been for one master to lecture to his students under the auspices of a cathedral and usually at some distance from the nearest rival master. Anselm and Ralph of Laon, two brothers, typify this kind of master, as do William of Champeaux at Paris and Bernard of Chartres. Abelard himself had been educated in schools like this, and until the 1130s his own school, however innovative in the content of instruction, had conformed to this model. In the 1130s, the masters' isolation from each other was ended by the development of a unique concentration of scholars and schools in Paris, where food and lodgings were abundant and where licences to teach were easy to come by. By 1140 there were perhaps fifteen masters with schools in Paris, including (in addition to Abelard himself) such luminaries as Thierry of Chartres and Gilbert of Poitiers.[1]

This concentration of scholars did not end resistance to the new forms of learning. Monks, especially, continued to express their opposition: in the 1140s, Bernard of Clairvaux targeted both Abelard and Gilbert. But it did mean that, for perhaps the first time, the immediate audience for new ideas was composed of people who were themselves experts and masters, and whose receptivity to the process of inquiry could be taken for granted. Doubtless, too, the situation encouraged a spirit of rivalry among the masters, who competed for reputation and students and who, in such close quarters, could hardly fail to have a detailed knowledge of each other's work. This combination of factors made Paris an ideal environment for work of the highest quality, and Abelard responded to the challenge by producing a series of original and ambitious treatises.

We can begin with the works on logic, the queen of sciences in the early twelfth century and the original source of Abelard's fame. We have already seen the origins of the interest in logic in the collapse of argument from author-

ity that occurred in the mid-eleventh century. Then the study of logic had seemed a means by which scholars might discover what truths were demonstrable to the satisfaction of all comers—a phenomenon that has its parallels in the analytical philosophy of the early decades of this century. By 1100, logical studies had grown technical and exact, with scholars debating questions specific to logic instead of using logic (as, for example, St. Anselm had), principally as a means to religious truths.

Chief among the issues that dominated the early twelfth-century schools was the question of universals. This question, handed down to the Middle Ages by Boethius in his account of a famous dispute between Plato and Aristotle, concerns words that can be predicated of, or used to refer to, more than one thing. One such universal is the noun "man," which can be used together with the name of any human to form such sentences as

Socrates is a man.

Plato is a man.

In these sentences, the names *Socrates* and *Plato* are of unambiguous meaning for they clearly designate specific individuals. But it is by no means obvious what the word *man* refers to. Is there a thing called *man* and, if so, is that thing something which is present in all individual men or does it have an existence independent of them? At this point the logical issue, defining the property of words like *man*, tends to blur into a metaphysical one. Plato, for example, was led to enunciate his theory of ideas or forms in order to defend the position that universals refer to things distinct from tangible objects.

Writing in the sixth century, Boethius summarized the disputes of Plato, Aristotle, and their followers in these terms:

Everything that the mind thinks of either is an item built into the nature of things, which it conceives by an idea and describes for itself by a definition, or is an item that does not exist and which it depicts for itself by an empty imagination. Thus we ask about the ideas of genera and the like whether we think of species and genera in the way we think of items which exist and of which we grasp true ideas, or whether we delude ourselves by forming for ourselves with invalid imaginings items which do not exist.[2]

So the matter stood until the late eleventh

---

1. For an elegant account of the rise of Paris, see R. W. Southern, "The Schools of Paris and the School of Chartres," in *Renaissance/Renewal*, 113–37.
2. *PL* 64: 82. The translation is by Martin Tweedale.

century when, with the generation of Abelard's teachers, the revival of interest in logic made universals once again a live issue. The terms of debate had changed in important ways since classical times, when it had been generally assumed that universals must refer to some existing thing, and many eleventh-century masters were prepared to argue the contrary. Roscelin, for example, one of Abelard's masters, became famous for the opinion that universals were "mere breath" (*flatus vocis*)—the sound produced by the larynx. But this position, although defensible if one looked for evidence that there existed actual things to which words like *man* referred, left unexplained the incontestable fact that sentences such as "Socrates is a man" conveyed meaning to the listener. Other masters, therefore, including William of Champeaux, were led to the position that a universal term refers to a material essence shared among the various individuals of the genus or species described by the universal.[3]

For both Roscelin and William, the nature of universals had been a *quaestio*. They accepted the formulation of the question pretty much as it came to them from Boethius, and they devised answers to the question without attempting to see their answers in relationship to their positions on other issues. Abelard, however, characteristically shifted the grounds of discussion to a plane where the role of universals was considered part of a general logical theory.[4] Instead of treating the *quaestio* of whether universals had an existence independent of the mind as an independent problem, Abelard conceived of it as impinging upon (and being itself influenced by) the answers one proposed to problems, such as what meaning is conveyed by the verb *to be* and what is the nature of mental entities.

Put another way, instead of trying to explain what *man* referred to in sentences such as "Socrates is a man," Abelard saw the objective as understanding how the whole sentence, or indeed any possible sentence, conveyed meaning. Because he perceived these issues as all interrelated, when in the course of his career he modified his position on one he often had to adapt other positions as well, setting for himself and his audience the standard of treating logical theory as a structured whole.

Tracing Abelard's theory of language would be a vast project, requiring a book far longer than this one. But we can grasp the mental work that made his theory different from that of his masters by focusing on the evolution of his position on universals over the twenty years or so covered by his surviving works on logic. His earliest statement, probably from around 1120, treated universals as vocal utterances (*voces*). At first glance, this position is reminiscent of Roscelin. But Abelard had in mind not specific sounds but meanings or significations, for, as he explained immediately upon offering his definition, one word of variable meaning could stand for two or more universals, whereas two distinct words or phrases that have the same meaning might represent one universal. Universals, then, are meanings or significations, not words or strings of words.

By distinguishing meaning from grammatical structure, Abelard had already broken with the tradition in which universals had been treated before. He then defended his position, and added complications, by insisting that the ideas represented by universals are not simply sensory images of external reality. As Abelard observed, we understand the meaning of the proposition,

---

3. For a summary of the eleventh- and twelfth-century discussion of universals, see Martin M. Tweedale, *Abailard on Universals* (Amsterdam, 1976), 91–140, and Norman Kretzman, "The Culmination of the Old Logic in Peter Abelard," in *Renaissance/Renewal*, 488–511; a basic introduction can be found in D. Knowles, *The Evolution of Medieval Thought* (New York, 1964), 107–16. In our treatment, we have avoided the terms *nominalist* and *realist*, usually applied to Roscelin and William respectively, because these terms date from a later, fourteenth-century, controversy that really centered on different problems.

For a suggestion about the reason the twelfth-century debate on universals centered on different issues than in classical times, see C. M. Radding, *A World Made by Men* (Chapel Hill, 1985), 207–9.

4. Abelard's extensive logical works include (in rough chronological order): *Logica "Ingredientibus"* and *Logica "Nostrorum petitioni sociorum,"* both ed. by Bernhard Geyer, Beiträge zur Geschichte der Philosophie und Theologie des Mittelalters, vol. 21, nos. 1–4 (Münster 1919–1921, 1933), and the *Dialectica*, ed. L. M. de Rijk, 2d ed. (Assen, 1970).

A man is sitting in this house.
even though only Socrates sits there, but (since he is not mentioned by the words of the proposition) we have no mental image of him. (See Text 7.) The idea conveyed by the word *man* is, therefore, not an idea of any physical thing, a condition that Abelard argued is true of mental images in general. One can have an image of a four-sided tower that is not itself four-sided, that can exist when the tower has ceased to exist, or even if the tower has never existed. Abelard's point was that mental images (including universals) exist even though they are not to be understood as things, that the universals subsist even when they are bare ideas, thus staking out a third position that Boethius had thought impossible.[5]

One need not be able to follow the technical details of Abelard's reasoning to see that, even in his earliest work on logic, he was not only aware of the interrelationship of a number of different philosophical problems but was also trying to coordinate his positions on those issues so that they mutually reinforce each other. The summary in Text 7, for example, is not the creation of the historian, assembling ideas scattered throughout several chapters or books, but is drawn from one five-page section at the beginning of the first gloss in the *Logica "Ingredientibus"*. Abelard's efforts to establish a systematic approach to logic became still more apparent when, in later works, he altered some of the elements of his earlier theory. Instead of leaving the other elements intact, he reworked his analysis of them as well so that the interrelationships between the doctrines was preserved.

The weak point seems to have been Abelard's position on the significance of the verb in propositions where the particular is joined to the universal by the verb *to be*. Abelard himself illustrated this kind of proposition by the following sentence:
Socrates is white.
When Abelard first discussed this question

in a later section of the *Logica "Ingredientibus,"* he argued that *is* in such sentences has two meanings: that Socrates exists and that *Socrates* and *white* are alike in essence, that is, that *Socrates* and *white thing* are interchangeable terms. Already in the *Logica "Ingredientibus"* it is possible to see the problems in this position, for Abelard went on to discuss the proposition "A chimera is a non-man."[6] The proposition is clearly true, but since chimeras do not exist, *is* in the proposition cannot be asserting their existence.

Abelard initially avoided the difficulty by asserting that the verb *to be* in such propositions has a different meaning than in other propositions: it is to be interpreted as naming, as in statements like "A chimera is thinkable." In later works, however, he adopted the more radical solution of arguing that in every sentence the words in the predicate must be interpreted as a unit, and indeed that every predicate has to be interpreted in light of the subject. The advantage of this approach, as he showed in elaborate detail, is to render comparable sentences whose grammatical structure is different. "Socrates is running," for example, becomes the equivalent of "Socrates runs." It also becomes possible to test the validity of propositions that differ from a true statement only in tense. Similar considerations led logicians early in this century to a position very like Abelard's in its handling of predicates and propositions.

For our purposes, however, the important feature of Abelard's revised theory of predication is that it meant, as Abelard himself knew, that his original definition of a universal as an utterance could not stand. Indeed, since words were liable to change meanings subtly depending on the sentence, the whole problem of universals became far less central than they had seemed to Abelard's masters. Abelard therefore reworked his definition to point directly to the *sermo*, the expression that by the conventions of language was suitable for use as a universal whether or not it was actually uttered and whether or not there truly existed any actual things describable by

---

5. *Logica "Ingredientibus,"* 16–21. Tweedale observes (*Abailard on Universals*, 173) that Abelard's analysis of mental images "is extraordinary and has, so far as I know, no precedents in the history of western philosophy."

6. *Logica "Ingredientibus,"* 361.

About these universals some questions have been raised because there are problems especially as to their signification, since they do not seem to have any subject thing nor to establish any valid idea. There do not seem to be things to which universal nouns are applied, since all things subsist distinctly in themselves and do not agree, as we showed, in any thing which would serve as that in virtue of which universal nouns are applied. . . .

For since "man" is applied to singulars on account of one and the same cause, viz. that they are mortal rational animals, this commonness of its application prevents anyone from understanding it like the noun "Socrates" which is understood to be of just one person and thus is said to be singular. In a common noun like "man" neither Socrates nor some other man nor the whole collection of men is rationally understood via the force of the utterance. Nor is Socrates, even in so far as he is a man, indicated by this noun, as some want to say. For even if Socrates alone were sitting in this house and for him alone this proposition were true:

A man is sitting in this house.
still in no way does the proposition mention Socrates by the subject noun "man" not even in so far as he is a man; for otherwise we could reasonably gather from the proposition that sitting belonged to him, and we could infer from this fact that a man is sitting in this house that Socrates is sitting in it. Likewise, no other man can be understood through this noun "man," and neither can the whole collection of men, since the proposition is true of only one. Thus it seems that neither "man" nor any other universal word signifies anything, since it establishes an idea of no thing. And neither does it seem that there can be an idea which does not have a subject thing which it grasps. Thus Boethius in his Commentary says: "Every idea is made from a subject thing either as the subject thing itself is or as it is not. An idea cannot be made from no subject thing." Therefore, universals seem to be totally divorced from signification [trans. Tweedale, *Abelard on Universals*, 162–63].

Text 7. An excerpt from Abelard's *Logica "Ingredientibus"*. Abelard shows that, if universals do not refer to ideas, they do not refer to anything at all.

that expression. He explicity rejected his own previous position, that both *sermones* and *voces* were universals, refuting it in several pages of careful argument and counterargument.[7]

What one can see in Abelard's logical works is a conception of philosophy that regarded specific questions, not as ends in themselves, but as interrelated parts of intellectual systems. The same attitude can be seen, perhaps with greater clarity, in his *Ethics*. This work, which dates from Abelard's last years in Paris, takes as its central thesis the idea that the

measure of morality is intention rather than action. This position is not as obvious as it may seem. In the early Middle Ages there had been little concern with intention or psychological states in any context, with the result that layperson and cleric alike tended to conceive of morality as external behavior that conformed to a rule. This tendency is most marked in moral codes of the widest circulation, for instance, Germanic law and Christian penentitials, but it was not confined to the illiterate or poorly educated. Even men such as Gregory the Great and Peter Damian, who greatly surpassed their contemporaries in their interest in interior life, regarded internal

7. *Logica "Nostrorum petitioni sociorum,"* 522–24.

obedience as a heightening of good actions rather than a primary good itself.[8]

The heightened concern with intention, apparent by the middle of the eleventh century in the new attitudes masters brought to ancient authorities, was by 1100 finding a variety of cultural and social expressions. The most conspicuous, perhaps, was the surge of interest in an intense spiritual life that fueled the sudden prominence of Cîteaux and the other new religious orders of the century. But the scholars also shared in this trend, and ethical problems are prominent among the glosses and *quaestiones* of the period.

The character of these early approaches toward an ethics based on intention may be illustrated by the *sententiae* attributed to another of Abelard's teachers, Anselm of Laon. As with most works of this genre, Anselm's *sententiae* are invariably short; rarely do they fill a printed page, and many are only a sentence or two in length. One of the longer and more theoretical is the following, in which Anselm strives for a definition of virtue and vice:

Virtue is the habit of a well-ordered mind, and vice is the habit of a badly ordered mind. It is asked whether it is possible to be both at once. . . . If one loves God, and loves virtue, even if one falls in with something criminal, either from the custom of sinning or the fragility of the flesh, and yet grieves for what he has done and prays and gives alms that God thus absolve him, then he retains the root of charity and does not cease to be just. . . . But it is otherwise for one who is obstinate in some evil . . . for he does not act out of the root of charity. Any good works he does out of natural piety or habit will never be vivifying.[9]

Others deal with specific practical situations—whether, for example, one can engage in commerce without sin, or in what situation one can lie without fault.[10] But nearly everywhere, Anselm's awareness of the moral significance of psychological states is unmistak-

able, and his concerns were shared by other, anonymous *sententiae* of the period.

Abelard did not, therefore, invent or rediscover the interior and psychological dimensions of ethics. Yet it is nevertheless true that to move from these glosses to Abelard's *Ethics* is to pass from a mentality centered on cases to one that treated cases only in relationship to a systematically articulated theoretical structure. The difference in outlook is apparent from the first paragraphs of the *Ethics*. It begins:

We consider morals to be the vices or virtues of the mind which make us prone to bad or good works. However, there are vices or good things not only of the mind but also of the body, such as bodily weakness or the fortitude we call strength, sluggishness or swiftness, . . . Hence to distinguish these, when we said "vices" we added "of the mind." . . . There are also, however, some vices or good things of the mind which are separate from morals and do not make human life worthy of praise or blame, such as dullness of mind or quickness of thinking, forgetfulness or a good memory, ignorance or learning. . . . Hence rightly when above we presented "vices of the mind" we added, in order to exclude such things, "which make us prone to bad works," that is, incline the will to something which is not fitting to be done . . .[11]

The clarity of definition, as compared to Anselm's "habit of the mind," is noteworthy and no less than one would expect from a master logician. But Abelard was doing more in this passage than defining his terms. He was also introducing a psychology specific enough and subtle enough to bear the analytical weight of the rest of the treatise. The passage excerpted above thus leads directly to the further distinction that vice itself (for example, the irascibility that makes us prone to anger) is not itself sin but only that which "inclines the mind . . . to do something which is not at all suitable." It is only this consent to vice that "we properly call sin."[12] Later in the

---

8. For details, see Radding, *World Made by Men.*

9. Odon Lottin, *Psychologie et morale aux XIIe et XIIIe siècles* (Louvain and Gembloux, 1959) 5:no. 68, p. 59. However, many of the sentences Lottin attributed to the school of Laon in the same volume in fact seem to represent the views of scholars from many other places as well, including perhaps monks not associated with the schools at all. For details, cf. Valerie I. Flint, "The 'School of Laon,'"

RTAM (1976): 89–110. See also Marcia Colish, "Another Look at the School of Laon," *Archives d'histoire doctrinale et littéraire du Moyen Age* (1986): 7–22.

10. Lottin, no. 14, p. 24, and no. 66, pp. 57–58.

11. Abelard, *Ethics*, ed. and trans. D. E. Luscombe (Oxford, 1971), 1.

12. Abelard, *Ethics*, 1, 2.

treatise, Abelard tied penance into the same conception, arguing that since sin is contempt of God expressed by inner consent rather than by deeds, penance must be similarly internal, taking the form not of confession but of contrition.

Having a clearly articulated psychological theory did more than add precision to Abelard's doctrine. It also enabled him to treat cases, not as isolated *quaestiones* as Anselm of Laon had done, but as applications of his general thesis. To illustrate the difference between willing and doing, for example, he invited his readers to consider an innocent man pursued by his lord, who means to kill him; the man flees as far as he can until, cornered and without other resort, he kills in self-defense. The fact that the man, at the end, acted intentionally Abelard did not deny, arguing instead that the will was not to kill his lord but to save his own life.[13] Similarly, to distinguish between the willed sin and the act that results, he remarked that "it often happens that when we want to lie with a woman whom we know to be married . . . we by no means want to be adulterous with her—we would prefer that she was unmarried." And to argue that sexual pleasure itself is not sinful, he invited us to consider the case of a monk, bound in chains on a bed with a woman on each side, and so brought to pleasure but not to consent. "Who may presume to call this pleasure, made necessary by nature, a fault?"[14]

As they are used in the final text of the *Ethics*, such cases both prove and illustrate Abelard's general thesis. Yet they are interesting in another way, as evidence of the reasoning he doubtlessly followed in the course of working out his theory. Abelard's psychology was not simply borrowed from someone else. St. Augustine, for example, had argued that

sin lay in the will alone. In determining which distinctions needed to be made, Abelard doubtless worked back and forth between theory and cases, testing one against the other until he had established the principles that could support the intellectual structure he was building. The mental effort involved in treating several issues at once, holding each in mind until solutions suitable to all had been found, set Abelard apart from those who had previously written on ethics as it had previously set him apart as a logician. The same kind of cognitive processes, as we shall see, went into the planning and design that set Saint-Denis apart from Romanesque styles.

SAINT-DENIS

Saint-Denis is situated less than twenty miles from the center of Paris, in what is today a working-class suburb of the capital, but in the twelfth century that distance was sufficient to insulate the monastery from the turbulent world of the Parisian schools. It is that insulation, perhaps, that led Abelard briefly to join the community after his castration in 1119, although he did not stay there long. Another attraction was surely the high status of the monastery which, already in the twelfth century, was very old and very distinguished. Founded in the seventh century by the Merovingian king Dagobert I at the chapel built by St. Genevieve to mark the burial site of Denis (Dionysius), Apostle to the Franks, Saint-Denis had over the succeeding centuries established itself as the royal abbey *par excellence* in France. Many princes received their education in the school of Saint-Denis; Charles the Bald and Hugh Capet had been its titular abbots; and over the centuries the abbey church had become the favored burial place of many French kings.

Shortly after Abelard's brief stay, Saint-Denis reached the peak of its influence under the abbacy of Suger (1081–1151). Elected abbot in 1122 when already in middle age, Suger brought to his office not only a boyhood friendship with King Louis VI and substantial adult experience as a royal emissary to Rome but a tireless energy in promoting

---

13. Abelard, *Ethics*, 6–9. The logician shows himself again in the conclusion of this discussion: "If perhaps someone says that he wanted to kill his lord for the sake of avoiding death, he cannot therefore infer that he wanted to kill him. For example, if I were to say to someone: 'I want you to have my cap for this reason, that you give me five solidi,' or 'I gladly want it to become yours at that price,' I do not therefore concede that I want it to become yours."
14. Abelard, *Ethics*, 16, 20.

both Saint-Denis and the Capetian house. The confidant of Louis VI, Suger placed the full authority of Saint-Denis behind the king. For example, when Louis faced an invasion in 1124, Suger laid out the relics of the abbey as the host gathered at Saint-Denis (they were later restored to the crypt by the king himself) and provided Louis with the Oriflamme— originally the emblem of a fief that Louis held of Saint-Denis—to use as a banner. In return, the grateful king confirmed the abbey's right to all the revenues of the Lendit, a fair held in honor of St. Denis and his companions in the evangelization of France.[15]

Suger's activities in support of his king, which lasted throughout his life, culminated in his biography of Louis VI and a tenure as regent when Louis VII (against Suger's advice) answered St. Bernard's call to the Second Crusade. But our present concern is with the substantial rebuilding of the abbey church that Suger undertook between circa 1135 and 1144. The existing building, which dated back to the eighth century (though Suger thought it was Dagobert's own building), was now too small to handle the crowds that gathered on feast days.

Often on feast days (Suger later wrote) completely filled, the church disgorged through all its doors the excess of the crowds as they moved in opposite directions, and the outward pressure of the foremost ones not only prevented those attempting to enter from entering but also expelled those who had already entered. At times one could see, a marvel to behold, that the crowded multitude offered so much resistance to those who strove to flock in to worship and kiss the holy relics, the Nail and Crown of the Lord, that no one among the countless thousands of people because of their very density could move a foot. . . . The distress of the women, however, was so great and so intolerable that you could see with horror how they, squeezed in by the mass of strong men as in a winepress, exhibited bloodless faces as in imagining death; how they cried out horribly as though in labor;

how several of them, miserably trodden underfoot [but then] lifted by the pious assistance of men above the heads of the crowd, marched forward as though upon a pavement.[16]

However gratifying such spectacles were as evidence for the esteem in which Saint-Denis was popularly held, the thought that inadequate space prevented worshippers from properly admiring the many wonders of the abbey could only have been a source of frustration to the proud abbot and community.

The initial plan for expansion provided for two additions: a new west facade joined to the eighth-century nave and a new east end where a substantially enlarged crypt would support a raised relic display platform, or feretory, surrounded by an ambulatory and radiating chapels. Both of these additions were completed under Suger's abbacy and, largely, still stand (Figure 40).[17] Originally, the transept, nave, and side-aisles between the two additions were to be retained, posing for the builders the task of harmonizing the new with the old parts of the building, though when the success of the additions was apparent, Suger decided to replace the rest of the eighth-century church as well. Preparations, in the form of foundations for the aisle walls, were begun before Suger's death, but the work was later abandoned and taken up again only in the thirteenth century.[18]

Work on the west end began circa 1135. The first builder employed by Suger and the monks constructed the ground floor of the new western block and the three portals of the facade.[19] He had perhaps worked previously in the Seine valley west of Paris, for his work at Saint-Denis was well within the Ro-

15. For details of Suger's career, see Erwin Panofsky's introduction to *Abbot Suger on the Abbey Church of St.-Denis and Its Art Treasures*, 2d ed. by Gerda Panofsky-Soergel (Princeton, 1979); Otto von Simson, *The Gothic Cathedral*, 2d ed. (Princeton, 1962), chap. 3; and the volume of papers from the 1981 symposium, *Abbot Suger and Saint-Denis*, ed. P. Gerson (New York, 1986).

16. Panofsky, *Abbot Suger*, 87–89.
17. The central section of the upper level was rebuilt on a taller scale in the thirteenth century, and the present hemicycle columns were made at that time. Some of them rest, however, on the twelfth-century base blocks, and all contain the twelfth-century abacus plates.
18. On the thirteenth-century church, see the analysis of Caroline Bruzelius, *The Thirteenth-Century Church at St.-Denis* (New Haven and London, 1986).
19. Sumner McKnight Crosby, *The Royal Abbey of Saint-Denis from Its Beginning to the Death of Suger, 475–1151*, ed. and completed by Pamela Z. Blum (New Haven and London, 1987); S. Gardner, "Two Campaigns in Suger's Western Block at St.-Denis," *Art Bulletin* 66 (1984): 574–87; J. Bony, "What Possible Sources for the Chevet of

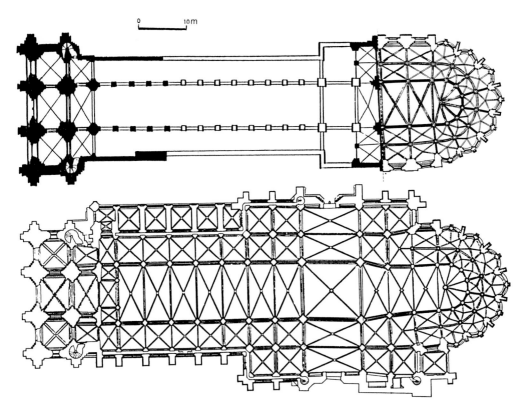

40. Saint-Denis, Abbey Church, plan of the church in Suger's time and curent plan.

manesque tradition current in Normandy and the Vexin.[20] With the second builder, however, we get something distinctly different. This builder's previous career cannot be precisely traced, though the character of his vaulting techniques suggests that he probably came from the area around Paris. He may well have come from the work site at Saint-Denis itself. But tradition and training do not account for this man's accomplishments. Wherever his work is found—in the upper levels of the facade, the upper stories of the west end, and, especially, in the crypt and feretory of the east end—this builder broke from his models by creating interconnections between separate sections to give the effect of a unified, articulated whole. This aesthetic achievement, moreover, was possible only because the

Saint-Denis," in *Abbot Suger and Saint-Denis*, ed. P. Gerson (New York, 1986), 131–43; W. Clark, "Suger's Church at Saint-Denis," in *Abbot Suger and Saint-Denis*, 105–30; J. van der Meulen and A. Speer, *Die fränkische Königsabtei Saint Denis: Ostanlage und Kulturgeschichte* (Darmstadt, 1988); C. Radding and W. Clark, "Abélard et le bâtisseur des Saint-Denis: Etudes parallèles d'histoire des disciplines," *Annales, économies, sociétés, civilisations* 43 (1988): 1263–90; R. Suckale, "Neue Literatur über die Abteikirche von Saint-Denis," *Kunstchronik* 43 (1990): 62–80;

and D. von Winterfeld, "Gedanken zu Sugers Bau in St.-Denis," *Martin Gosebruch zu Ehren* (Munich, 1984), 92–107.

20. S. Gardner, "The Influence of Castle Building on Ecclesiastical Architecture in the Paris Region, 1130–1150," in *The Medieval Castle, Romance and Reality*, ed. K. Reyerson and F. Powe, Medieval Studies at Minnesota, no. 1 (Minneapolis, 1984), 97–123; see also Jean Bony, "The Genesis of Gothic," *Australian Journal of Art* 2 (1980): 17–31; and Panofsky, *Abbot Suger*, 50–51.

builder was capable of mentally manipulating various architectural details simultaneously until he achieved a combination in which the various elements worked together successfully as an integrated design. More than any particular technical or stylistic device, what distinguishes his work from his predecessors is this ability to work back and forth between different elements.

The changes in cognition between the first two builders are apparent in their approaches to the facade (Figure 41). The first builder erected only the three portals, the strongly projecting pier buttresses between them, and the horizonal molding across the top of the central portal. The molding is revealing of the thought processes of the first builder because it is not perfectly horizontal but some 20 centimeters higher on the south side. This was not a chance error. Crosby has argued that the builder first planned the doorways using dimensions based on those taken from the eighth-century nave and transept, and then, to disguise the fact that the heights of the portals differed, accommodated the molding to the portals. He worked, in short, as the philosophical masters had worked before Abelard, taking each problem sequentially, with the solution to one defining a context to which the next had to be adapted.

This sloping molding is the only non-horizontal line on the west facade. On the upper levels of the facade, the second builder regularized the other molding lines to the horizontal even while preserving the minor dimensional discrepancies between the two lateral sections. This interest in creating a sense of visual regularity despite minor differences is an important clue to his method of thinking. Whereas the first builder worked from problem to problem, the second builder in planning his design evidently worked back and forth between the different architectural and sculptural elements until he achieved a combination that produced a logic and organization that subordinated the parts to the whole. The regularity of horizontal lines was thus for him an important part of the whole, and the effect was enhanced by the use of bands of acanthus foliage that establish the horizontal divisions and make up the elabo-

41. Saint-Denis, Abbey Church, west façade.

rate, multiple-arched framing around the window openings. The design of the facade, in fact, is articulated by this ornament, whose motifs and patterns are repeated in a manner that ties the whole scheme together. For example, the windows are single openings, but the fact that they are surrounded and then flanked by arcading means that they do not float as abstract holes punched through a surface. They are fixed in place by ornamental moldings and arcading as part of a complete system of wall articulation. The changes between the facade of Saint-Denis and those precedents with which it is often compared (for example, facades in Normandy or in the southwest of France, particularly in the Poitou and Saintonge) resulted in nothing less than the creation of the Gothic facade.

The second builder's handling of interior space was no less remarkable than his work on the facade. The problem here was not to bind together different linear elements but to find a means of bridging the modules that defined

Romanesque space in order to give the impression of a single, spacious volume. He did this, moreover, using not just one device but several, demonstrating again his ability to mentally coordinate a number of design elements.

This can be seen, for the first time at Saint-Denis, upstairs in the center chapel of the western block (Figure 42). The space was formed by two bays, following the plan already in place at ground level, but instead of emphasizing the boundaries between them, as the first builder would have done, the second master fused them. The compound piers between the two units were composed of pilaster strips with bevelled edges allowing the eye to slide around their complex polygonal shapes and to merge them with the wall surface rather than see them as supports separating the units. In the arched openings that communicate to the tower chambers, he set detached shafts in niches cut into the masonry; the shafts effectively mask surface transitions and, together with the center colonnette, create a layered effect to deemphasize thickness. The extension of the abaci into wall moldings and their linkage to the arch moldings heightens the surface linearity. In this upper chapel, the treatment of wall surfaces expressed neither the sense of heavy mass seen at ground level, nor the defining surface plasticity of such Romanesque examples as Saint-Sernin of Toulouse.

The fusion of these two vault units into a single space is the first indication of the spatial attitude that dominates the work of this unnamed master builder in the eastern end. This addition, said to have been begun in 1140 and completed for Suger and the monks in three years and three months, comprised two levels: the crypt and the upper level or feretory, where the relics of Denis and his martyred companions were to be displayed for the admiration of worshippers. In each of these levels, the builder had the problem of harmonizing the new work with the old, a desire Suger expressed several times in his writings and doubtless impressed on his builder. Suger may also have asked the builder to maximize the amount of light that entered the building, perhaps even out of respect for the theology

42. Saint-Denis, Abbey Church, upper chapel in west façade complex. The coordination of all the decorative elements in a total scheme anticipates the eastern end. The end wall was originally open into the nave of the eighth-century church.

attributed to Denis that stressed light as the link between the material and celestial worlds. But the talent of the builder evidenced in the visual logic of organization in the east end of Saint-Denis cannot have been dictated by the patron. However remarkable Abbot Suger might have been and however much he might have appreciated the church, he was not a professional builder, and only a man expert in building techniques could have conceived and executed the complex series of interrelated spatial units framed by floors, walls, and vaults found in the east end of Saint-Denis.

First to be built was the crypt, which had to be enlarged and expanded to the east in order to serve as the foundation for the upper level (Figure 43). Many aspects of the crypt, notably the seven radiating chapels, mirror the plan of the feretory. In fact, as the exterior (Figures 44 and 45) demonstrates, the number of correspondences and dependencies between the two blocks proves that the design of the entire east end was established before work began.[21] The central chamber of Hilduin's chapel, a ninth-century extension east of the eighth-century apse and caveau around

21. William W. Clark, "Suger's Church at Saint-Denis," in *Abbot Suger and Saint-Denis*, 105–30.

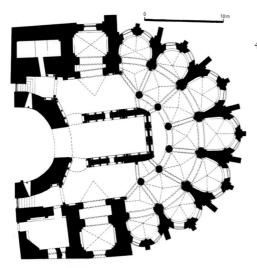

43. Saint-Denis, Abbey Church, restored plan of the crypt.

44. Saint-Denis, Abbey Church, exterior of east end. The integrated design of the exterior grid suggests the builder had the plan of the entire east end worked out in detail when he began building the additions to the crypt.

45. Saint-Denis, Abbey Church, east end, south side.

the burial site of Denis and his companions, was retained, and its walls were reinforced inside and out with blind arcading, as were the outer walls of the eighth-century apse. The barrel vault of Hilduin's chapel was apparently also reinforced, since it would form part of the platform supporting the upper level. The two lateral hall-like spaces parallel to it were decorated with new arcading and barrel-vaulted at the same height as the center chapel. Groin sections were inserted in these lateral vaults to mark the entrances to the new rectangular side chapels that precede the radiating chapels. These groin sections and the chapels that open from them soften the abruptness of the shift to the new ambula-

tory and radiating chapels added around the east end of Hilduin's crypt.

It was in the new ambulatory and chapels of the crypt that the builder faced the problem of creating a sense of inner spaciousness (Figures 46, 47, and 48). Unlike the western bays and facade, and even the central upper chapel, the builder now had to design a sequence of units of different sizes and shapes. More important, he had to establish visual continuity in the ambulatory, while keeping each of the chapels separate but accessible. The plan he devised was complex and depended, as had the facade, not on one element but on the interaction of several. One aspect of his plan involved the careful repetition of ornament, especially the

46. Saint-Denis, Abbey Church, crypt ambulatory. Although the builder used round arches and groin-vaults here in the crypt, he achieved the complete integration of architectural elements that is the most important feature of the new style we call Gothic.

47. Saint-Denis, Abbey Church, crypt ambulatory from a chapel.

48. Saint-Denis, Abbey Church, crypt chapel.

49. Saint-Denis, Abbey Church, crypt chapel vault.

large foliage capitals. To give focus and continuity to the ambulatory, the capitals were the same size and height there, whereas in the chapels the capitals were smaller and set higher up. Another aspect involved the faceted surfaces of the groin vaults, whose use is certainly to be understood as part of the process of harmonizing the new with the old. These vaults create a feeling of surfaces folded around complex spaces. The effect does not, however, result from the vaults alone, but also from the way the builder avoided sharp, projecting right angles that would interrupt the spatial continuity from ambulatory and chapels by champering the vault arches, the piers at the entrance to the chapels, and the pilasters against the chapel walls (Figure 49). The regularity of the repeated units, lit by double windows in the outer walls, creates a sense of lateral spaciousness rarely encountered in earlier crypts, but which is a clear forerunner to the spatial configurations in the upper chevet.

The upper or feretory level of the east end was even more radical in its departure from traditional designs. The space was organized by two hemicycles of free-standing columns: the first defined the border of the central space, or feretory proper, and ambulatory; the second marked the border between the ambulatory and the ring of radiating chapels (Figure 50). The use of free-standing columns, doubtless intended to harmonize with the columns in the eighth-century nave (of which the feretory was to be the upper-level extension) was surely encouraged by Suger who had considered having columns and capitals brought from Rome.[22] Suger's interest in light, if that was indeed part of the commission he gave to his builder, may also have inspired the careful ordering of the columns that left the chapel windows unobstructed so that in fact light could flood into the space (Figures 51 and 52). Whether or not Suger specifically asked for light, he was certainly pleased with the result, commemorating the effect with verses for the new building. "The church shines with its middle part brightened. For bright is that which is brightly coupled with the bright. And bright is the noble edifice which is pervaded by the new light."[23]

But although Suger's influence is undeniable in certain features of the new feretory, other aspects of the design clearly reflect the builder's own interest in fusing the different sections to create a sense of unified spaciousness. Indeed, the success of the upper level of the east end of Saint-Denis depends less on any single architectural element than on the

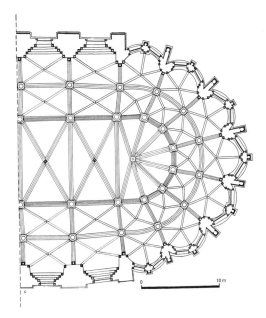

50. Saint-Denis, Abbey Church, restored plan of the upper chevet.

directly comprehensible expression of a visual logic in the arrangement of several design features. Unity of space is achieved through the interpenetration and multidirectionality of the parts, each of which is intentionally subsumed within the dominant expression of the whole. First to be noticed is the builder's daring elimination of wall sections between the ambulatory columns and chapels, for this serves to open up the interior space by removing all partitions (Figures 53 and 54). The key both to the clarity and the complexity of the east end lies in the visual role played by the columns with their square bases and strongly defined capitals. The columns punctuate the space without giving or restricting direction to the view. The omnidirectional column, consciously borrowed from the eighth-century church, here becomes the means of opening up the spaces, of overriding the sense of individual units—chapels and ambulatory bays—in favor of the total space.[24] The thinness of the shafts further emphasizes the openness of the east end and enhances the interweaving, multidirectional lines of the arches and vault

22. Panofsky, *Abbot Suger*, 90–91, 100–101; S. Crosby, *Royal Abbey of St.-Denis*, 251–56; Clark, "Suger's Church"; and J. Bony, "What Possible Sources for the Chevet of Saint-Denis?" in *Abbot Suger and Saint-Denis*, 131–42.
23. Panofsky, *Abbot Suger*, 50–51.

24. Crosby, *Royal Abbey of Saint-Denis*, 127–30.

51. Saint-Denis, Abbey Church, interior of the central space.

52. Saint-Denis, Abbey Church, chapels seen from the central space, north side.

53. Saint-Denis, Abbey Church, feretory ambulatory. This figure is taken from the same angle as Figure 47, the crypt ambulatory. Comparing the two dramatizes the variety of means the builder used to distinguish the spaces. Figure 53 and 54 together illustrate the openness of the upper level.

54. Saint-Denis, Abbey Church, feretory chapels.

ribs springing from the broad abacus blocks above the capitals. One sees from one side of the peripheral wall all the way across to the other, unimpeded even by changes in the level of floor or height of the vaults.

Important as the columns are, however, they do not alone account for the success of Suger's feretory—a fact understood by the builders of the next generation who, even when influenced by Saint-Denis, did not always employ similar columns. The builder's real genius lay in coordinating a number of details in the walls and vaults to enhance and to echo the effects of the columns. For example, the sections of wall that do remain are disguised by multiple colonnettes and arches that flank and frame the windows to reflect the multiple lines in the vaults, but also to deny the mural surface as an enclosing, limiting plane (Figure 55). Detached colonnettes, set in niches cut into the wall masonry, are placed to respond to the window moldings

and to the ribs of the vaults. Horizontal moldings continue and link the bases and abaci of the colonnettes, further denying a mural effect (Figure 56). Because the architectural decoration thus continues the lines of the ribs and appears to support the vaults, the walls function visually as curved compound piers rather than as mural surfaces. They become, in fact, clusters of separated shafts serving as the framing elements for the large windows and as the "background" for the freestanding columns of the ambulatory and the original hemicycle. This approach is all the more remarkable because in the crypt the builder treated walls in an entirely different way, emphasizing the mural surface by using moldings and plinth to define the top and bottom of the wall. Again we are reminded that what mattered to the master builder of Saint-Denis was not this or that stylistic feature but the context into which each particular feature was placed.

55. Saint-Denis, Abbey Church, pier at chapel entrance.

56. Saint-Denis, Abbey Church, chapel interior.

The architectural ornament also helps create and maintain the precise visual distinctions throughout the east end. One example has already been mentioned, the use of colonnettes as wall responds to echo the lines of ribs and moldings. Another is the carefully ordered and maintained sequence of positioning for the wall shafts, which provides clear visual distinctions between the different kinds of arches and responds (Figures 55 and 56). The transverse arches lead to responds— wall shafts—that are taller than those of other arches, have a greater diameter, and stand in front of the walls between the chapels. The responds of the transverse vaulting ribs that are centered between the windows in each chapel likewise stand away from the surface of the peripheral wall, but in contrast to the transverse arches they have the same diameter as the single torus vault ribs they appear to support. The responds of the diagonal ribs, like the shafts of the arches framing the

windows, do not stand away from the wall but are set back in niches cut into the wall fabric and are topped by moldings that, like those at the bottom, follow the curve of the chapel walls. The builder thus leads us to perceive and to understand the complex visual logic by which the whole space is ordered.

A comparable effect is achieved in the vaulting, where the contrast between the thin vault ribs, with their slight projection from the surface, and the smooth curving surfaces of the vaults themselves creates a sense of lightness and delicacy (Figures 57, 58, 59, and 60). The unity of the visual expression in the east end is enhanced by these vaults, in which the boundary between ambulatory and chapels disappears in spite of differences in the vault profiles. Three different molding profiles are used in the rib vaults, and the distinctions between, for example, the simple torus-molded diagonal rib and the more complex transverse arch moldings, are as rigorously

57. Saint-Denis, Abbey Church, ambulatory columns and vaults.

58. Saint-Denis, Abbey Church, ambulatory vault unit.

59. Saint-Denis, Abbey Church, ambulatory and chapel columns and vaults.

60. Saint-Denis, Abbey Church, chapel vault.

maintained as the separate visual roles of the various colonnettes used against the peripheral wall. Here, each profile serves a differing but specific visual purpose. Taken together, the ambulatory and chapel vaults form a delicate armature of arches and arcs, built of small stones held in compression by skillful coun-terbalance, that rests lightly on the network of thin shafts unrelated to mural surface. The slender columns lift the eye to the vaults where the articulation of the ribs and the relatively even height of the ambulatory and chapel contribute to the sense of standing in a single, unified space. The architectural tools—pointed arches and rib vaults—were not themselves sufficient to produce this effect until a builder appeared who was capable of mentally organizing the elements into a coherent spatial whole.

The architectural achievement of the east end of Saint-Denis speaks for itself: it is unquestionably the most elegant platform constructed for the display of relics in the twelfth century. The builder's cognitive achievement is less immediately accessible, but one can perhaps grasp the processes involved by comparing Saint-Denis to Romanesque buildings. The builders in the earlier style worked sequentially, first designing the floor plan, then the walls and windows, finally the vaults—all without having to reconsider what had already been decided. Wall decorations and sculpture may have been left entirely to other masters, such as Giselbertus at Autun, because their efforts were not closely coordinated with those of the builder. At Saint-Denis, in contrast, because all those elements had to work together to produce the coordinated effects the builder desired, they all had to be designed together and each decision constantly reevaluated in light of decisions made on other elements. Despite the differences in subject matter, the parallels between this builder's reasoning and that of Abelard are thus extremely close.

Just as intellectual historians have tried to trace the intellectual achievements of the twelfth century to new translations from Greek and Arabic, architectural historians have tried to explain the origins of Gothic style purely in technical terms, as a combination of specific engineering and stylistic features.[25] Seen in context, however, the story is far more complex. It was not the materials they had at their disposal, but the ways in which they thought about and ordered their materials that set Abelard and the master builder of Saint-Denis apart from their predecessors. For both of them, subtlety of detail resulted, not from the desire for refinement for its own sake, but from the need to integrate individual sections of their work into a larger whole. If their accomplishments do not stand out as distinctly from our perspective as

they did at the time, that is in part because their examples inspired their successors not to imitate specific features of their works, but to construct paradigms of philosophy and architecture. Since much of later twelfth-century culture results from those efforts, it is to that story that we now turn.

25. See also the discussions in P. Frankl, *The Gothic*. The tendency to define Gothic architecture purely in terms of stylistic and technical features persists: J. Harvey, "The Building of Wells Cathedral, I: 1175–1307," in *Wells Cathedral: A History*, ed. L. S. Colchester, esp. 53, writes, "in its complete rejection of the round arch and of the system of supports based on the Roman orders, Corinthianesque capitals and square piers and responds, Wells is the first building in the world, not merely in Britain, to proclaim the emancipation of the new Gothic style."

PART III

THE LATER TWELFTH CENTURY

Bourges, 1195

5 · An Age of Experiment

he period between circa 1140 and circa 1220 has traditionally been a complex one for historians of learning and architecture, because it provides neither a direct elaboration of the innovations of the 1140s nor a progression toward the synthesis of the thirteenth century. Panofsky described the problem as it applies to architecture in these terms:

To reach its classic phase the Gothic style needed no more than a hundred years—from Suger's Saint-Denis to Pierre de Montereau's; and we should expect to see this rapidly and uniquely concentrated development proceed with unparalleled consistency and directness. Such, however, is not the case. Consistent the development is, but it is not direct. On the contrary, when observing the evolution from the beginning to the "final solutions," we receive the impression that it went on almost after the fashion of a "jumping procession," taking two steps forward and then one backward, as though the builders were deliberately placing obstacles in their own way. And this can be observed not only under adverse financial or geographical conditions as normally produce a retrogression by default, so to speak, but in monuments of the very first rank.[1]

Setting aside the question of whether there was a "classic" phase of Gothic architecture, much less whether it existed in the mid-thirteenth century, analysis of Panofsky's remark reveals an assumption of progression that resulted from his habit of reading the history of Gothic architecture from the thirteenth back to the twelfth century. But the historiography of the schools is not much different. A typical view is that of David Knowles, who remarked that the later twelfth century appears "as an interlunary period containing few signs of important development or change, and witnessing few movements of thought." Knowles was, however, perplexed by this assessment, because although "it is certainly true that for more than sixty years after the death of Gilbert de la

1. *Gothic Architecture and Scholasticism* (Latrobe, Pa., 1951), 60–61. Robert Branner was closer to the mark when he wrote that "[t]he line between Sens and St. Denis to Chartres was not direct, . . . and the years between 1140 and 1190 were filled with a bewildering number of experiments" (*Gothic Architecture*, 24).

Porrée no thinker or theologian of the first rank appeared in Western Europe, . . . underneath this surface of tradition and mediocrity, a whole culture was changing, and the world of 1210 was a very different one from that of 1155 both in its institutional forms and in its interior spirit."[2]

The paradox is only apparent if instead of focusing on individual works, we look at late twelfth-century architecture and learning as disciplines, in which the participants were exercising their ability to explore in different directions, it becomes obvious that the seeming lack of direction is intimately related to processes that eventually made European culture circa 1220 different from what it had been in 1140. In the mid-twelfth century, neither builders nor masters felt bound by the models of their predecessors, with the result that the varieties of architectural elements, not to mention decoration and ground plans, matched experiments in the format and subject matter of philosophical works. It can be said of both the master builder of Saint-Denis and of Abelard that although they inspired many, they were copied by none. In the thirteenth century, however, genius and originality came to be expressed within fairly established forms: thirteenth-century *summae* and thirteenth-century cathedrals generally impress but they rarely startle. Simply stated, the difference in architecture and learning between circa 1140 and circa 1220—as measured by comparing, for example, Abelard with Albert the Great, or Saint-Denis and Reims—lies less in the skill or maturity of individual works than in the clarity with which traditions of architectural design and scholarly inquiry had come to be laid down.

In this part, then, we shall treat the late twelfth century as a period when scholarly and architectural traditions were widely explored for the first time. Although this exploration was accomplished by individuals, as all intellectual or artistic work is, the process was also in a sense a collective endeavor. The builders and masters of the later twelfth century were more obliged than Abelard or the master builder of Saint-Denis had been to take into account the activities of their peers, not because their own individual abilities were less ("the absence of geniuses" asserted by Knowles) but because the higher general level of accomplishment that existed was impossible to transcend by genius alone. Just as builders could no longer treat vaulting, buttressing, or moldings as separate problems, masters had to couch their discussion of the eucharist in terms consistent with what they would say about the other sacraments or the incarnation of Christ. The competition, no longer of individual ideas or design features but of entire aesthetic or intellectual structures, was unavoidably intense, and the achievement of consensus about those structures produced "gothic" and "scholastic" styles as they came to exist in the thirteenth century.

---

2. D. Knowles, *The Evolution of Medieval Thought* (New York, 1964), 223–24.

6 · Learning and the Schools in the Later Twelfth Century

n institutional context is not always necessary for disciplines to prosper. Architecture did not assume an institutional form until much later than the Middle Ages, and other disciplines—for example, seventeenth-century mathematics—also thrived without even a clear career path. But when historians have written about the Parisian schools of the later twelfth century, they have usually focused on the origins of the university—the corporate structure of masters that took shape around 1200 and eventually gave its name to institutionalized higher education.[1] From the modern perspective, this emphasis is warranted by the continuing importance of universities into the present time. Not only have most medieval universities survived, with their example being copied throughout the world, but the institutionalization of higher education in universities has spared medieval and modern learning the kinds of interruptions and losses that make the history of ancient science or ancient philosophy a story of repeated discontinuities and re-starts.[2]

Yet in the Middle Ages, the *universitas* or corporate structure was secondary to the *studium* or *studium generale*, as large conglomerations of masters and students were known. The studium of Paris existed as a social reality by the 1130s, well before one can find any evidence for a university corporate structure. Indeed, in an important sense the university

1. The basic work on medieval universities is still Hastings Rashdall, *The Universities of Europe in the Middle Ages*, ed. Frederick M. Powicke and Alfred B. Emden, 3 vols. (Oxford, 1936). Other works include Gérard M. Paré, A. Brunet, and P. Tremblay, *La Renaissance du XIIe siècle: Les Ecoles et l'enseignement* (Paris and Ottawa, 1933); Emile Lesne, *Histoire de la propriété ecclésiastique en France*, 6 vols. (Lille, 1910–43), vol. 5: *Les Ecoles de la fin du VIIIe siècle à la fin du XIIe*, Mémoires et travaux des Facultés Catholiques de Lille no. 50 (1940); Philippe Delhaye, "L'Organisation scolaire au XIIe siècle," *Traditio* 5 (1947): 211–68; and John W. Baldwin, "Masters at Paris from 1179 to 1215: A Social Perspective," in *Renaissance/Renewal*, 138–72. Despite its title, S. Ferruolo, *The Origins of the University* (Stanford, 1985) concerns the critics of the schools more than the masters, the scholarly community, or the course of study.
2. See, for example, G. E. R. Lloyd, *Greek Science after Aristotle* (New York, 1973).

grew out of the studium and the sense of shared interests it created. The process was not unique to Paris. Bologna, the only other twelfth-century studium of European importance, followed a very similar path to arrive at a very different corporate structure. Understanding the intellectual world of later twelfth-century Paris, therefore, means first of all understanding the studium and the people who comprised it.

SCHOLAE TO STUDIUM

We may take as a point of departure John of Salisbury's well-known account of his own education. In 1136 he came to Gaul as a youth, he tells us, studying logic with Abelard and, after Abelard's departure, remaining on Mont Ste.-Geneviève to hear Alberic and Robert of Melun for two years. (John's chronology, it should be noted, is only approximate.) After studying for three years with the "grammarian" William of Conches, John then followed Richard Bishop, and studied rhetoric with Thierry of Chartres and Peter Helias; during the same period he also earned money by working as a tutor and, though not formally a student of Adam of the Petitpont, profited from Adam's friendship and discussions on Aristotle. Need for money then necessitated an interruption of his studies, during which he worked as a teacher, but after an interval of three years he returned to Paris to hear Gilbert of Poitiers on logic and theology. Finally, after Gilbert's departure, John completed his formal training by hearing lectures on theology given by Robert Pullen and Simon of Poissy.[3]

John's account has generally been read for the purpose of determining which masters were located in Paris in the 1140s. By combining the *Metalogicon* with two other sources— William of Tyre's remarks about his own student years and the *Metamorphosis Goliae*

written in lament of Abelard's death[4]— Southern compiled a list of fourteen masters active in Paris between 1135 and 1150, including nearly all of the most famous names in the arts and theology.[5] These sources do not mention the masters at the nearby community, the regular canons of Saint-Victor, an omission that should be taken seriously; although occasional students may have studied at Saint-Victor, and works of Victorine masters certainly circulated at Paris, Saint-Victor was not on the usual academic circuit of the 1140s.[6] Yet even without counting Saint-Victor, the numbers and quality of masters leave no doubt that "by 1140 Paris was in the full tide of its progress toward scholastic dominance over all other schools in northern Europe."[7]

Dominance was not yet monopoly. As late as the 1160s, Peter the Chanter could receive a first-rate theological education in Reims, while *ars dictaminis* thrived at Orléans until after 1200.[8] But after 1140 students who sought the greatest variety of masters would inevitably be drawn to Paris, and the number of students in Paris—perhaps two to three thousand by 1140—meant that aspiring mas-

---

3. John of Salisbury, *Metalogicon*, ed. C. C. I. Webb (Oxford, 1929), bk. 2, sec. 10. A complete translation of the *Metalogicon* was published by Daniel D. McGarry (Berkeley, 1962); this particular passage was also translated by Lynn Thorndyke in *University Records and Life in the Middle Ages* (New York, 1944).

4. R. B. C. Huygens, "Guillaume de Tyr étudiant," *Latomus* 21 (1962): 811–29; Huygens, "Mitteilungen aus Handschriften," *Studi medievali*, 3d ser. 3 (1962): 747–72 at 764–72; John F. Benton, "Philology's Search for Abelard in the *Metamorphosis Goliae*," *Speculum* 50 (1975): 199–217.

5. R. W. Southern, "The Schools of Paris and the School of Chartres," in *Renaissance/Renewal*, 128–33. Note that the captions "Probably Elsewhere" and "Certainly in Paris" have been reversed in the table given in appendix 1, p. 133.

6. For references to teaching at St. Victor, see Ferruolo, *Origins*, 29–30, although he somewhat overstates Robert of Melun's teaching at St. Victor. Robert certainly had some connection to St. Victor, as appears from the letter of congratulation from Ernisius abbot of St. Victor on Robert's election as bishop of Hereford (*PL* 190: 687), but the bulk of the evidence (including the *Metalogicon*) suggests that most of Robert's teaching was done on Ste.-Geneviève. See Lesne, *Histoire*, 228–30.

7. Southern, "Schools of Paris," 128.

8. On Peter the Chanter and Reims, see J. Baldwin, *Masters, Princes and Merchants* (Princeton, 1970), 7; for examples of the work done at Orléans, see Richard H. Rouse, "Florilegia and Latin Classical Authors in Twelfth and Thirteenth-Century Orléans," *Viator* 10 (1979): 131–60; and Richard H. Rouse and Mary A. Rouse, "The Florilegium Angelicum," in *Medieval Learning and Literature* (Oxford, 1976), 66–114.

ters had no choice but to go there as well. Precise numbers are impossible to obtain, but the growth of the studium can be charted in the expansion of Paris on the left bank of the Seine: by the 1170s, tenements to house scholars were replacing vineyards on the south side of the Seine, and by 1200 settlements extended as far as the once distinct abbey of Sainte-Geneviève.[9]

In effect, the supermarket had driven out the corner store, offering an increase in variety and standardized quality at the expense of personal attention. This too can be seen in the *Metalogicon*. John had come to Paris to study with particular masters, most of whom were the preeminent scholars in their fields; indeed, it is the masters he stressed in the *Metalogicon*, generally omitting mention of where they taught. But John's ability to support himself by teaching suggests that by the 1140s the schools of Paris were already being subsumed into a more impersonal studium. Students were drawn to Paris more by the reputation of the academic community as a whole than by the fame of specific individuals, and after arriving they often began their studies with younger men of limited expertise, such as John himself was in the 1140s. So far as the students were concerned, such masters must have been more or less interchangeable.

Another consequence of this shift from schools to studium may be seen in the shape of teaching careers. Masters with teaching careers extending over three or four decades on the model of Berengar of Tours, Anselm of Laon, or Abelard, certainly did not cease to exist in the later twelfth century. The most prominent masters of the period, men such as Alan of Lille and Peter the Chanter, spent many years teaching in Paris despite the demand for their services from ecclesiastical and secular officials, and they were responsible for the most challenging and original works of the period. But although these long-term masters continued to dominate the Parisian intellectual world, they must have been considerably outnumbered by scholars who were younger and less experienced than earlier masters had been. Typical of many must have been Peter of Blois, who studied in Paris in the mid-1140s (perhaps with John of Salisbury), then went to Bologna to study law, but was probably still in his early twenties when, after returning to Paris in the mid-1150s, he supported his theological studies by teaching grammar.[10] Still less seasoned in the schools was Gerald of Wales, who had only recently arrived from Britain and was in his early twenties when he taught the trivium at Paris circa 1170.[11] In practice, there appear to have been few restrictions on who could teach at Paris in the later twelfth century.

The relative absence of great names from the schools of the later twelfth century is not, therefore, entirely an illusion induced by the poverty of our sources. Rather, we should imagine the schools of Paris from the mid-twelfth century on as a crowd including many very young masters. There were some complaints about this. Those relatively hostile to the schools—men such as Bernard of Clairvaux and Stephen of Tournai—were, of course, particularly vocal, but senior masters

9. Peter Classen, "Die Hohen Schulen und die Gesellschaft im 12. Jahrhundert," *Archive für Kulturgeschichte* 48 (1966): 155–80; Adrien Friedmann, *Paris: Ses rues, ses pariosses du Moyen Age à la Révolution* (Paris, 1959), 233–76; Jacques Boussard, *Nouvelle Histoire de Paris de la Fin du siège de 885–886 à la mort de Philippe Auguste* (Paris, 1976), 179–96; for details on the growth of the studium of Paris, see Stephen Ferruolo, "Parisius-Paradisus," in *The University and the City*, ed. Thomas Bender (Oxford, 1988), 22–43; Jacques Verger, "A propos de la naissance de l'université de Paris," in *Schulen und Studium im sozialen Wandel des hohen und späten Mittelalters*, ed. Johannes Fried (Sigmaringen, 1986), 69–96; and John O. Ward, "Gothic Architecture, Universities and the Decline of the Humanities in Twelfth-Century Europe," in *Principalities, Powers and Estates*, ed. L. O. Frappell (Adelaide, 1979), 65–75.

10. R. W. Southern, "Peter of Blois: A Twelfth Century Humanist?," in *Medieval Humanism and Other Essays* (Oxford, 1970), 109n.
11. "*Processu vero temporis causa studii majoris atque profectus ter in Franciam transfretando, tresque status annorum plurium Parisius in liberalibus disciplinis faciendo, summosque praeceptores demum aequiparando, trivium ibidem egregie docuit, et praecipuam in arte rhetorica laudem obtinuit*" (*De Rebus a se Gestis i.2 (p. 23)*, in *Giraldi Cambrensis Opera*, ed. J. S. Brewer, J. F. Dimock, and G. F. Warner, vol. 1 (*Rerum Britannicarum Medii Aevi Scriptores*, no. 21) (London, 1861). Gerald was born about 1147 (p. x) and returned to England about 1172, so this would have been ca. 1169. This visit to Paris was distinct from the later episode (before 1180) when he lectured to fellow students on law, *De gest.* ii.5.

also expressed concern. Peter the Chanter, for example, advised students to "believe only the bearded master";[12] and Robert of Courson (in his 1215 statutes for the university of Paris) set twenty-one years as a minimum age for masters of arts, who were also to have spent at least six years in the schools.[13] Further in a major departure from the practice of earlier schools, in which Abelard and other prominent masters taught dialectic, rhetoric, and grammar throughout their careers, the consensus was growing that the study of the arts was mainly for the young. Now the older scholars who concentrated on Priscian and Cicero rather than abandoning them for theology were generally subject to ridicule.[14]

For our present purposes, however, the important point is the changing nature of the studium in which the learned disciplines were practiced. In the first place, from as early as the 1140s much of the teaching at Paris was in the hands of those for whom teaching was an interlude rather than a career. John of Salisbury, Peter of Blois, and Gerald of Wales looked back with pleasure on their years at the studium, but they all left scholarship behind them to pursue careers in ecclesiastical and government service. Still the claim to have studied to the point of being able to teach others appears to have been worth a great deal; indeed, after 1135 one finds the title *magister*—previously applied only to men presiding over a school—used more and more as an honorific by men not currently engaged in teaching.[15] But this must also have meant that the turnover of personnel within the studium was quite rapid—a pattern that continued into the later Middle Ages.

The impact on the rest of society of this outflow of educated people from the schools can be seen in the steady construction of government and ecclesiastical institutions that characterizes the late twelfth century: the ability to learn details and analyze problems that makes a good student also makes a good bureaucrat or administrator. The effect on the studium of this trend, although it is more elusive, must also have been considerable. There may have been a tendency, in the arts at least, to concentrate on problems that did not require a lifetime's study but could be solved in a few years; thus one sees interest in general theories of language and meaning replaced by analysis of fallacies and terms.[16] It also seems probable that masters who expected to pursue careers outside of the schools were somewhat indifferent to their scholarly reputations, a circumstance that perhaps explains the curious fact that most later twelfth-century works in the arts come down without a clue to authorship.[17]

A final observation concerns the relationship of scholars to other specialists in their discipline. Because masters of the late eleventh and early twelfth century were few in number, unless they were unfortunate enough to attract the attention of someone outside the schools like Bernard of Clairvaux, they could be immune to serious criticism for years. This situation may have permitted some mediocre teachers to survive unchallenged, but for masters such as Abelard, William of Conches, and Gilbert of Poitiers, it also meant that they had the time to develop their ideas into distinctive and individual systems of thought. By 1140, however, the age of scholastic heroes was past, and if there was less originality during the rest of the century, the doctrinal results proved more enduring, becoming permanent parts of the curriculum. In both the arts and theology, individual genius found expression within a context defined by the criticism of peers.[18]

12. See John W. Baldwin, *Masters, Princes and Merchants* (Princeton, 1970), 130–31 and notes for references to late twelfth-century complaints about the youthfulness of masters.

13. The statutes are given in H. Denifle and E. Chatelain, *Chartularium Universitatis Parisiensis* (Paris, 1889–1897), 1:78–79. On the legal aspects of the university, see Gaines Post, "Parisian Masters as a Corporation, 1200–1246," in *Studies in Medieval Legal Thought* (Princeton, 1964), 27–60.

14. See, for example, Peter of Blois, epistle 6, *PL* 207: 91, cited by Delhaye, "L'Organisation scolaire," 264–65.

15. Southern, "Schools of Paris," 134–35; Baldwin, "Masters at Paris," 151–58; Julia Barrow, "Education and the Recruitment of Cathedral Canons in England and Germany 1100–1225," *Viator* 20 (1989): 117–38.

16. See, for example, the works published by L. M. de Rijk, *Logica Modernorum* (Assen, 1962–67).

17. Baldwin, "Masters at Paris," 145, 148.

18. For valuable observations on the self-awareness of medieval masters, see Jacques Le Goff, "How Did the Medieval University Conceive of Itself," in *Time, Work, and Culture in the Middle Ages* (Chicago, 1980), 122–34.

CURRICULUM

The significance of the later twelfth century for intellectual life is suggested by the subsequent history of teaching texts: whereas works by masters working before 1140 fell out of use very quickly, many of those written in the 1150s and 1160s remained standard into the thirteenth century. This difference was not entirely or even mainly a matter of content. It has recently become clear, for example, how much Peter Helias's commentary on Priscian owes to that of William of Conches, it was Peter's commentary that became the standard for the next century.[19] Conversely, Peter Lombard's *Sentences* remained a standard teaching text throughout the later Middle Ages, well after some of his doctrine had become outdated.

The durability of these textbooks in the medieval curriculum is sometimes explained by the fact that they took the form of commentaries on ancient texts or collections of patristic quotations. The commentaries and sentence collections, it is argued, were appropriate for a period "in which ancient texts were held to be the source of all knowledge"; by extension, medieval scholarship consisted of "building up a body of knowledge from the conflation and criticism of many texts."[20] The error of this opinion is easily shown, by the frequency with which the opinions of modern masters are cited, and by the confidence with which the views even of Aristotle are discarded.[21] Perhaps the most telling example of this attitude, however, is to be found in Peter the Chanter's gloss to Num. 3:18. The front teeth of theology, he wrote, were the apostles, while the canine, or middle teeth, were the expositors of Scripture who barked against

heretics. But the molars, "which were the most necessary," were the modern doctors who prepared sacred doctrine to nourish the faithful.[22] The confidence of the modern masters in the authority of their own views could hardly be plainer.

The enduring popularity of many texts written between 1140 and 1170 must be ascribed to a crystalization of the intellectual content of the arts and theology, an event that at once limited subsequent generations' choices and concentrated their energies on specific topics. We can understand this consolidation of the curriculum by considering the masters' developing relationship to their disciplines. Masters of the 1120s and 1130s could hardly feel the weight of tradition when their own teaching differed so extensively from that of their teachers. To their contemporaries, the doctrines of Abelard or William of Conches would have seemed to reflect their own personal views. By the 1140s, however, many of their ideas and even more of their methods had lost their personal associations and had become familiar to all specialists, and in the hands of their successors became the common property of all members of the discipline. The process did not stop there, of course. For some disciplines, the work of several more generations of masters was needed before masters arrived at a general consensus on concepts and working methods. But it was the twelfth-century construction of this working consensus—what Kuhn calls a disciplinary matrix[23]—that prepared the way for the more obviously original work of the thirteenth-century schools.

The last point concerns the character of the learning that made up the curriculum. The systematic cross-linking of issues that Abelard had originated in the first decades of the twelfth century was, by his death, a widely accepted standard. The change is marked by the deliberate employment of consistent categories and language: Gilbert of Poitiers transferred the terminology he developed to dis-

19. On William of Conches's commentary on Priscian, see K. M. Fredborg, "The Dependence of Petrus Helias' *Summa super Priscianum* on William of Conches' *Glose super Priscianum*," *CIMAGL* 11 (1973): 1–57. We await the work of Teresa Gross-Diaz that will show that Gilbert of Poitiers's Psalm commentary met a similar fate at the hands of Peter Lombard.
20. R. W. Southern, *Platonism, Scholastic Method and the School of Chartres* (Reading, 1979), 8, 6.
21. See for example, Abelard's discussion of the verb *to be* in his commentary on Aristotle's *De Interpretatione* in *Logica "Ingredientibus,"* 358–63. The subject is thoroughly discussed by M.-D. Chenu, *Nature, Man, and Society in the Twelfth Century,* chap. 8.

22. Baldwin, "Masters at Paris," 161.
23. See the discussions in his "Postscript" to *The Structure of Scientific Revolutions,* 2d ed. (Chicago, 1970), and "Second Thoughts on Paradigms," in *The Essential Tension* (Chicago, 1977).

cuss universals into ontology and theology,[24] and the revisions either Adam of the Petit Pont or a follower made to Adam's *Ars Disserendi* standardized the vocabulary used to discuss technical issues.[25] Later scholars either had to develop their ideas within these intellectual structures or devise entirely new ones. The parallel between this process and the process of architectural design, where a variety of design elements had to be integrated into an aesthetic whole, is the same.

In what follows, we shall explore the consolidation of the curriculum in two disciplines in the arts—grammar and logic—and in the related field of theology.

Grammar

In the early twelfth century, grammar, like logic, was principally concerned with assessing the relationship between language and reality.[26] This had been Berengar's purpose in bringing grammatical issues into the eucharistic controversy, and the same concerns also run through the *Glosule* from the later eleventh century. The association with logic meant that glossators had tended to discuss grammatical concepts in logical terms, writing on nouns, for example, with an eye to distinguishing their substantial and accidental qualities.[27] Both Priscian's own text and the fact that masters taught all the subjects of the trivium encouraged them to approach grammar this way, and as a method it had the advantage of permitting each word to be tack-

led in isolation, without commentators needing to juggle too many issues at once.

The process of disentangling grammatical issues from those that belonged to logic was begun by William of Conches, one of the great masters of Abelard's generation. William is remembered today principally for his works on natural philosophy—the *Philosophia Mundi* of circa 1120 and the *Dragmaticon* from the later 1140s—in which he asserted the importance of studying natural forces.[28] But during his teaching career, from perhaps 1115 to the late 1130s, much of William's reputation rested on his lectures on grammar; thus, for example, John of Salisbury went to William in the late 1130s to study grammar, as he recalls in the *Metalogicon*. William was obviously as original a thinker in grammar as he was in natural philosophy, and in both the *Philosophia* and the *Dragmaticon* he criticized his predecessors and contemporaries for failing to go beyond Priscian and take up grammatical questions that Priscian himself had not discussed.

William's program is revealed by his glosses on Priscian, which exist in two versions, one from before 1125 and a revised version from the 1140s.[29] William's sources were the same as his contemporaries—Boethius and Aristotle as well as Priscian—and he dealt with questions involving universals, accidents, and substance as his predecessors had done.[30] But even as he worked within this tradition, William introduced and elaborated on discussions of a wide range of issues that had previously been neglected. His innovations were often highly technical: the *causae inventionis* of the parts of speech (roughly, an analysis of primary and secondary meanings of words), systematic study of the relationship between nouns and the things to which they refer, and

24. John Marenbon, "Gilbert of Poitiers," in Dronke, *Philosophy*, 228–52. Note especially how Gilbert applies his concept of something which makes it so (*quo est*) across a variety of philosophical issues.
25. L. Minio-Paluello, "The *Ars Disserendi* of Adam of Balsham 'Parvipontanus,'" *Medieval and Renaissance Studies* 3 (1954): 140–46.
26. The essential works on later twelfth-century grammar include R. W. Hunt, "Studies on Priscian in the Eleventh and Twelfth Centuries I," *Medieval and Renaissance Studies* 1 (1941–43): 194–231, and "Studies on Priscian in the Twelfth Century II," *Medieval and Renaissance Studies* 2 (1950): 1–56; J. Pinborg, *Die Entwicklung der Sprachtheorie im Mittelalter* (Münster and Copenhagen, 1967); K. M. Fredborg, "Speculative Grammar," in Dronke, *Philosophy*, 177–98.
27. On William of Conches, see Hunt, "Studies on Priscian I," esp. 211–14; de Rijk, *Logica Modernorum*, 2: 95–125; and Fredborg, "Dependence."

28. See, for example, the discussion of William by Dorothy Elford in Dronke, *Philosophy*, 308–27, which also gives references to earlier literature. For William's teaching career, we follow Southern's account in *Platonism, Scholastic Method, and the School of Chartres*, 16–17; the question of whether William was or was not at Chartres during much of his career is irrelevant to our purposes.
29. E. Jeauneau, "Deux Rédactions des gloses de Guillaume de Conches sur Priscien," *RTAM* 27 (1960): 212–47. Neither commentary has been edited.
30. See, for example, the long excerpts printed by de Rijk, *Logica Modernorum*, vol. 2, pt. 1, pp. 221–23.

the beginning of the study of syntax or how words in the same statement relate to each other. Yet his achievement can be understood in terms of what has already been said about Abelard because his general method was to study words in sentences where their meaning was modified by their relationship with other words and by the general context of human discourse.

An example may make this clear. One of the distinctions William regularly employed was between the *significatum* of a word—its primary meaning—and the *nominata* or objects to which the word refers.[31] Although familiar with the distinction, the eleventh-century author of the *Glosule* (see Text 5) had done little with it:

popularization of the doctrines of William and his predecessors."[32] Nevertheless, it was Peter's *Summa* that became the standard textbook of grammar, being included in the thirteenth-century *Speculum doctrinale* of Vincent of Beauvais. Yet it would oversimplify developments to suggest that the *summa* can be used to define twelfth-century grammar.[33] Often, as Hunt showed, commentators considered Peter's views only to differ with him— the fate of any medieval textbook. Other scholars went off in their own direction, and several freestanding treatises on syntax were written in the later twelfth century. There were, finally, various *quaestiones* on grammatical issues, continuing the tradition dating back to the eleventh century but with more

significata		*nominata*
man	signifies the substance of individual men, by determining their quality	refers to the substance of individual men
white	signifies whiteness	refers to a body

In contrast, William of Conches uses the distinction both more exhaustively and with greater awareness of how verbal context can affect meaning.

man	signifies a substance, by determining a general quality	refers to individuals only *or* to the form in "man is a species" *or* to itself in "man is a noun"
Socrates	signifies an individual substance and individual quality	refers to the substance itself, in "Socrates runs" *or* to itself in "Socrates is a name"

William's interest in verbal context is similarly revealed by his pioneering analysis of Latin syntax, in which he tried to describe the relationships between the different parts of a sentence.

In the 1140s, William's doctrines were restated by Peter Helias's *Summa super Priscianum*. According to K. M. Fredborg, Peter's work "added perhaps little new grammatical doctrine but is a convenient and much used

detailed analysis and critique of opposing views.[34]

31. This paragraph is based on Fredborg, "Speculative grammar," 183–95; the table appearing on pp. 183–85 provides the basis for the one used here.

32. "Speculative grammar," 179; see also Fredborg, "Dependence."

33. Later twelfth-century works on grammar are still being sifted and published, most notably by Fredborg and others in *CIMAGL* and by C. H. Kneepkens, esp. *Het Iudicium Constructionis*, 4 vols. (Nijmegen, 1987). In writing this paragraph we have also used Hunt, "Studies II," and "Absoluta," *Historiographia Linguistica* 2 (1975): 1–22 [repr. *Collected Papers*, pp. 95–116].

34. See, for example, C. H. Kneepkens, "The Quaestiones Grammaticales of the MS Oxford, Corpus Christi College 250," *Vivarium* 23 (1985): 98–123.

Logic

Although the originality and sophistication of Abelard's logic would seem to have provided at least as firm a foundation for further development as William of Conches's glosses on Priscian, logic veered into an apparently entirely different direction in the later twelfth century.[35] There is no mystery why this occurred. The renewed study of Aristotle's *Logica Nova* or "New Logic"—the *Sophistical Refutations*, *Topics*, *Prior Analytics*, and *Posterior Analytics*—introduced logicians to new problems that (even apart from their intrinsic interest) provided them with an opportunity for making a reputation that they were quick to seize. The earliest response to the *Logica Nova*, the *Ars Disserendi* of Adam of the Petit Pont, dates from the 1130s, thus overlapping Abelard's career, and by the 1140s the process of assimilating the new works into the curriculum was already advanced. Once the interest of logicians was focused in another direction, the works of Abelard and his contemporaries fell out of currency, and it was not until the reinvention of linguistic logic in the twentieth century that their works again received much attention.

Yet the recovery of the *Logica Nova* was not an instance of the rediscovery of ancient learning inspiring a medieval "renaissance," but the result of the maturation of logic as a discipline. To begin with, it was not a chance occurrence: the works were searched for and found (that the works existed was known from some of Boethius's remarks), and some were newly translated from the Greek. Moreover, once the works were available, masters traveled great distances to study the new translations.[36] We know from the *Metalogicon*

that Alberic de Monte journeyed from Paris to Bologna to study the new texts and that after his return to Paris he incorporated this knowledge into his teaching (much to John of Salisbury's distress).

Most telling, however, was the very different fate of the various books of the *Logica Nova* in the twelfth century. Of the four works, only Aristotle's study of fallacies, the *Sophistical Refutations*, received much attention before 1200. At first glance, this seems a peculiar choice; today the *Sophistical Refutations* is among the less read of Aristotle's logical works and certainly is seen as less important than the *Prior* and *Posterior Analytics*. But as a study of fallacious inferences, the *Sophistical Refutations* dealt with questions already current in the mid-twelfth century as a result of the shift into studying words in the context of complete sentences; indeed, although Abelard had said relatively little specifically concerning fallacies, examining how and when one sentence was logically equivalent to another had been one of his main analytical techniques.[37] In concentrating their attention on the *Sophistical Refutations*, therefore, later twelfth-century masters chose the Aristotle that fit into their existing interests, leaving the rest for subsequent generations.

John of Salisbury denounced the logicians of his time for excessive concern with logic for its own sake—another clue that masters were specializing more than they had been earlier. But Klaus Jacobi is surely right when he argues that the very features which disturbed John can better be seen as evidence of the appearance of a "research mentality" in the middle decades of the twelfth century.[38] Particularly significant in this regard is the general consensus about subject matter among the various doctrinal schools.

Parvipontani, Montani, Porretani, and Melidunenses are not as easily distinguished by their method of posing questions as had been the case with Adam [of the Petit Pont], Alberic, Gilbert, and Robert of

35. For a perceptive discussion of developments in logic in the later twelfth century see Klaus Jacobi, "Logic (ii)," in Dronke, *Philosophy*; also good is John Marenbon, *Later Medieval Philosophy* (London and New York, 1987). More detailed discussions of many points can be found in L. M. de Rijk's introductions to the pioneering editions of these works in *Logica Modernorum*.

36. C. H. Lohr, "The Medieval Interpretation of Aristotle, in *Cambridge History of Later Medieval Philosophy*, ed. Norman Kretzmann, Anthony Kenny, Jan Pinborg (Cambridge, 1982), 83; Jacobi, "Logic (ii)," 233. On the translations and their translators, see George Lacombe, et. al., *Aristoteles Latinus* (Bruges and Paris, 1939–76).

37. For Abelard's work on fallacies, see de Rijk, *Logica Modernorum*, vol. 1, pp. 49–61, 109–12; but see also the discussion in Martin M. Tweedale, *Abailard on Universals* (Amsterdam, 1976), 213–304.

38. "Logic (ii)," 234–35; the following quotation is from p. 235.

We say that the same term can be taken in two ways and that nothing prohibits the same term from signifying several things in different locutions with different adjoining phrases. Nor will it signify different things in a simple manner, since that which signifies so much depending on adjoining phrases does not signify. . . . On this account, there are not equivocal nouns but nouns taken equivocally. To be equivocal and to be taken equivocally are distinct, since a certain expression is equivocal because it signifies different things from different conventions; an expression is said to be taken equivocally because it is said in another manner from one case to another. Thus, "healthy" (*sanum*) is said of an animal in a manner other than of a bee or of urine [from de Rijk, *Logica Modernorum*, vol. 2, pt. 1, p. 298; trans. Radding].

Text 8. An excerpt from the *Ars Meliduna*. Notice how the basic argument, that meaning depends on context, develops the line of analysis worked out by Abelard in dealing with universals.

Melun, from whom the schools took their names. . . . In their approach to problems they had come to resemble one another; the differences lie in their responses to specific individual questions. The Ars Meliduna, *for example, and the* Compendium logicae Porretanum . . . *are both divided into four books which deal respectively with terms, with what is signified by terms, with propositions, and with what is signified or asserted by propositions. And within the individual books the individual topics succeed one another in more or less the same order.*

The consistency in the order of presentation is especially noteworthy since it did not derive from ancient authorities but rather represents a twelfth-century consensus.[39]

To illustrate this research mentality, we may take as an example the *Ars Meliduna* written in the third quarter of the twelfth century (see Text 8). The text itself often lays down rules and definitions, for example this one about implications:

We deny implications in which . . . propositions about things (res) proceed to statements about language (dicta). For if "Socrates is a man," then it cannot be inferred "That Socrates is a man is true."[40]

The author was not simply being perverse; modern logicians arrived at very similar conclusions. But students did not merely commit the rules to memory. They were expected to test the rules by counterexamples or instances known as *instantiae*, the proof of any one of which would invalidate the rule. Much ingenuity went into constructing and arguing these instantiae, with the already specialized character of these arguments enhanced by the fact that they often addressed other members of the same school rather than challenging the doctrine of those with different approaches.[41]

Although work of this kind confirms John of Salisbury's judgment that logicians of his time had become enmeshed in technicalities, not all students may have seen this as a fault. Technical details are not necessarily forbidding: one thinks of the comparatively young age of computer prodigies today. And the very narrowness of the concerns of twelfth-century logic probably facilitated acquisition of expertise. With the changing character of the studium, in which few students planned on teaching logic for long, the tight focus on particular details must have meant that they

39. de Rijk, *Logica Modernorum*, vol. 2, pt. 1, pp. 539–40.
40. de Rijk, *Logica Modernorum*, vol. 2, pt. 1, p. 347.

41. On instantiae see the work of Y. Iwakuma, "Instantiae" *CIMAGL* 38 (1981): 1–91; "Instantiae Revisited," *CIMAGL* 44 (1983): 61–80; and, with S. Ebbensen, "Instantiae and 12th Century 'Schools,'" *CIMAGL* 44 (1983): 81–85.

could display their intelligence and originality after a much shorter period of study than would have been needed to attack broader questions.

In any case, the clear definition of the field did not result in logic being cut off from other disciplines as John of Salisbury had thought. Among the propositions mentioned in logical treatises were some—for example, Antichrist is a future man—that were theological in content, and what discussion of such propositions by logicians might look like is suggested by Peter the Chanter's treatise *De Tropis Loquendi*. The Chanter is best known for his work in moral theology, but that reckons, as Gillian Evans observes, without this treatise. Not only did the Chanter borrow the framework of such late twelfth-century logical treatises as the *Fallacie Londonienses* when discussing equivocations and superficial contradictions in theology. He also employed a variety of technical terms, showing "clearly that he expected his students to come to him already equipped with a knowledge of the grammatical and dialectical rules and terminology they would need." It was in this intellectual context that the Chanter dealt with the then-current questions on the *natura* and *essentia* of Christ that are missing from his better-known and more popularly directed works (see Text 9).[42] Peter the Chanter was by no means unique in these interests, which appear to run through late twelfth-century theology.[43]

Theology

Theology found its textbook in the late 1150s, with the appearance of Peter Lombard's *Sentences*.[44] The idea of collecting authoritative statements or sentences was not entirely new; monastic *florilegia*, in which monks copied excerpts from their readings for future study, go back to the early Middle Ages. But twelfth-century sentence collections differed from florilegia in that the selection and arrangement of excerpts was done not for contemplation but to permit analysis and comparison of often opposing views on controversial or difficult topics.[45] Readers were not necessarily expected to read the whole work from start to finish; thus the Lombard made a point of providing a table of contents—still a new feature in the twelfth century—"so that which is sought may be easily found."[46] Peter Lombard's was not the only sentence collection of the time, but as the most complete and best organized it found a lasting place in the schools.[47]

42. G. R. Evans, "A Work of 'Terminist Theology'?" *Vivarium* 20 (1982): 40–58; the quotation comes from p. 44. See also de Rijk, *Logica Modernorum*, vol. 1, pp. 163–78; F. Guisberti, "A Twelfth Century Theological Grammar," in *Materials for a Study on Twelfth Century Scholasticism*, History of Logic, vol. 2 (Naples, 1982).

43. See, for example, N. M. Häring, "Petrus Lombardus und die Sprachlogik in der Trinitätslehre der Porretanerschule," in *Miscellanea Lombardiana* (Novara, 1957), 113–26; Philip S. Moore and Marthe Dulong, *Sententiae Petri Pictaviensis* (Notre Dame, 1943), 1: xvii. Often even the propositions discussed by Peter of Poitiers are presented using the vocabulary of twelfth-century logic; for example, 1.5 (An huiusmodi nomina *aliquis, unus,* masculine accepta, sint in eadem regula) and 1.6 (De illis terminis complexis qui constat ex una dictione significante substantiam, et alia que significat relationem, ut *potens generare*).

44. This essay deals only with theology in the schools. For an introduction to monastic theology of the same period, see Jean LeClerc, "The Renewal of Theology," in *Renaissance/Renewal*, 68–87.

45. Other important sentence collections include that of Robert of Melun and Hugh of St. Victor's *De Sacramentis,* but Robert's was incomplete and in any case later than the Lombard's and, although Hugh's work was widely read, being at St. Victor meant that he was somewhat off the circuit of the Paris schools. Robert of Melun, *Oeuvres,* ed. R. Martin, Spicilegium sacrum lovaniense nos. 13, 18, 21, 15 (Louvain, 1932–52); Hugh of St. Victor, *De Sacramentis, PL* 176; and *On the Sacraments,* trans. R. J. Deferrari (Cambridge, Mass., 1951).

46. Prologue, quoted by Richard H. Rouse and Mary A. Rouse in their important study of twelfth-century research tools, "Statim Invenire," in *Renaissance/Renewal*, 206–7. The significant point here is that the Lombard views his readers as inquirers and scholars who need quick access to materials, in effect conceding that theological study consists as much of ongoing inquiry as of definitive answers. See also M. B. Parkes, "The Influence of the Concepts of *Ordinatio* and *Compilatio* on the Development of the Book," in *Medieval Learning and Literature* (Oxford, 1976), 115–41.

47. On Peter Lombard and his role in systematizing theological studies, see Marcia Colish, "Systematic Theology and Theological Renewal in the Twelfth Century," *Journal of Medieval and Renaissance Studies* 18 (1988): 135–56. A different perspective on theology in the mid-twelfth century is provided by David Luscombe, *The School of Peter Abelard* (Cambridge, 1969), a work that covers more ground than its title might suggest.

On the Eucharist

§65. It is asked whether it should be conceded that the body of Christ is seen on the altar. It does not seem that it should be conceded and this is shown first by simile. For it is not said that the Holy Spirit was seen in the dove, although the dove was a kind of sign of the Spirit descending and remaining over Christ. For the Holy Spirit was not dressed in the body of another creature, nor was the Father. Nor is it said that the Holy Spirit was *indovate* (*incolumbatus*), as Christ is said to have been incarnate or made human. . . .

Further. It is asked if it may be said that the body of the Lord is white, or that the priest sees a white thing on the altar since he sees whiteness. It seems rather that he does not see a white thing, since there is no subject of that whiteness which is there. Similarly it follows that the body of the Lord is not white. But would it not be said that a man is white, who is all in whiteness, and the foot black which is immersed in black dirt? And is it not said that mountains are white when they are covered by clouds?

The truth of the aforesaid locutions is not certain, but even if it were conceded, it would nevertheless not be necessary to concede it in regard to the body of Christ, since clothes adhere to men much more closely and familiarly than these extrinsic accidents adhere to the body of Christ. Since thanks to this kind of accident the body of Christ may seem concealed, as we say, one could proceed to ask if accidents of this kind (such as whiteness, roundness, flavor, even that substantial property that could be called breadness) are in any subject and in what. And there are those who say that they are in the confused air as in a subject, but it seems to us better that they are in no subject, remaining miraculously after conversion [no. 4, pt. 1, pp. 166–68; trans. Radding].

Text 9. An excerpt from Peter the Chanter's *Summa de Sacramentis*. In this passage, Peter the Chanter worked through a number of *quaestiones* about the character of the eucharist, many of which had been previously explored in the literature thanks to the works of earlier scholars (see, for example, Peter Lombard, *Sentences*, bk. 4, dist. 12, c. 1). The use of the technical vocabulary of logic can be taken for granted, as can the objective of finding a conception of the eucharist sufficiently coherent to be applied consistently across a range of problems.

The durability of the *Sentences* as a text—it was the object of commentaries from the 1160s until the sixteenth century[48]—conceals the extent to which the discipline was transformed between 1140 and 1220. Even when subsequent masters often found commentaries on the *Sentences* a useful form for

48. For the earliest commentaries on the *Sentences*, see O. Lottin, *Psychologie et morale aux XIIe et XIIIe siècles* (Louvain and Gembloux, 1942–60), 6: 9–18.

the exposition of their own ideas, they did not feel particularly bound by the Lombard's opinions (see Text 10). It is possible that less of his doctrine survived into the thirteenth century than of William of Conches's grammar. Moreover, the discipline itself was, in many respects, new in the twelfth century. The very word *theology* goes back no further than 1100, having been coined by Abelard, and systematic exploration of the faith had

The contents of the old and new laws are made known, by diligent investigation and constant reflection on ourselves, the grace of God leading the way, when in treatises on the sacred matters one is occupied principally with things and signs; as the illustrious Augustine says in his book *On Christian Doctrine*, "All doctrine concerns either things or signs, but things are learned by signs. Strictly speaking, I have here called a *thing* that which is not used to signify something else; there are also signs whose whole use is in signifying." Of those there are some whose use is entirely in signifying, not in justifying; these we do not use unless for signifying something, as some sacraments of the old law. There are others which do not only signify but also confer that which sustains within, as the evangelical sacraments. From which it is obviously understood what are called signs here, that is, those things which are used to signify something. "Therefore, every sign is also some thing. For that which is not a thing," as Augustine says (in the same book and place), "is nothing at all." But the contrary is not truly, for "not every thing is a sign" because it is not used for signifying something [bk. 1, dist. 1].

Excerpt from *Glossae super sententias*

Circumcision justified . . . But other sacraments of the old law, also carried out with charity, did not justify, as Augustine said, but charity justified.

But it may be objected: those works were done in charity, and therefore were meritorious. Also *the merit of those works consists of the will*, which whether *good or bad has its own merit before it is brought to an effect*. But those were done from good intention and will. Therefore they were meritorious, especially since the authority says [Luke 11:34]: *if your eye is sound your whole body is full of light*. Therefore it is seen by some such as master Odo that sacraments of the old law justify.

Excerpt from *Summa Udonis*

Since therefore we made mention of signs, it should be known that some signs were instituted for signifying and sanctifying, as all sacraments of the new law; others however were for signifying but not sanctifying, as all sacraments of the old law, except circumcision which both signifies and sanctifies, i. e., it cleanses from sin; as Bede . . .

It also seems, however, that it can be proved that other sacraments of the old law not only signify but sanctify in this way: *the merit of those works* principally *consists of the will*, and likewise the merit of the work and will. *For whether good or bad the will or intention has its own merit before it is brought to an action* and the merits of a deed are computed accordingly . . . and further: *if your eye is sound your whole body is full of light* [both glosses from O. Lottin, *Psychologie et morale*, 6: 10–11; all trans. Radding].

Text 10. An excerpt from Peter Lombard's *Sentences* with two early glosses. Commentators extended the range of discussion by raising questions not explicitly treated in the Lombard's text and by noting the views of other scholars and commentators.

barely begun even by his death.[49] Patristic writers such as Augustine had discussed a wide range of issues, and individually had been generally consistent in their views, but none of them had attempted to construct an intellectual system free of inconsistencies by systematically studying problems from all possible angles. The physical character of the eucharist, which had provoked the eleventh-century debate between Berengar and Lanfranc, had been one issue not considered by the Fathers. But it was not unique, and as theologians began to collect and use topically arranged sentence collections, they discovered many other areas where the silence of the Fathers or their lack of agreement left much work to be done. Still other problems were posed by customs that had grown up rather casually over previous centuries and that now needed to be justified by theological arguments.

What was involved in this endeavor can be illustrated by the efforts to define the practice of penance. The work of deciding what was and was not a sin had begun quite early; some glosses of Anselm of Laon discuss specific cases, the questions apparently having arisen while he was commenting on the Bible; and the distinction between good action and good intention had been greatly clarified by Abelard's *Ethics*. Yet at midcentury much still had to be settled before the new ideas of penance could be applied generally throughout the church. Ordinary priests had to be instructed, for which purpose Alan of Lille—a Parisian master of extraordinary range—wrote the first confessor's handbook in the 1180s; it was followed by several others, also by Parisian masters, in the early thirteenth century. The success of the handbooks, moreover, depended on the analysis of a multitude of situations, a task that was taken up with enthusiasm by the Parisian master Peter the

Chanter and his associates in the late twelfth and early thirteenth centuries. Although the Chanter's *Summa de Sacramentis et animae consiliis* discusses all seven sacraments, its bulk consists of *quaestiones* regarding the appropriate penance for a wide range of instances.[50] The case of the thief who permits an innocent man to be convicted of his crime, of the master who accepts money for teaching, of Christian moneylenders: all these found their way into the Chanter's *Summa*.

Work of this kind was important, because it was through applying such new concepts as "venial" sin to cases that the masters clarified the implications of their doctrines. Yet at the same time that the masters were deepening their understanding of individual concepts, they were also seeking to establish links between concepts so that they would eliminate the possibility of contradictions within the faith. Their goal, as Chenu wrote quoting Alan de Lille, was to make of theology a "'well ordered arrangement' (*artificioso successu*), [that] entered into the structuring of the faith itself."[51]

The formation of the doctrine of purgatory, eloquently explored by Jacques Le Goff, provides an example of this process at work.[52] The ideas inherited by twelfth-century scholars were contradictory. Although the Fathers had made no mention of purgatory, discussing the afterlife solely in terms of heaven and hell, some had also allowed for the possibility that suffering after death or prayers by the living could after a time liberate certain souls from suffering. This latter theme had been taken up in visions—notably one reported by Gregory the Great—and in the practice of prayers for the dead; indeed, the prosperity of many monasteries came to depend on gifts to

49. Colish, "Systematic Theology," notes that in the early twelfth century Rupert of Deutz and Honorius Augustodunensis, both Benedictine monks, wrote commentaries intended to give an overview of the key issues of the faith. Although comprehensive in form, however, these commentaries were not *systematic* in the sense we use the term here, to describe a conscious effort to resolve apparent contradictions by integrating the concepts used in different aspects of theological studies.

50. On penitential theology, see Paul Anciaux, *La Théologie du sacrement de pénitence au XIIe siècle* (Louvain and Gembloux, 1949). Peter the Chanter's *Summa* has been edited by Jean-Albert Dugauquier, Analecta mediaevalia Namurcensia, nos. 4, 7, 16, 21. For a detailed discussion of Peter the Chanter's work, see Baldwin, *Masters, Princes and Merchants*.

51. M.-D. Chenu, "The Masters of the Theological 'Science,'" in *Nature, Man, and Society in the Twelfth Century*, ed. and trans. Jerome Taylor and Lester K. Little (Chicago, 1968), 280.

52. *La Naissance du Purgatoire* (Paris, 1981).

finance such prayers. It was hardly possible that such practices (by 1100 already centuries old) would be cast aside in the twelfth century. But neither was it clear how such practices could be reconciled with emerging ideas of sin and penance. At a time when some scholars were prepared to argue that contrition alone might be sufficient to win God's forgiveness, how could actions alone, especially the actions of those other than the sinner, be of any value?

We can pick up the trail of twelfth-century discussions of this problem in Peter Lombard's *Sentences.* The Lombard dealt with the issue twice, both in the discussion of sacraments that comprises the fourth book. At distinction 21, on whether sins can be forgiven after death, the Lombard quoted from book 21 of *The City of God,* glossing to refer to venial sins (*venialia peccata*) Augustine's remark that the earthly materials ("wood, hay, and straw") would be burned away in purgatorial fires. This established a link to twelfth-century conceptions of sin, for the distinction between venial and mortal sins was in the process of being established virtually as the *Sentences* were being written.[53] Distinction 45 discussed the various "receptacles" of the souls of the dead. Here the Lombard reasserted the three Augustinian categories of souls—the good, the bad, and the not altogether bad—adding two categories of his own: the not altogether good and the moderately bad.

The Lombard had to contend with the whole, disorderly mass of patristic writings. The next generation of masters, in contrast, could take advantage both of the focus on reasonably well-defined problems provided by the *Sentences,* and of the concentration of masters and expertise provided by the studium, which made it easier to coordinate concepts that originally belonged to different areas of theology. Peter of Poitiers, for example, in the sentence collection modeled on that of the Lombard, borrowed the notion that purgatorial fire burned away venial sins from the Lombard's discussion of the afterlife and asserted an equation between penance paid for venial sins on earth and in the after-

life. "Two persons culpable of equivalent venial sins deserve to be punished equally for those sins, although one is punished in this life and the other in purgatorial fire."[54] And as the concept of venial sin drawn from penitential theology gave definition to purgatory, theologians of penance began to borrow the idea of purgatory for their own purposes. Thus, in reply to a *quaestio* whether masses could reduce penance for venial sins, Peter the Chanter based his answer on the theology of the afterlife: just as masses could reduce time in purgatory, so they could also reduce the amount of terrestrial penance to be performed.[55] Theology of the afterlife thus became firmly linked to penitential theology.

Through such means, by 1200 the existence of purgatory was established as a separate place in the afterlife where souls could expiate venial sins and from which the prayers of the faithful could help the dead gain release. In a sermon for All Saints Day in 1202, Pope Innocent III expanded the received dichotomy (dating from Peter Comestor's work in the mid-twelfth century) between the Church Militant on earth and the Church Triumphant in heaven to include the souls in purgatory. Confessors' manuals from the early 1200s discussed purgatory in relationship to prayers for the dead. Magisterial discussion continued, of course, but on details such as whether the pain of purgatory was greater than the pleasure derived from the sin.[56] Not only was purgatory's place in theology secure; it had become a commonplace.

The careful coordination of doctrines across a number of fields that turned early medieval visions of purgatory into approved doctrine was typical of much of twelfth-century theology. The process of ordering the faith went on in every area, whether scriptural studies, sacramental theology, or even the theology of the Trinity. These were all enormously complicated fields: it was the often anonymous work of specialists to determine what the main issues were and what principles worked best to eliminate contradictions in the

53. Le Goff, *La Naissance du Purgatoire,* 293–98.

54. *PL* 201: 1064.
55. Peter the Chanter, *Summa,* vol. 3, pt. 2b, p. 264.
56. Le Goff, *La Naissance du Purgatoire,* 236–39, 308, 319–72.

handling of different cases. Once this was done, however, it became possible to perceive connections between previously distinct specialties, as Peter the Chanter and Peter of Poiters did with the theology of the afterlife and penitential theology.

The eventual result of this kind of work was a theology whose general principles moved with considerable consistency across a whole range of issues. This lent strength and stability to the whole intellectual structure. One could not, after the early thirteenth century, question the existence of purgatory without being prepared to deal with penitential theology as well. Thus, if thirteenth-century theologians often dealt with more interesting or difficult problems, that is due in large part to the consensus about the fundamentals of faith that had been achieved in the twelfth century. But if specialists in theology generally attained a higher degree of consensus about essentials than did masters of the liberal arts, this consensus resulted less from any personal tendency among theologians to compromise their differences than from the circumstances in which they worked. Unlike grammar and logic, where controversies had little impact beyond the masters involved, theology easily shaded over into the domain of canon law, dealing with daily practices such as sacraments and generally defining the boundary between orthodoxy and heresy.[57] Not only was the pressure on masters eventually to reach agreement correspondingly greater than in the liberal arts, but once definitions were arrived at, they tended to be enforced by the coercive power of the church, effectively ending discussion. Only the doctrines constructed by twelfth-century jurists—another field where the necessity of rendering judgment had the effect of cementing consensus—would prove to be as enduring as those of the theologians.

The work described in this chapter was not a collective project in the sense of committee work. Most twelfth-century masters worked alone, taking responsibility—and, one supposes, credit—for their achievements. But it was the collective enterprise, which we have

called disciplines, that provided direction and audience for the individual scholars as well as the disciplinary matrix or consensus into which successive generations were initiated. In a real sense, one of the remarkable features of the medieval studium was that it achieved the institutionalization of jobs in the university, assuring employment for future scholars, without requiring them to teach only what they themselves had been taught. The masters remained free to open new areas of inquiry as older ones were exhausted, continually revitalizing the disciplines.

Having spoken of studium and disciplines, we may be permitted in conclusion a word on their relationship to cognition. Universities today are often criticized for the excessively specialized character of their curriculum. Instead of teaching eternal truths, professors insist on introducing their students to the latest ideas in their fields and to the most current problems. But what we have seen in this chapter is that this specialized character of university education has been there from the beginning; indeed, it may even be an essential part of the success of universities as educational institutions. Twelfth-century students acquired the skills that made them good priests or effective administrators by examining often esoteric questions of logic, grammar, or theology where the truth was still uncertain. It was not just that the questions were so difficult that anyone capable of mastering them could go on to master others. Much of the difficulty, and the intellectual stimulation that resulted, derived precisely from the fact that the students were encountering questions to which the answers were not entirely settled. When the masters themselves disagreed, students could not succeed by memorizing the right answers: instead of learning *what* to think they found that they could decide among competing and often contradictory positions only by learning *how* to think. The social importance of universities, which has helped secure their place in western and now world civilization for the past eight hundred years, is thus an extension of the ability of disciplines constantly to find new areas worthy of debate when old ones have become settled or exhausted.

57. See, in particular, the fundamental work of J. de Ghellinck, *Le Mouvement théologique du XIIe siècle*, 2d ed. (Bruges, 1948).

7 · The First Half-Century of Gothic

he words *Romanesque* and *Gothic*, as used to describe buildings, were unknown in the Middle Ages. They are of modern coinage, used generally to contrast art and architecture before and after Saint-Denis, and we continue to employ them in this book because we believe there were genuine differences between art and architecture of the eleventh and early twelfth centuries and much of what was built after 1150. These differences did not, however, consist of a new stylistic vocabulary: the rib-vaults and pointed arches of Gothic replacing the low, round arches and groin-vaults of Romanesque. We have seen that the crypt at Saint-Denis itself used groin-vaults and round arches, and one can as easily point to Romanesque buildings conceived in modules that used rib-vaults and pointed arches— Durham Cathedral, for example. Likewise, round arches continued to be used in a Gothic context right through the end of the twelfth century. Romanesque and Gothic must be understood to reflect profoundly different attitudes toward architectural space and not simplistically limited to technical or stylistic features. When we use the term *Gothic*, we are directing attention to the diffusion of the design process, pioneered at Saint-Denis, by which builders integrated different design elements into an overall, unified conception of space. The familiar stylistic vocabulary that has come to identify Gothic architecture emerged only gradually, over more than half a century of experiments.

THE COMMUNITY OF BUILDERS

Although architecture changed greatly in the eighty years following Saint-Denis, little evidence exists by which one can trace changes in the social or occupational status of builders. Given medieval attitudes toward manual arts, there is nothing too surprising in this indifference; indeed, it was not until Alberti wrote about architecture in the fifteenth century that the builder's creative role in designing buildings began to be widely appreciated. Yet if the social position of builders remained essentially unchanged, the character of their work underwent a rapid development in two important areas: the builders took closer control of the work site by giving artisans more specific instructions for more complicated projects, and they paid closer attention to one another, exchanging information and techniques with remarkable rapidity. In modern terms, they moved from being contractors to architects, in both their cohesiveness as a group and their desire for technical and stylistic innovation.

The first detailed description of a major construction project comes from the later twelfth century, Gervase of Canterbury's account of the rebuilding of Canterbury cathedral after the fire of 1174.[1] Gervase mainly discusses the progress of the construction, giving the number of columns or arches erected each year, and modern research has confirmed the accuracy of his account. He does, however, also give us a valuable glimpse of the interaction between master builders and their employers, in this case the monks, in the passage where he discusses the advice the monks received as they tried to assess the damage caused by the fire:

French and English builders [artifices] were called in, but they disagreed in their advice. Some promised to repair the [damaged] columns without harm to the works above, but others contradicted this opinion, saying that the whole church would have to be demolished if the monks wished it to be safe. Such advice, if it were true, caused great sadness, since the monks could not hope that any human could complete such a great work in their time. But then among the other builders there came one named William of Sens, a very vigorous man and a builder extremely skilled in both wood and stone, whom the monks hired on account of the liveliness of his intelligence and the good reputation of his work, committing the work to him and God's providence. He spent many days with the monks, carefully inspecting the burnt walls above and below, inside and out, but for a long while he was silent about what would have to be done lest he too sharply upset those who were timid. Nor did he cease to prepare that which was necessary to be done for the work whether he did it himself or it was done by others. When he saw that the monks were somewhat consoled, he admitted that the pillars were harmed by the fire and that everything above would have to be destroyed if the monks wished to have a safe and incomparable work. Convinced by reason they agreed, desiring the work he promised to have the greatest safety.[2]

William of Sens brought the monks around to his ideas by taking them through the ruins of the chevet, so they could see for themselves the damage from the fire in detail, and by describing the building he planned—thus revealing a skill at dealing with patrons that architects have needed ever since.

When it comes to describing the builder's role during construction, Gervase's history is far less informative. We know that the builder closely supervised the work force because it was while directing work on the crossing in the fourth year of building (1179) that William of Sens fell some fifty feet to the floor. Although seriously injured, William continued to direct the work from his bed using a monk as an intermediary, for the remainder of the building season, but his health having failed to improve, William retired and returned to France. And we know that builders were able to understand one another's designs because William's replacement, William the Englishman, was able to continue the plan through the point where an expansion of the scheme marks the introduction of his own design. But for more detail on these important issues, it is necessary to supplement the written record with other kinds of evidence.

Perhaps the most interesting indications of the builder's management of the work site are provided by the evidence of molding templates. The control of artistic details apparent at Saint-Denis would in itself have led us to suspect the use of such templates, but in fact Gervaise mentions that one of William of

---

1. *Opera Historica*, ed. William Stubbs, *Rerum Britannicarum Medii Aevi Scriptores*, vol. 73, no. 1, pp. 3–29, but only pp. 6–7 and 19–22 discuss the construction itself. The most accurate English translation of Gervase's chronicle is still that by Robert Willis, *The Architectural History of Canterbury Cathedral* (London, 1845); reprinted in *Architectural History of Some English Cathedrals*, vol. 1 (Chicheley, 1972). Jean Bony made two minor but important corrections to the Willis translation in "French Influences on English Gothic Architecture," *Journal of the Warburg and Courtauld Institutes*, 12 (1949): 1–15.

2. *Opera Historica*, 6–7 (translated by Radding).

Sens's first acts was to give "forms" to his sculptors.[3] Templates from this period do not survive, although they could not have been greatly different from those drawn in the mid-thirteenth century by Villard de Honnecourt. The use of tracing floors, on which master builders sketched profiles at full size, or other convenient surfaces that could be used as templates may also date back to the twelfth century. At Soissons Cathedral there is both a full-scale engraving on the wall of the profile for a window and, adjacent to it, the window that was made from it.[4]

The real measure of the extent to which builders formed a discipline, however, is provided less by their control over artisans than by their communication among themselves.

Here, unsurprisingly, there is no direct written evidence at all. The builders neither wrote nor were written about. But the diffusion of information about flying buttresses, a new and still experimental technology in the later twelfth century, nonetheless attests to such communication.

At Notre-Dame-de-Paris flying buttresses were first used in the work on the nave that began circa 1170–75, as a device to support the gallery roof and the main vaults, which were then the highest that had been attempted. The basic idea, bracing the wall with quadrant arches to contain the outward thrust of the stone vaults and timber roof, probably had precedents in the chevet at Paris where arches hidden by the gallery roof were

3. "Formas quoque ad lapides formandos his qui convenerant sculptoribus tradidit" (*Opera Historica*, 7).
4. Lon R. Shelby, "Medieval Masons' Templates," *Journal of the Society of Architectural Historians* 30 (1971): 140–54; Shelby, "The 'Secret' of the Medieval Masons," in *On Pre-Modern Technology and Science*, edited by B. Hall and D. West, Human Civilitas, no. 1 (Malibu, 1976), 201–19; H. R. Hahnloser, ed., *Villard de Honnecourt*, 2d ed. (Graz, 1972); Carl F. Barnes, Jr., "Le 'Problem' Villard de Honnecourt," in *Les Bâtisseurs des cathédrales gothiques*, ed. R. Recht (Strasbourg, 1989), 209–23; Barnes, *Villard de Hon-*

necourt (Boston, 1982); Barnes, "The Gothic Architectural Engravings in the Cathedral of Soissons," *Speculum* 47 (1972): 60–64; P. du Colombier, *Les Chantiers des cathédrales* (Paris, 1953; new ed., 1973); J. Fitchen, *The Construction of Gothic Cathedrals* (Oxford, 1961); Jean Gimpel, *The Cathedral Builders*, new ed., trans. Teresa Waugh (New York, 1985); R. Mark, *Gothic Structural Experimentation*, (Cambridge, Mass., 1982); R. Mark, *High Gothic Structure*, (Princeton, 1984); R. Mark, *Light, Wind, and Structure*, (Cambridge, Mass., 1990).

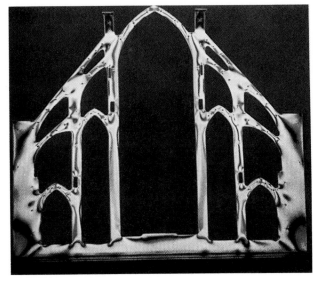

61. Paris, Notre-Dame, windloaded photoelastic model, nave section. In these three windloaded models, the areas of greatest stress are indicated by the concentration and density of contrasting patterns visible under polarized light.

62. Chartres, Notre-Dame, windloaded photoelastic model, nave section.

63. Bourges, Saint-Etienne, windloaded photoelastic model, chevet section.

intended to support the clerestory or high window wall. But the flying buttresses of the nave were both higher than those quadrant arches of the chevet and fully exposed, permitting the builder to contain the greater thrusts produced by the wider span of flatter vaults and the roof of the nave, while at the same time reducing the weight of the walls by opening wider clerestory windows. As an elegant solution to the problem of building on a grand scale without massive walls, this innovation spread rapidly. The Paris designs were almost immediately imitated at Saint-Martin at Champeaux, a church owned by the bishop of Paris, and other buildings further afield.[5]

As it happened, experience revealed faults in the original design ca. 1220–25. Photoelastic modeling of the original Paris buttresses has shown that under heavy wind loading, such as would occur in a storm of a severity likely to occur once or twice in a forty-five-year period, the compressive stress would

have produced readily apparent cracking of the mortar at the two points where the buttresses met the walls (Figures 61, 62, and 63). It was probably in response to such cracking that a major redesigning of the buttresses of Notre-Dame was undertaken in the 1220s, and these are the buttresses that (rebuilt by Viollet-le-Duc) are still seen today. Yet the important point is that work on flying buttresses was not confined to Paris. News of problems at Paris evidently spread quickly. Within a few years of the new buttressing having been begun at Paris, similar projects were begun at Bourges, Chartres, and Reims, among other sites, and even as far away as Spain in anticipation of the same problem that had developed at Paris. This rapid diffusion of technical information, which could have been accomplished only by communication among the builders themselves, is the best imaginable evidence of the extent to which the builders formed a community.

Technical information was not, of course, the only subject on which builders communicated with one another. They were also acutely aware of one another's designs, responding to experiments elsewhere with in-

5. William W. Clark and Robert Mark, "The First Flying Buttresses," *Art Bulletin* 66 (1984): 47–65; for the next paragraph, see Mark and Clark, "Gothic Structural Experimentation," *Scientific American*, Nov. 1984, 176–85.

novations of their own. The character of the discipline of architecture thus gave direction to the development of architectural style in the twelfth century, and it is to this subject that we now turn.

SAINT-DENIS TO CHARTRES

Interaction between twelfth-century master builders is, of course, best illustrated by the history of architectural style in the half century after Saint-Denis, for the builders responded to the innovations of their peers in much the same way as the masters.[6] As was also the case with the masters, however, the path of development between Saint-Denis and Chartres was by no means direct, and not simply because the builders were interested in experimentation. Later Gothic styles were by no means implicit in Saint-Denis itself, anymore than later twelfth-century logic was implicit in Abelard. Rather, if we are to understand the buildings, we must imagine each major architect as having before his eyes both existing buildings as well as other buildings under construction as he set about to solve the particular design and engineering problems he faced. The challenge was then not to copy those previous buildings as much as it was to integrate specific ideas or features used elsewhere into an essentially original composition. Thus the basic process of design remains similar to that of the builder of Saint-Denis, although the actual buildings that resulted were necessarily shaped by the particular historical moments in which their designs were decided.

In this section, therefore, instead of organizing our exposition around specific design

6. Recent general treatments of early Gothic architecture include Jean Bony, *French Gothic Architecture of the 12th and 13th Centuries* (Berkeley, 1983); Dieter Kimpel and Robert Suckale, *Die gotische Architektur in Frankreich 1130–1270* (Munich, 1985). Examples of the complexity of early Gothic are discussed in Robert Branner, "Gothic Architecture 1160–1180 and Its Romanesque Sources," *Acts of the Twentieth International Congress of the History of Art, New York, 1961. Studies in Western Art* (Princeton, 1963) 1: 92–104. Bony's book updates some of Branner's hypotheses and should be consulted for discussions of all the buildings mentioned in this chapter.

features such as windows or vaults, we have adopted a strictly historical approach, breaking the later twelfth century into four architectural generations: the period immediately after Saint-Denis, including an aside on sculpture; the mid-1150s to 1160s as represented by Paris and Laon; the response to Paris and Laon in the 1170s and 1180s; and finally Bourges and Chartres from the 1190s. Our treatment of each generation will necessarily be selective. We cannot discuss every important building or every significant question regarding even the buildings we do discuss. Our purpose, rather, is to trace the shifting conditions in which the builders worked and the process by which they developed Gothic style.

Following Saint-Denis

One of the curiosities of the 1140s is the apparent disappearance of the builder who designed the east end of Saint-Denis. Saint-Denis was probably the builder's first independent project, placing him at an early stage in his career, and the east end itself was completed by 1144. Moreover, many of the stonecutters who worked for him at Saint-Denis can be traced through work they did around Paris in the 1140s and 1150s. Yet the builder himself seems to have simply disappeared. Suger may have kept the builder on at Saint-Denis until nearly 1150 for work on the transept, completed by 1148, and on the nave that was planned and begun but not completed. But after that date there is no surviving work that can be attributed to his hand.

The fate of the Saint-Denis master is of particular interest because of the cautious response to Saint-Denis in those buildings constructed immediately after it in the 1140s and early 1150s. Nowhere in this period was a building attempted that was quite as ambitious as Saint-Denis, even by other builders who had worked under the Saint-Denis master. Two builders—those for Saint-Maclou of Pontoise and Saint-Germer-de-Fly—borrowed specific elements of Saint-Denis's east end for their own buildings, whereas the builders of Saint-Germain-des-Prés and Sens showed some skill at adapting the complex design strategies of Suger's builder. But on the whole this generation of architecture is probably best understood as one in which the standards of design gradually rose as builders struggled with the intellectual problems of applying the lessons of Saint-Denis to practical problems.

The builders of Saint-Maclou of Pontoise and Saint-Germer-de-Fly knew Saint-Denis well enough to borrow from it ideas about organizing the east end of their own buildings, but their innovations consisted chiefly of incorporating aspects of the regional styles within which they worked into simplified versions of Saint-Denis's plan.[7] At Saint-Maclou of Pontoise, for example, although the ambulatory and radiating chapels are vaulted together in imitation of the vaulting scheme of Saint-Denis, the builder, who had worked at Saint-Denis, retained a clear distinction between the two parts of the chevet instead of erasing it as at Saint-Denis (Figures 64 and 65). The wall, moreover, is still that of the regional style with round-headed windows and simple moldings that relate to the wall and not to the wall shafts or vaulting. The builder at Saint-Germer-de-Fly, who had certainly seen Saint-Denis but who had probably not worked there, also tried to simplify the complexities of Saint-Denis, this time within the context of the rich Anglo-Norman regional style. One might say that the problem presented here was how to combine the spatial achievement of Saint-Denis while retaining the Oise valley compound pier instead of adapting the column. Yet the compromise is only partially successful. The lines of the vaults here do drop to the floor, although rather awkwardly, and do, through the wall

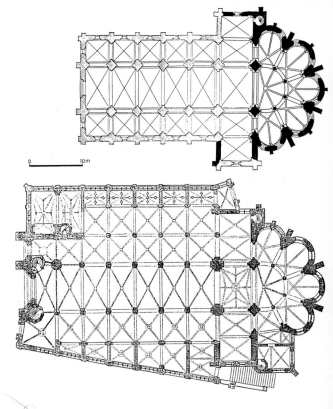

64. Pontoise, Saint-Maclou, restored plan and current plan.

65. Pontoise, Saint-Maclou, interior of ambulatory and chapels. Although much altered, vestiges of the original design of the chapel windows and wall remain in this east end where the vaulting of the ambulatory and chapel together is derived from the chapel vaults of Saint-Denis.

7. For Pontoise, see Eugène Lefèvre-Pontalis, *Monographie de l'église Saint-Maclou de Pontoise* (Pontoise, 1888); and Lefèvre-Pontalis, "Pontoise, église Saint-Maclou," *Congrès archéologique (Paris)* 82 (1919): 76–99. For Saint-Germer-de-Fly, see Maryse Bideault and Claudine Lautier, *Ile-de-France gothique*, vol. 1: *Les Eglises de la vallée de l'Oise et du Beauvaisis* (Paris, 1987); A. Besnard, *L'Eglise de Saint-Germer de Fly et sa Sainte-Chapelle* (Paris, 1913); P. Héliot, "Remarques sur l'abbatiale de Saint-Germer et sur les blocs de façade du XIIe siècle," *Bulletin monumental* 114 (1956): 81–114; J. Henriet, "Un édifice de la première génération gothique," *Bulletin monumental* 143 (1985): 93–142; and M. Pessin, "The Twelfth-Century Abbey Church of Saint-Germer-de-Fly and Its Position in the Development of First Gothic Architecture," *Gesta* 17 (1978): 71.

responds, create a continuous interweaving along the outer wall, but these features do not open the space (Figures 66 and 67). As at Pontoise, the attempt to simplify Saint-Denis and to retain elements of regional styles resulted in a building that was far less radical than the original.

At Saint-Germain-des-Prés, in Paris, the builder's strategy took a different approach. His commission may have made innovation a necessity. Unlike Pontoise and Saint-Germer, Saint-Germain was a rival of Saint-Denis as a royal abbey and burial site of kings. In itself this fact may have made an obvious copy of the plan of Saint-Denis impossible. The monks of Saint-Germain would not have wished to offer Suger the compliment of imitating him, and in any case Saint-Germain lacked relics important enough to justify a dramatic, elevated platform. Liturgical practice may also have been different at Saint-Germain-des-Prés, requiring more individualized chapels. The basic plan of the new chevet was thus comparatively conservative, with chapels, ambulatory, and central space each clearly marked out from the other (Figure 68). Yet the builder's handling of details within each area shows clearly that he, at least, understood what had been accomplished at Saint-Denis, down to the planned harmonization of architectural elements from earlier periods with the new work.[8]

The chapels illustrate the Saint-Germain builder's complex response to Saint-Denis, which involved not simply borrowing specific ideas but freely reworking elements from Saint-Denis into an original, coordinated design (Figure 69). Although the chapels were treated more as distinct units than the feretory chapels at Saint-Denis, having both smaller windows and a clear boundary with the ambulatory, the builder articulated the wall with much the same decorative vocabu-

lary of detached and coursed shafts as that employed by Suger's builder (Figure 70). The result is a space that in its internal unity owes something to both the crypt and upper-level chapels of Saint-Denis while imitating neither. The deliberate organization of architectural elements, moreover, makes it plain that the overall effect, as at Saint-Denis, was planned from the beginning. The capitals and bases of the piers at the chapel entrances are particularly instructive in this regard. Those within the chapels are positioned on the diagonal facing in, preparing visually for the rib to be carried from the capital to the keystone of the chapel, whereas those on the outside of the chapel follow the plan of the ambulatory wall. Using two types of capital and base positioning on the same pier is without precedent either at Saint-Denis or the other buildings immediately derived from it. Its appearance here indicates the extent to which the builder was looking ahead to the total effect even as work was proceeding on the lower courses of stone.

In the design of the ambulatory and the central space at Saint-Germain-des-Prés, the builder similarly incorporated means both borrowed from Saint-Denis and original with him. The columns of the hemicycle and the outer piers line up as at Saint-Denis, but since the ambulatory was simply to be a passageway, he minimized projections that might interrupt the eye's movement along the walls (Figure 71). Many of the capitals resemble those of Saint-Denis and not surprisingly so: the same craftsmen carved them. The borrowings in the central space go still further. Thus, although the thirteenth-century replacement of the upper levels at Saint-Denis prevents direct comparison, the general effect of the upper levels of the chevet of Saint-Germain-des-Prés—including a three-level elevation and the use of wall-shafts and formerets to create a surface pattern—was similar to that of Saint-Denis (Figure 72). Yet the builder also knew how to innovate to accommodate the more conservative floor plan of Saint-Germain. For example, because the choir was to be visually cut off from the ambulatory and chapels, he moved the keystone of the hemicycle vault about one meter east of the geo-

8. William W. Clark, "Spatial Innovations in the Chevet of Saint-Germain-des-Prés," *Journal of the Society of Architectural Historians* 38 (1979): 348–65. References to earlier work are given there. See also L. Grodecki, *Saint-Germain-des-Prés* (Paris, 1945); E. Lefèvre-Pontalis, "Etude historique et archéologique sur l'église de Saint-Germain-des-Prés," *Congrès archéologique (Paris)* 82 (1919): 301–66; and P. Plagnieux, "Le Portail de XIIe siècle de Saint-Germain-des-Prés à Paris," *Gesta* 28 (1989): 21–29.

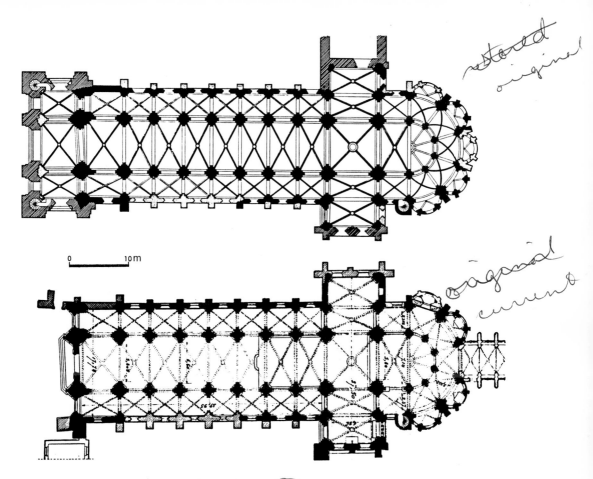

[handwritten: restored / original]

[handwritten: original / current]

66. Saint-Germer-de-Fly, restored plan and current plan.

67. Saint-Germer-de-Fly, ambulatory piers from the east. The adaptation of rib vaults to the design of the compound pier, reflecting both new and older preferences, resulted in some awkward visual joinings at the level of the capitals.

[handwritten: 1150]

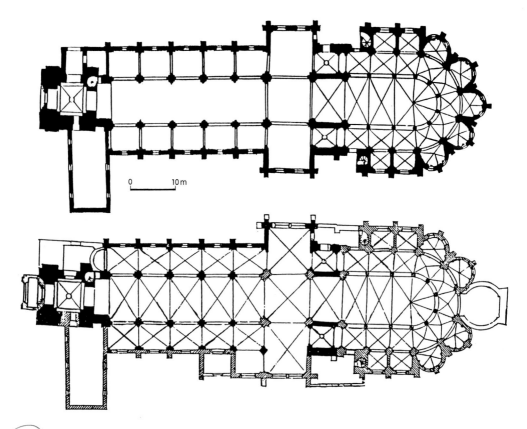

68. Paris, Saint-Germain-des-Prés, restored plan, ca. 1163, and current plan.

69. Paris, Saint-Germain-des-Prés, chevet exterior.

70. Paris, Saint-Germain-des-Prés, chapel interior. The chapel originally had two large windows, but their openings have been filled in with masonry in this example.

71. Paris, Saint-Germain-des-Prés, ambulatory.

metric center according to which the ambulatory and chapels were laid out. The intention, clearly, was to emphasize the spatial unity of this central liturgical area, and it was in this area that the new tombs of the founder and other Merovingian royalty were placed.

Although the builder of Saint-Germain-des-Prés showed both a thorough understanding of Saint-Denis and an ability to employ the same systematic planning, Saint-Germain-des-Prés itself contained no major innovations. The last building we have to consider, however, both offers a more radical response to Saint-Denis and indicates some of the potential of the new style. The cathedral of Sens was certainly begun before 1140 (possibly as early as the late 1120s),[9] and in its earliest parts it was a very traditional building. Thus, the chapel of Saint John on the north side has the massive wall and half-dome vault typical of the regional style in the early twelfth century, and the very wide nave may originally have been intended to have a wooden roof (Figures 73 and 74). Yet as construction proceeded, the design changed, apparently under the impact of Saint-Denis (Figures 75 and 76). The innovations are particularly significant because the new features—the wall was increased in height, the windows were enlarged, and rib vaults were added—were not so much borrowed from Saint-Denis as arrived at by the Sens builder as a means to achieve the spatial integration of Saint-Denis's east end in the different and much larger scale of the Sens nave. (The single aisle at Sens is nearly as wide as the double aisle at Saint-Denis [6.70 versus 7.30 meters], and the height of the ambulatory is 12.10

9. Bony, *French Gothic Architecture*, 66, notes that the Chronicle of Saint-Pierre-le-Vif lists the rebuilding of the cathedral as one of the first acts of Archbishop Henri le Sanglier (1122–42). For the size of Sens compared to St.-Denis, see p. 475, n. 21. On Sens, see Kenneth W. Severens, "The Early Campaign at Sens, 1140–1145," *Journal of the Society of Architectural Historians* 29 (1970): 97–107; Severens, "The Continuous Plan of Sens Cathedral," *Journal of the Society of Architectural Historians* 34 (1975): 198–207; Severens, "The Cathedral at Sens and Its Influence in the Twelfth Century" (Ph.D. diss., Johns Hopkins University, 1968); Jacques Henriet, "La Cathédrale Saint-Etienne de Sens," *Bulletin monumental* 140 (1982): 81–168; and L. Bégule, *La Cathédrale de Sens* (Lyon, 1929).

72. Paris, Saint-Germain-des-Prés, chevet interior. The enlargement of the clerestory windows downward in the seventeenth-century changed the proportions of this three-story elevation but did not alter the character of the unified space.

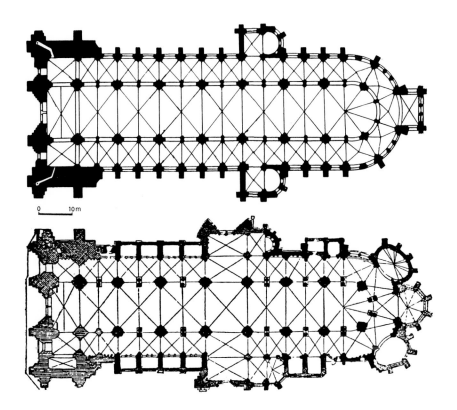

73. Sens, Saint-Etienne, restored plan and current plan.

74. Sens, Saint-Etienne, chapel of Saint-Jean, interior.

75. Sens, Saint-Etienne, ambulatory.

76. Sens, Saint-Étienne, chevet interior. The plan was
changed several times in the early phases of the construction with the result that the chevet of Sens became the first Gothic essay in colossal size.

1140

meters against 7.60 at Saint-Denis.) The results were not always felicitous. Bony observes that the earlier outer walls "are in striking disagreement with the central structure of the choir and nave." And the engineering depended almost entirely on using walls thick enough to contain the forces created by the weight of the vault without further buttressing. But in struggling to cope with the large volumes that made up the central space, the 1140s builder devised a system that used alternating compound piers and double columns linked by moldings to the aisle wall and to the main elevations that had the effect of integrating the separate, Romanesque-style modules into the first large, organized space. This achievement was to mark the point of departure for the next generation of builders.

Early Gothic Sculpture

One of the main issues in the study of early Gothic sculpture has been the attempt to define the moment when the change from Romanesque to Gothic occurred. This problem has arisen because all attempts to differentiate the two have focused on purely stylistic issues and, as with architecture, there are stylistic similarities between the two periods, particularly in the sculpture at Saint-Denis.[10] If, however, we seek the differences in the relationship between sculpture and architecture, or in the changing emphasis from the threat of damnation to the promise of salvation, then the change can be understood in terms that transcend style. Because of the damage to Saint-Denis's sculptures during the French Revolution, however, early Gothic sculpture is most easily studied not there but at Chartres.

The three western portals of Chartres, known collectively since the thirteenth century as the royal portal, were originally planned shortly after the facade of Saint-Denis was completed in 1140 (Figure 77).[11] The first plan was for a wider location, probably the front of the eleventh-century cathedral. The three portals were erected, however, in their present location circa 1145–1150, between the two west towers, both begun by 1142. Like the three lancet windows above them, the towers and portals survived the 1194 fire and, with the addition of the giant rose window, were retained as the west facade of the new cathedral.

According to the most recent analysis, the royal portal, which is unquestionably the best known example of early Gothic sculpture, is the work of three major artists, each of whom worked about the same length of time and each of whom created about the same amount of sculpture. The stylistic interconnections of the works attributed to each is an indication that they were all working at the same moment.[12] Indeed, the iconographic program, salvation through Christ, provides another link among all three portals. The central portal tympanum shows Christ enthroned in Majesty, surrounded by the symbols of the Four Evangelists, with angels and the twenty-four Elders of the Apocalypse in the archivolts, while the Apostles occupy the lintel (Figure 78). Taken in its entirety, the tympanum represents the Second Coming of Christ and symbolizes the triumph over death. The north portal tympanum, traditionally identified as the Ascension of Christ, might also represent Christ's First Coming, which would be appropriate with the Second Coming in the central portal and the Incarnation or earthly life of Christ shown in the south portal. The presence in the archivolts of the lateral portals of

10. P. Z. Blum, "The Lateral Portals of the West Facade of the Abbey Church of Saint-Denis," in *Abbot Suger and Saint-Denis*, ed. P. Gerson (New York, 1986); S. McK. Crosby and P. Z. Blum, "Le Portail central de la façade occidentale de Saint-Denis," *Bulletin monumental* 131 (1973): 209–66; W. Sauerländer, *Gothic Sculpture in France 1140–1270* (London and New York, 1972); F. Joubert, "Recent Acquisitions, Musée de Cluny, Paris. Tête de Moïse provenant du portail droite de Saint-Denis," *Gesta* 28 (1989): 107; and New York, Metropolitan Museum of Art, *The Royal Abbey of Saint-Denis in the Time of Abbot Suger (1125–1151)*, ed. S. Crosby, J. Hayward, C. Little, and W. Wixom (New York, 1981).

11. W. Sauerländer, *Das Königsportal in Chartres* (Frankfurt, 1984); O. Nonfarmale and R. R. Manaresi, "Il Restauro del "Portail Royal" della Cattedrale di Chartres," *Arte Medievale*, 2d ser. 1 (1987): 259–75; A. Lapeyre, *Des Façades occidentales de Saint-Denis et de Chartres aux portails de Laon* (Mâcon, 1960); and W. Stoddard, *Sculptors of the West Portals of Chartres Cathedral* (New York, 1987).
12. W. Stoddard, *Sculptors of the West Portals of Chartres Cathedral* (New York, 1987).

77. Chartres, Notre-Dame, royal portal.

78. Chartres, Notre-Dame, tympanum of the central door of the royal portal.

79. Chartres, Notre-Dame, statue-columns of the left jamb of the central portal.

80. Chartres, Notre-Dame, statue-columns of the right jamb of the central portal.

the labors of the months and the signs of the zodiac lends terrestrial and celestial significance to the whole.

The arrangement of these figures in relation to each other and to their architectural setting exhibits none of that inner tension and dynamic animation that characterizes Romanesque sculpture. In the tympanum at Saint-Lazare in Autun the figures present a terrifying vision of the threat of damnation and suffering awaiting unrepentant sinners at the end of the world. The teeming, crowded tympanum space is filled with attenuated twisting figures, many of them writhing in fear from the threat of a last judgment explicit in its depictions of tortuous punishments. In contrast, the majestic version of the central portal at Chartres relieves much of the crowding by removing the Elders and Apostles to the archivolts and lintel and replaces the threat of damnation with the promise of salvation—an eternal existence as ordered, peaceful, and harmonious as the composition itself, centered on the supremely confident figure of Christ.

The New Testament scenes in the upper part of the portal are visually supported by the tall, thin statue-columns of Old Testament Kings, Queens, and Prophets set in the door splays (Figures 79 and 80). Here we see the new relationship between architecture and sculpture that first appeared at Saint-Denis elevated to new heights of expression. In fact, statue-columns were probably first used on the portals at Saint-Denis, but those were unfortunately removed in the late eighteenth century.[13] In contrast, most of the statue-columns at Chartres survive in excellent condition: of the twenty-four original statue-columns, sixteen remain in place in the portals, another became the sundial on the south tower in 1564, and three were replaced with modern copies in the 1970s.[14] These calm, grand figures seem to float serenely in space in front of their supporting columns, touching neither top nor bottom. Yet their slim vertical proportions, like their tightly positioned arms, are dictated by the architectural framework behind them. An underlying abstract conception of the composition governs the placement of all the heads at the same level, in spite of the obvious differences in height, and the repetitive positioning of their arms, the right one raised, the left one lowered, in spite of the differences in gestures, attributes, and even rank and gender. At the same time, the figures are remarkably free from that tension between architecture and sculpture that is so characteristic of the Romanesque period.

Early Gothic sculpture shows the same extraordinary stylistic variety and technical experimentation as early Gothic architecture in the period from the completion of the west facade of Saint-Denis in 1140 right through the sculptures of the great cathedrals of the early thirteenth century, from Laon, Mantes, and Sens to the transepts of Chartres, Paris, Reims, and Amiens. There is considerable technical experimentation with the actual structure of a portal, such as the form and treatments of the door splays in relation to the statue-columns or the placement of the lintel or, more difficult to study owing to the losses, the presence or absence of a trumeau. We find influences from a wide variety of sources, from metalwork and ivories (at Laon and Mantes) to newly imported Byzantine art (at Senlis and Paris). Indeed, in the later twelfth century, whole new modes of seeing and ways of signifying meaning make their appearance, some of these are only now being investigated.[15] All of these experiments in style, meaning and structure are analogous to the experimentation taking place in architecture and in the other visual arts.[16]

Paris and Laon

In the mid-1150s the first buildings that clearly went beyond Saint-Denis were finally begun: Notre-Dame of Paris and Notre-Dame of Laon. The builders of Paris and Laon saw their tasks in very similar terms. Learning from Sens, they built on a large scale, with Paris being the highest and longest building so far attempted. Both builders, moreover, sought to integrate these large volumes by using ornament that was visually logical and suggested lines of construction. At Laon, for example, the ornament consists of detached shafts creating a vertical grid on the wall, yet these shafts were mounted with the grain of the stone vertically positioned so that it would have sheared off had it actually been required to bear much weight. In the working out of details, the master builders of Paris and Laon made decisions very different from one another, a variety that can remind us that for twelfth-century builders Saint-Denis was less a design to be imitated or adapted than a standard that could be lived up to in many different ways, a system of thinking rather than an artistic model.

13. F. Joubert, "Recent Acquisitions, Musée de Cluny, Paris. Tête de Moise provenant du portail droite de Saint-Denis," *Gesta* 28 (1989): 107.
14. On the recent cleaning, see Nonfarmale and Manaresi, "Il Restauro." See also, M.-C. Chadefaux, "Le Portail Royal de Chartres," *Gazette des Beaux-Arts* 6th ser. 76 (1970): 273–84; M.-A. Chevallier and L. Pressouyre, "Fragments récemment retrouvées du Portail Royal de Chartres," *Revue de l'art* 57 (1982): 67–72; W. Sauerländer, *Das Königsportal in Chartres*; and W. Stoddard, *Sculptors of the West Portals of Chartres Cathedral*.

15. Madeline H. Caviness, "Images of Divine Order and the Third Mode of Seeing," *Gesta* 22 (1983): 99–120, is one of the more perceptive investigators. See also Caviness, " 'The Simple Perception of Matter' and the Representation of Narrative, ca. 1180–1280," *Gesta* 30 (1991): 48–64.
16. See New York, Metropolitan Museum of Art, *The Year 1200*, ed K. Hoffman (New York, 1970), and the continuing discussions.

Despite the fact that construction required many decades under the supervision of a succession of master builders, the basic plans of both buildings were implicit in the work done by the first builder on each site. Of the two, Paris is closer to Saint-Denis.[17] As conceived by the first builder, who directed work on the chevet from around 1155 until perhaps 1170, the plan called for a five-aisled building culminating in a double ambulatory—perhaps reflecting, as Branner remarked, the plan Suger had intended for the nave at Saint-Denis that he did not live to complete, although equally inspired by the five-aisled plan of the Merovingian cathedral of Saint-Étienne (Figure 81). But the differences from Saint-Denis are

17. In addition to the articles cited in note 5, see Jean Bony, "Essai sur la spiritualité de deux cathédrales," *Chercher Dieu*, Rencontres 13 (Paris, 1943): 150–67; William W. Clark, "The Early Capitals of Notre-Dame-de-Paris," *Tribute to Lotte Brand Philip* (New York, 1985), 34–42; Clark and Franklin M. Ludden, "Notes on the Archivolts of the Sainte-Anne Portal of Notre-Dame-de-Paris," *Gesta* 25 (1986): 109–18. Caroline Bruzelius, "The Construction of Notre-Dame de Paris," *Art Bulletin* 69 (1987): 540–69 offers important insights into the thirteenth-century work at Notre-Dame, but her hypotheses for the twelfth-century chevet fail to explain all of the facts or to consider all of the evidence. See William W. Clark and Robert Mark, "Le Chevet et la nef de Notre-Dame de Paris," *Journal d'histoire de l'Architecture* 2 (1989): 69–88; F. Salet, "Notre-Dame de Paris, état présent de la recherche," *La sauvegarde de l'art français* 2 (1982): 89–113; C. Wright, *Music and Ceremony at Notre Dame of Paris 500–1550*, Cambridge Studies in Music (Cambridge, 1989); Annie Blanc and Claude Lorenz, "Observations sur la nature des materiaux de la cathédrale Notre-Dame de Paris," *Gesta* 29 (1990): 132–38; and Chantal Hardy," Les Roses dans l'élévation de Notre-Dame de Paris," *Bulletin monumental* 149 (1991): 163–99.

81. Paris, Notre-Dame, restored plan and current plan.

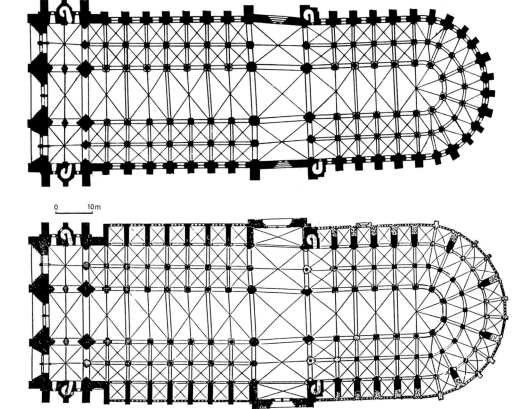

0 10m

82. Paris, Notre-Dame, ambulatory.

plex vaulting scheme for the ambulatory ceilings that eliminated divisions between the bays. Finally, in what Bony has aptly characterized as a stroke of genius, he planned a transept that, although not projecting and disrupting the lines of the wall, nevertheless dramatically opened up the entire east end to a viewer in the nave (Figures 83 and 84). In effect, the builder sacrificed the compact unity of the chevet in order to achieve a wonderful sweep of space around the east end, visually linking it to the western extension of the cathedral.

Beginning with the upper stories of the chevet that date from the early 1170s, direction of the construction passed to a second builder. This builder began the nave, increasing its height to over 100 feet, and he also faced the problems imposed by the technical demands of the more ambitious design. He was a master engineer. Although stone vaults had never been attempted at such heights, these vaults are among the finest and most accomplished medieval stonework—quite

83. Paris, Notre-Dame, nave aisles.

even more important. In the first place, the first builder chose not to have the columns marking off the double ambulatory align with one another or with the windows. Instead of visually merging with the choir, the ambulatories thus became layered spaces beyond it (Figure 82). This was not an error on the builder's part, but part of a conception that stressed continuity of rhythm and space over regularity. Indeed, that this was the builder's objective becomes apparent whenever we compare the chevet of Notre-Dame with that of Saint-Denis. On the peripheral wall of the east end, for example, which was the earliest part of the construction, the builder eliminated the gentle bulges of the Saint-Denis chapels in favor of a smooth continuous curve punctuated on the inside by wall responds and on the outside by buttresses. Further, in a conception that looked ahead to the plan for the nave, he preserved a regularity of spacing between the columns, even devising a com-

84. Paris, Notre-Dame, chevet wall. New evidence suggests that the original elevation was somewhat different from the way in which Viollet-le-Duc restored it in the bays adjacent to the crossing in the nineteenth century.

85. Paris, Notre-Dame, nave wall. The design of the nave, which was correctly restored to four stories by Viollet-le-Duc in the bays adjacent to the transept, was wider, taller, and more open than that of the chevet, reflecting the incorporation of the flying buttresses.

different in that regard from the chevet, where changes in the vaulting from bay to bay reveal that the masons were experimenting with ways to achieve this vaulting even as they constructed it (Figure 85). The nave builder also used flying buttresses first to carry the ramped up gallery roof and to brace its wall, then to support the high vaults without obscuring the windows (Figure 86). But apart from the increased height and expanded width, the basic schema followed that laid out by the first builder (Figure 87). Sculpture completed in the mid-twelfth century, apparently for the first builder's design of the west facade that may have been partly built before the decision was made to extend the length of the nave, was used in the present west facade

that was built only after 1200. Even the molding profiles for the nave were clearly based on those originally used in the chevet.

The basic plan and constructional style of Paris, as well as the intricate coordination of details, link Paris to Saint-Denis, but Laon drew on very different sources.[18] In contrast to the compact plan of Paris, Laon stretched

18. For Laon, see William W. Clark and Richard King, *Laon Cathedral, Architecture (1)*, Courtauld Institute Illustration Archives, Companion Text 1 (London, 1983); Clark, *Laon Cathedral, Architecture (2)*, Courtauld Institute Illustration Archives, Companion Text 2 (London, 1986); E. Fernie, "La Fonction liturgique des piliers cantonnés dans la nef de la cathédrale de Laon," *Bulletin monumental* 145 (1987): 257–66; and E. Lambert, "La Cathédrale de Laon," *Gazette des Beuax-Arts*, 5th ser. 13 (1926): 361–84.

86. Paris, Notre-Dame, restored and current nave sections.

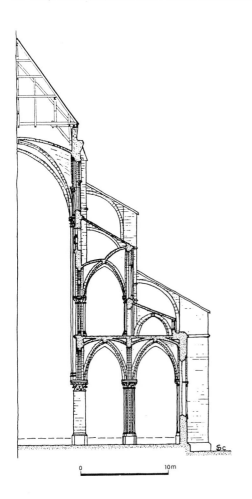

87. Paris, Notre-Dame, interior.

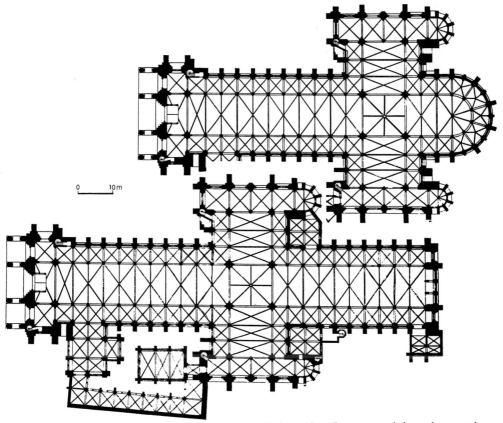

88. Laon, Notre-Dame, restored plan and current plan.

out to the four points of the compass. Its most distinctive conception, the crossing tower or lantern, was a feature the builder of Laon would have known from northern French and English Romanesque buildings such as the cathedral of Tournai (Figure 88). The heavier, deeply carved moldings were also inspired by regional sources, especially neighboring Noyon. But the builder transformed these ideas by placing them in a very different context, using them not to mark out divisions between units but to give a sense of ordered spaciousness to the whole building.

As at Paris, the basic scheme for Laon is apparent from the earliest construction on the chevet and eastern wall of the transept (Figures 89 and 90). The crossing tower, which was elevated above both transept and nave and equipped with windows on all sides, was to provide the spatial focus for the entire building. The light streaming from the cross-

ing tower onto the altar area below would by itself have made this the dramatic center of the building, but the builder enhanced the importance of the crossing tower by making the two transept arms equal in width, length, and height and ending the arms with rose windows and lancets similar to those later used on the west facade. The viewer is thus led to see the main volumes of the building as expanding from the central space—an effect enhanced in the thirteenth century by the extension of the original chevet to form a space that visually duplicated the volume of the nave.

The diversity in the approaches used by the builders of Paris and Laon went beyond the plans and elevations (where doubtless the needs of the respective chapters had to be satisfied) to the ornament chosen to articulate the interior spaces. This was an important issue because the length and height of both

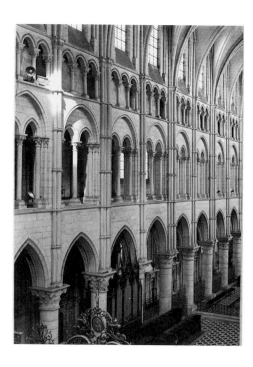

89. Laon, Notre-Dame, view across transept. The lantern tower over the crossing is the center point of the spatial organization at Laon.

90. Laon, Notre-Dame, nave wall.

1155

buildings meant that the builders had to deal with a huge expanse of wall, balancing horizontal and vertical lines in a grid so that neither overpowered the other. Both builders found the solution in devising a system of ornament that created a sense of structural lines, but the ornament they used for this purpose was entirely distinctive. At Laon, the builder chose clusters of separate shafts attached to the wall. These lend a sense of depth to the wall, and despite the fact that the lines of the shafts reached vertically, the thick clusters are so prominent—with their importance emphasized by the builder's use of similar decoration in the arches and in other moldings—that their repetition along the length of the wall creates a sense of lateral

movement as well (Figure 91). The imposed visual lines thus become the chief means of looking at the wall, and they are so integrated with the other elements of the elevation that we see the wall as a series of projections and recessions framing openings since so little surface remains.

At Paris, in contrast, the moldings and arches are exaggeratedly thin, but not because the builder wished them to be overlooked: he had the ornament undercarved to produce thin shadows emphasizing their presence (see Figures 83 and 85). Rather, the thin ornament was part of a general strategy of emphasizing the wall surface instead of concealing it as at Laon or the chevet of Saint-Denis, and the builder sought this effect in

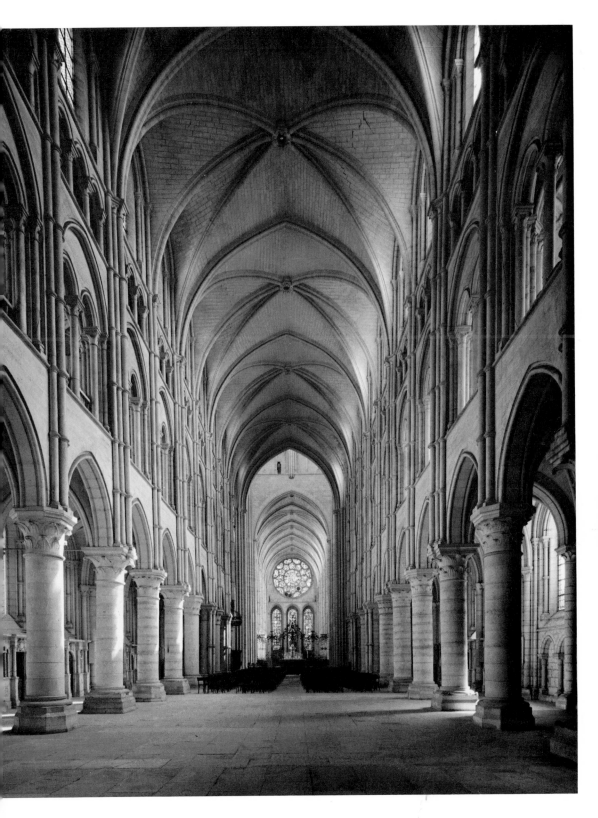

91. Laon, Notre-Dame, interior. A comparison of Laon with Notre-Dame de Paris, Figure 87, reveals not only the very different approaches to the treatment of the wall, but also the greater illusion of height at Laon, which, in reality, is only about three-quarters as tall as Paris.

other details as well. Before the window were enlarged downward in the thirteenth century, the elevation of Notre-Dame had four stories. Above the aisles and galleries, which formed the lower two stories, were a series of tracery oculi at the third story and a single window at the top level. Relatively large areas of blank wall surface were left around the oculi and windows. This wall did not suggest mass or thickness, however, because the very thin moldings created the impression of a delicate, thin wall, a membrane stretched between wall shafts, a smooth surface with little sense of depth. This implied thinness of wall is one of the most important aesthetic aspects of Notre-Dame, and one that was continued and exaggerated still more by the second master.

This brief discussion does not exhaust the list of points on which a comparison of Paris and Laon is instructive, nor did Paris and Laon hold a monopoly on architectural innovation in the third quarter of the twelfth century. Yet the variety may itself be the main point. At this stage of the development of architecture as a discipline, the specific features used mattered little. Saint-Denis itself was low with round arches and groin vaults in the crypt—Romanesque features according to most style sheets of medieval architecture. Moreover, once rib vaults, pointed arches, and other "Gothic" features became common, they could be employed even by builders whose approach to design was essentially that of Saint-Sernin. Lisieux Cathedral, a Romanesque structure "disguised" as Gothic, is one example.[19] What distinguished the builders of Laon and Paris (apart from their talent) was not their sources so much as their conception of a building as an integrated space and their attempt to coordinate design elements into a coherent plan. Only after the success of those buildings became apparent in the last quarter of the twelfth century did a distinctive vocabulary of forms, the Gothic style as we now know it, begin to take shape.

19. William W. Clark, "The Nave of Saint-Pierre at Lisieux," *Gesta* 16, no. 1 (1977): 29–38.

The Third Generation of Gothic

Paris and Laon were far from complete in 1170. Many important features—the nave with flying buttresses and the famous facade at Paris, the west facade with its rose window at Laon—still lay in the future, not to be finished until after 1200. But the innovations of even the unfinished buildings were apparent to the expert eye of master builders, who drew upon them to create freely in the buildings under construction in the 1170s and 1180s. The important point about this period, however, is not the importance of Paris or Laon or any single building as a source of ideas. Rather, it is the way builders of these decades responded to one another's innovations, not only freely borrowing specific design features and combining them in new ways, but finding original means to achieve the overall aesthetic effect they saw elsewhere and wanted to accomplish. From the perspective of the history of disciplines it is this intensity of interaction among the builders that commands attention, for it demonstrates the extent to which they looked beyond their own work sites to the activities of their professional peers.

This is not to diminish the patrons' impact. Indeed, chapters and bishops must have responded favorably to, and even encouraged through their commissions, the intensity of experimental activity among the builders. The patrons still made the basic decisions about the main features they wanted in consultation with the master builders; about the presence or absence of separate chapels and the number needed, as well as their location; about the needs and size of the liturgical area; about whether or not to have a transept and how prominent it should be. If Canterbury is an accurate indication of other projects, the chapter interviewed several builders before making a decision. But the translation of the requirements, the shaping of space around liturgy to the satisfaction of the clergy was the exclusive sphere of the master builders.

Notre-Dame of Mantes, which was begun about 1170, illustrates the expertise and intelligence needed even to adapt ideas found else-

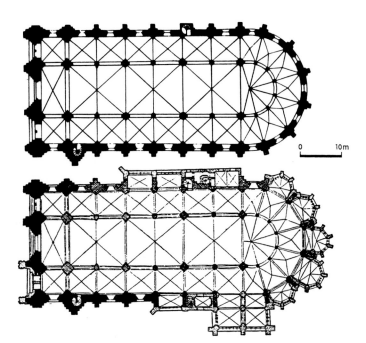

92. Mantes, Notre-Dame, restored plan
and current plan.

where.[20] The builder preserved Notre-Dame's sweep of space around the east end in a simplified plan with a single side aisle and ambulatory, no transept, and—as at Paris—no radiating chapels (Figure 92). This compact plan, combined with the thin, Parisian-style moldings and large expanses of undecorated wall, served only to enhance the impression of a central volume enclosed by a thin shell of stone. Yet Mantes is less a small-scale copy of Paris than a rethinking of the Parisian aesthetic of thin walls and compact spaces for a smaller, simpler building (Figure 93). The builder obviously understood which elements had to be retained and which could be changed without harming the overall effect; thus, although he borrowed his molding styles from Paris, he chose to use compound piers and columns in alternation, rather than col-

umns alone, and capitals that were markedly different from those at Notre-Dame. Also striking was his adaption of the east end. With only a single ambulatory, the builder was able to align ambulatory columns with the windows as at Saint-Denis, and he vaulted the choir with a keystone over the point of convergence. Even though the aesthetic objective of Mantes was clearly inspired by the nave of Paris, the builder knew how to achieve it by using specific design elements different from those used at Notre-Dame.

The Mantes builder showed the same intelligence in his use of flying buttresses. His earliest walls, built before flying buttresses were introduced at Paris were substantial: about four feet thick at the base. But when the breakthrough in buttress design was achieved, the Mantes builder not only incorporated them quickly into his design, he understood their significance. Beginning with the second story of the gallery, the walls shrink dramatically in thickness, to less than eighteen inches (Figures 94 and 95). Later, when the Parisian flying buttresses proved

20. J. Adams, *An Architectural Analysis of Mantes-la-Jolie* (M.A. thesis, Tufts University, 1976); R. Bailly, *La Collégiale Notre-Dame a Mantes la Jolie* (Mantes, ca. 1980); J. Bony, "La Collégiale de Mantes," *Congrès archéologique (Paris-Mantes)* 104 (1946): 163–220; and J. Bony, *Notre-Dame de Mantes* (Paris, 1947).

93. Mantes, Notre-Dame, interior. The aesthetic pref-
erence for flat surfaces and the resulting sense of thinness reveal, as does the actual plan, that Mantes is a
smaller-scaled "copy" of the nave of Notre-Dame de Paris.

1170

94. Mantes, Notre-Dame, chevet exterior.

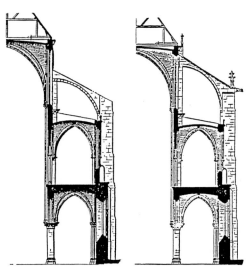

95. Mantes, Notre-Dame, restored and current nave sections. The dramatic thinning of the wall, made possible by the introduction of the flying buttress, is visible in the difference between the outer wall's thickness in the first and second stories.

problematic in the 1220s, the builder then in charge of Mantes responded quickly to the crisis by devising distinctive buttress arches positioned on top of the vertical supports. This increase in height caused the arches to abut the wall at a higher point and thus support the vaults and roof more directly.

If the builder of Mantes simplified the design of Notre-Dame, the builder of the chevet of Saint-Remi of Reims returned to Saint-Denis and the several copies made after it.[21] The rebuilding of Saint-Remi was at least in part a response to the attempt by Saint-Denis to claim the royal coronation from Reims because, as keeper of the miraculous oil and the relics of Saint Remi, the monastery played an important role in the coronation ceremony. Between 1160 and 1165 abbot Pierre de Celle initiated the rebuilding with a new western

facade; an elaborate mosaic was also installed in the floor around Saint Remi's tomb. Construction on the east end began around 1170, leaving the older nave intact as at Saint-Denis.

This east end was one of the most distinctive designs of this generation. Where the chevet joined the existing nave, the builder provided for two side aisles, with the inner side aisle leading to an ambulatory rimmed with columns (Figures 96, 97, and 98). These

21. The most recent work on Saint-Remi is A. Prache, *Saint-Remi de Reims*, Bibliothèque de la Société française d'archéologie, no. 8 (Geneva, 1978); Prache, *Reims* (La-Pierre-qui-Vire, 1984); and Prache, "Saint-Remi de Reims," *Congrès archéologique (Champagne)* 135 (1977): 109–21. See also the new book on the stained glass of Saint-Remi by Madeline H. Caviness, *Sumptuous Arts at the Royal Abbeys in Reims and Braine* (Princeton, 1990).

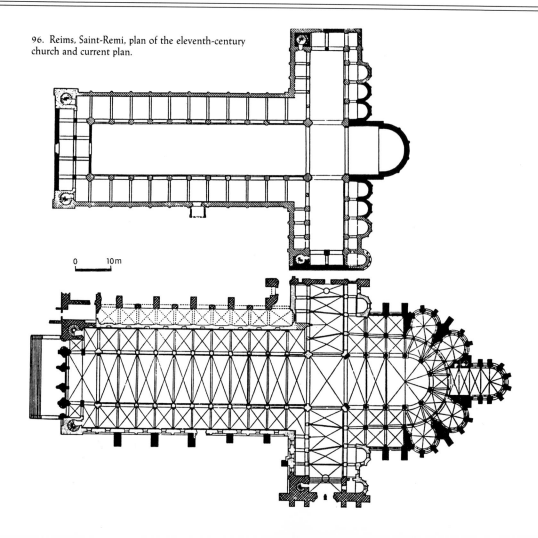

96. Reims, Saint-Remi, plan of the eleventh-century church and current plan.

0   10m

97. Reims, Saint-Remi, exterior of the chevet. The dramatic double volley of flying buttresses around the chevet of Saint-Remi probably results from the desire to increase the number of windows in the gallery and clerestory walls.

98. Reims, Saint-Remi, ambulatory.

1170

99. Reims, Saint-Remi, chevet interior. The builder's
fascination with multiple window openings contributes
to a light-filled interior that glows with stained glass
and a reduced wall space.

1170

columns play a double role, for they both support the vaults and form a screen through which the five radiating chapels are partially seen. The chapels themselves are laid out as perfect circles with the keystones of the vaults positioned directly over the centers. It hardly needs to be added that all these details had to be completely planned before construction began; even the complex vaulting for the ambulatory must have been part of the original conception. All in all, Saint-Remi is the most integrated design of its generation.

Sources can be found for many features at Saint-Remi. The general plan for a five-aisled chevet structure may have derived from Notre-Dame if not from Saint-Denis. The Saint-Remi builder also drew upon the twelfth-century cathedral of Reims, the chevet of which was dated from the 1150s and 1160s and was probably inspired directly by Saint-Denis: it may have been from Archbishop Samson's chevet that the builder took some of the richness of the moldings he used in the east end, for these are carved far more deeply than those of Paris. But even where the influence of earlier buildings is apparent, the builder was not content simply to copy them. In designing the ambulatory, for example, the Saint-Remi builder may have had in mind the way the builder of Notre-Dame devised a special vaulting plan to produce the effects he wanted for his east end; but whereas the vaulting of Notre-Dame uses diagonal ribs to create patterns in the trapezoidal bays, that of Saint-Remi uses square bays within the trapezoids, the outer sides resting on the columns that screen the chapels, with small expanding triangles to fill out the space (Figures 81 and 96). Similarly, although the builder's use of flying buttresses was probably inspired by the example of Paris, the actual shape of the buttress and windows are original to Saint-Remi. If anything, the Saint-Remi builder pushed the implications of flying buttresses further than did the nave builder of Paris, because the tribune and clerestory levels are now almost entirely windows (Figure 99). Everywhere the builder used multiple window openings, but the triplets of the gallery and clerestory are unquestionably the most complex of his designs.

The last building we will consider is Canterbury cathedral, which Gervase's text permits us to date exactly to the years between 1175 and 1184 (Figures 100, 101, and 102).[22] At Canterbury, as at Saint-Remi, an existing building had to be considered. But the first builder of Canterbury, William of Sens, also faced a problem unknown at Mantes and Saint-Remi, that of reconciling the stylistic details he learned from his previous experience—probably in Flanders and northern France, as well as the Ile-de-France—with local traditions and a local work force. For example, although William probably got the idea of using contrasting stone for shafts and capitals from buildings such as Tournai cathedral, the actual moldings he used to implement that idea were adapted from English precedents.

Because of William's injury, from 1179 construction was in the hands of a second builder, known as William the Englishman. This William had probably worked under William of Sens, and the general schema that he carried out—including such concepts as a progressive enrichment of ornamentation as one approached the shrine and tomb of Thomas Becket—continue that of the first builder. Other aspects of William the Englishman's work are of special interest for documenting the extent to which builders engaged on one project paid attention to their colleagues' work at other sites. It seems a reasonable guess

22. On Canterbury, see Jean Bony, "French Influences," with additional comments and references in Bony, *French Gothic Architecture*, 159–61. Also see P. Draper, "William of Sens and the Original Design of the Choir Termination of Canterbury Cathedral 1175–1179," *Journal of the Society of Architectural Historians* 42 (1983): 238–48; P. Kidson, "Canterbury Cathedral: The Gothic Choir," *Archaeological Journal* 126 (1969): 244–46; Y. Kusaba, "Some Observations on the Early Flying Buttress and Choir Triforium of Canterbury Cathedral," *Gesta* 28 (1989): 175–89; *Medieval Art and Architecture at Canterbury before 1220*, ed. N. Coldstream and P. Draper, British Archaeological Association Conference Transactions 1979 (London, 1982); K. W. Severens, "William of Sens and the Double Columns at Sens and Canterbury," *Journal of the Warburg and Courtauld Institutes* 33 (1970): 307–13; Robert Willis, *Architectural History of Canterbury Cathedral* (London, 1845), reprinted in *Architectural History of Some English Cathedrals*, vol. 1 (Chicheley, 1972); and F. Woodman, *The Architectural History of Canterbury Cathedral* (London, 1981).

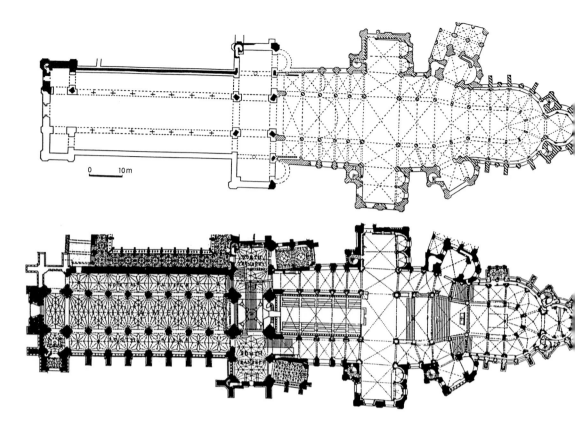

100. Canterbury Cathedral, restored plan, ca. 1185, and current plan.

101. Canterbury Cathedral, exterior of Trinity Chapel.

102. Canterbury Cathedral, interior. The rising floor
levels and increasing richness of decoration, which
rivals Saint-Denis, direct the worshipper to the site of
the tomb of the martyred archbishop, Thomas Becket.

that the English William spent every winter in Paris, because almost as soon as details were first employed at Notre-Dame in Paris, Mantes, and Saint-Remi at Reims, among others, they appeared at Canterbury. Indeed, given the precise dating of each pier possible from Gervase's account of the construction, Canterbury cathedral itself provides important evidence for establishing the dates of the corresponding work at Paris and Saint-Remi. Several capitals, for example, copy specific capitals at Notre-Dame and Saint-Remi, even down to details such as the use of the drill and undercutting, details that could not be transmitted by patterns. To effect such close copies, William would have either brought a sculptor with him or imported one from France to England to do the carving. William also copied the flying buttresses at Paris, although less successfully than the builders of Mantes and Saint-Remi, since his buttresses do not actually resist any outward pressures. Evidently William imitated the form without fully understanding the purpose.

Looking at the third generation of Gothic from the modern perspective, we can easily see influences and derivations from previous buildings. Yet even allowing for the extent to which this understanding is correct—and we must not underestimate the creativity that went into the apparently simple reworking of Notre-Dame of Paris at Mantes—this generation's work meant that the builders of 1190 faced a set of challenges very different from their own. With Mantes, Saint-Remi, and other buildings now added to Paris, Laon, and Saint-Denis, the range of available models was far greater, and the possibility of creating a distinctive design with a simple variation correspondingly less. But the breadth of experiment also opened up the possibility of synthesis, so much so that the last decade of the twelfth century saw not one synthesis but two.

Bourges and Chartres

Begun almost simultaneously in the mid-1190s, Bourges and Chartres cathedrals provide very different summations of the experience of the previous half century: whereas Bourges offered the ultimate complexity in an elaborately engineered and designed plan of great subtlety, Chartres achieved a radical simplification of previous designs. Yet the differences between the two buildings should not disguise the builders' shared participation in the architectural milieu of the late twelfth century. The comprehensive approach to design, so revolutionary when it first appeared at Saint-Denis, had now become completely standard for major buildings. Both Bourges and Chartres were thought through completely, down to the last detail. Both builders also realized that the flying buttress was the major technological innovation of their time. Although earlier buildings, such as Laon and Saint-Remi, had used flying buttresses to bolster designs of a type previously conceived without them, the builders of Bourges and Chartres planned buildings that would have been impossible without the new buttressing systems. Both builders, finally, responded to the experiments in spatial organization of the previous half century, sharing, as Bony observed, "an overall vision . . . of an intelligible and perfectly ordered universe."[23]

Begun in 1195, Bourges combines the late twelfth-century taste for intricate design with extraordinary sophistication in engineering. The builder who planned Bourges was, in both respects, the equal of the master who built Saint-Denis (Figure 103 and 104).[24] At thirty-six meters, Bourges was the tallest building of the twelfth century, but the height was achieved with remarkable efficiency. Although the flying buttresses are quite steep and light, containing relatively little weight of stone, photoelastic modeling has shown that

23. Bony, *French Gothic Architecture*, 245–46.
24. The principal works on Bourges are R. Branner, *La Cathédrale de Bourges et sa place dans l'architecture gothique* (Paris and Bourges, 1962) and Branner, *The Cathedral of Bourges and Its Place in Gothic Architecture*, ed. by Shirley Prager Branner (Cambridge, 1989). Other important works include A. Blanc, P. Lebouteux, J. Lorenz, and S. Debrand-Passard, "Les Pierres de la cathédrale de Bourges," *Archéologia* 171 (1982): 22–35; R. Branner, "Encore Bourges," *Journal of the Society of Architectural Historians* 25 (1966): 299–301; J. Michler, "Zur Stellung von Bourges in der gotischen Baukunst," *Wallraf-Richartz Jahrbuch* 41 (1980): 27–86; and M. Wolfe and R. Mark, "Gothic Cathedral Buttressing: The Experiment at Bourges and Its Influence," *Journal of the Society of Architectural Historians* 33 (1974): 17–27.

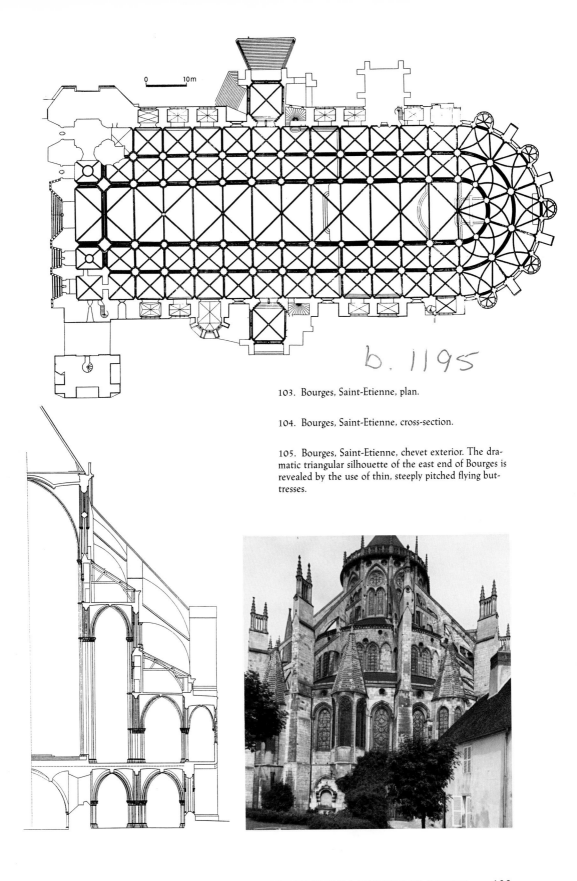

b. 1195

103. Bourges, Saint-Etienne, plan.

104. Bourges, Saint-Etienne, cross-section.

105. Bourges, Saint-Etienne, chevet exterior. The dramatic triangular silhouette of the east end of Bourges is revealed by the use of thin, steeply pitched flying buttresses.

the stresses borne by the chevet flyers are one-half to two-thirds as great as in comparably large buildings (Figure 105). What the builder designed was a building nearly as wide as it is tall and almost triangular in cross section because the inner aisle is dramatically higher than the outer aisle. In effect, the forces from the main vaults and roof stepped successively down to the vaults of the inner and outer aisles, with the steep arches of the flying buttresses helping to convey the forces directly to the ground.

It is the mark of the sophisticated planning of the Bourges builder that some of the same features that contributed to the efficiency of the buttressing also worked to enhance the open spaciousness that is the building's special achievement. In the absence of a transept, the sweep of wall along the nave around the chevet turns it into a single, vast space in which all of the bay divisions are subsumed into the whole; yet the height of the inner side aisle permits the viewer to see through to the windows of the exterior wall despite the building's great width (Figures 106, 107, 108, and 109). Thus, from the outer wall on one side it is possible to see all three levels of the main elevation, as well as all three levels of the outer wall of the inner aisle, and, at the lowest level, the windows of the outer aisle (Figures 110, 111, and 112), giving the visual impression of five stories with three levels of windows and two wall-passages, an audacious visual scheme.

Chartres cathedral was begun in 1194, following a fire that left intact only the west facade and the crypt of Fulbert's church (Figures 113 and 114.[25] Construction of the new

106. Bourges, Saint-Etienne, outer ambulatory.

107. Bourges, Saint-Etienne, inner ambulatory.

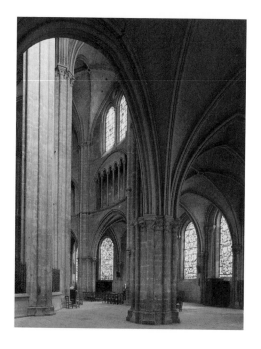

25. On Chartres see, in addition to Bony, André Chédeville, *Chartres et ses campagnes XIe–XIIIe siècles* (Paris, 1973). Important recent bibliography includes B. Klein, "Chartres und Soissons," *Zeitschrift für Kunstgeschichte* 49 (1986): 437–66; C. Lautier, "Les Peintres-verriers des bas côtés de la nef de Chartres au début du XIIIe siècle," *Bulletin monumental* 148 (1990):7–45; N. Levis-Godechot, *Chartres* (La-Pierre-Qui-Vire, 1987); J. van der Meulen and J. Hohmeyer, *Chartres, Biographie der Kathedrale* (Cologne, 1984); J. Michler, "La Cathédrale Notre-Dame de Chartres," *Bulletin monumental* 147 (1989): 117–31; J. W. Williams, "The Windows of the Trades at Chartres Cathedral" (Ph.D. diss., University of California at Los Angeles, 1987).

108. Bourges, Saint-Etienne, chevet piers. The extraordinary height of the piers at Bourges opens the aisles and reveals the multiple levels of the lower elevations.

109. Bourges, Saint-Etienne, ambulatory piers seen from above.

110. Bourges, Saint-Etienne, chevet interior.

111. Bourges, Saint-Etienne, nave from ambulatory.

112. Bourges, Saint-Etienne, full elevation.

ing was double or even triple the norm, it must have been considerably larger than the average.

Although Chartres is an exceptionally well documented building, the master builder, as usual, is neither named nor mentioned. Nevertheless, his artistic personality emerges clearly from the building itself. He was an experienced builder, for he knew what corners could be cut to achieve more rapid construction. His whole scheme is simplified with this aim in mind, as well as with an awareness that the scale of the project obviously limited his ability to oversee every detail. The most radical simplifications concerned the reduction of elevation to three stories and the enlargement of the components to colossal size. The design involves both repetition and regularity, from the bases of the piers through the rectangular rib-vaults (Figures 115 and 116). In addition, each element has been rethought. The builder used only three levels—tall windows of equal size (fourteen meters) in the aisle and clerestory separated by a narrow wall passage or triforium—to achieve the great height of nearly thirty-five meters. Bourges, in contrast, uses five levels, in which windows alternate with tall wall-passages, to reach an only slightly greater height.

More obviously aesthetic concerns can be seen in the Chartres builder's choice of pier form for the main arcades: in the *piliers cantonnées* the core is surrounded by four axially disposed shafts that lend immediate visual emphasis to the vertical lines of the elevation. Interestingly, the piers alternate octagonal cores with round colonnettes and round cores flanked by octagonal colonnettes, a rather old-fashioned detail to be found in such an otherwise regular building. Many of the piers were irregularly aligned and roughly cut—a sign of rapid work—and some capitals appear

building was lavishly financed. In the first place, the building was planned to contain large expanses of stained glass. Even in the twelfth century stained glass was an expensive material, so the decision to employ it on such a scale must have been made by the chapter in consultation with the bishop, Pierre de Celle. (Pierre had been abbot of Saint-Remi when construction was undertaken there, so he was well-informed in such decisions.) Construction, moreover, proceeded at a great pace and on an enormous scale, with work going on simultaneously throughout the site. As a result of these efforts, the whole building was complete by 1221—an astonishingly short period for so large a project.[26] There is no reliable way to estimate the size of the work force needed to maintain this pace of construction, but since the scale of the undertak-

26. We cannot subscribe to the notion put forward by John James, *Chartres, les constructeurs*, 3 vols. (Chartres, 1979–82) that there was no architect, no animating artistic genius, who designed the cathedral of Chartres. Nonetheless, James's order, sequence, and perhaps even the time periods for the construction are acceptable. See L. Shelby, "The Contractors of Chartres," *Gesta* 20 (1980): 173–78. Anne Prache's forthcoming analysis of the documents suggests construction proceeded even more quickly.

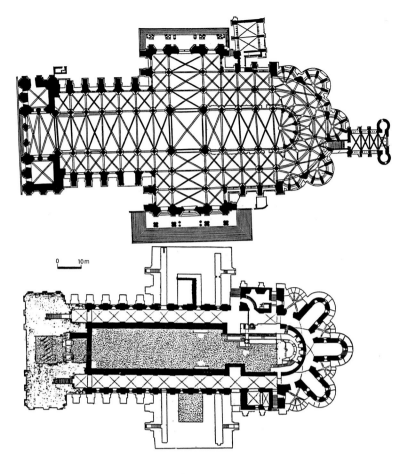

113. Chartres, Notre-Dame, current plan and crypt plan.

114. Chartres, Notre-Dame, section of chevet, interior and exterior nave elevations, and nave section.

115. Chartres, Notre-Dame, nave wall. Use of the flying buttresses allows the three-story elevation at Chartres to include clerestory windows as tall as the main arcades, and the four-part vaults permit regular repeating units in the bays.

clearly in his handling of engineering problems (Figures 117 and 118). Unlike the flying buttresses at Bourges, those of the nave at Chartres are massively overbuilt, with far more stone than is really necessary. Even the thinner buttresses of the chevet are overbuilt, as photoelastic modeling has shown, and too flat in their slope to be very efficient. This may indicate excessive caution on the builder's part, or he may merely have allowed for the fact that with the building going up so fast there was no time to watch how the first bays settled before building the rest.

Although Chartres and Bourges are comparable achievements, their influence was disproportionate: the direct influence of the Bourges scheme can be seen in only five buildings, whereas that of Chartres, with the modifications in its basic design introduced at Reims, became the standard model for most thirteenth-century construction. The reason is not hard to find. Precisely because of the intricate complexity of its design, Bourges was difficult to modify; the dimensions afforded too little leeway for builders to reduce or otherwise adapt them and to still preserve the spatial magnificence. Chartres, on the other hand, with its simplified elevation and less exacting engineering could be modified more easily to accommodate larger or smaller buildings.

The development of Gothic style is usually analyzed in terms of specific elements: round or pointed arches, rib vaults, elevations, plans, and the like. More important than such shifts in design features, however, was the change in the way builders worked within their architectural vocabulary. In the eleventh century, builders could simply borrow ideas, more or less unchanged, from other buildings, placing them in the corresponding place in a new structure. For example, in most instances it made little difference whether half-columns or pilaster strips divided one module from another, so long as the usage was consistent throughout the building. Twelfth-century builders, or at least the best of them, proceeded differently. Even when borrowing elements from other buildings, as at Mantes or even Saint-Remi, builders had to integrate

not to have been cut from a single piece of stone but to be carved slabs placed to imitate a capital. Such work was tolerable, however, because the builder knew that the stained-glass windows would produce a low level of interior lighting in which it would be impossible for viewers to scrutinize the quality of the stonework in detail. The interior painting, with its network of visually regular joints, also concealed irregularities.[27] The size of the piers made it easier and faster to build, as well as tending to subsume any irregularities in workmanship into big, bold architectural lines that lend a sense of power. In effect, the builder increased the size of individual components such as piers, windows, and buttresses while reducing the variety of the parts.

The builder's experience shows more

27. J. Michler, "La Cathédral Notre-Dame de Chartres," *Bulletin monumental* 147 (1989): 117–31.

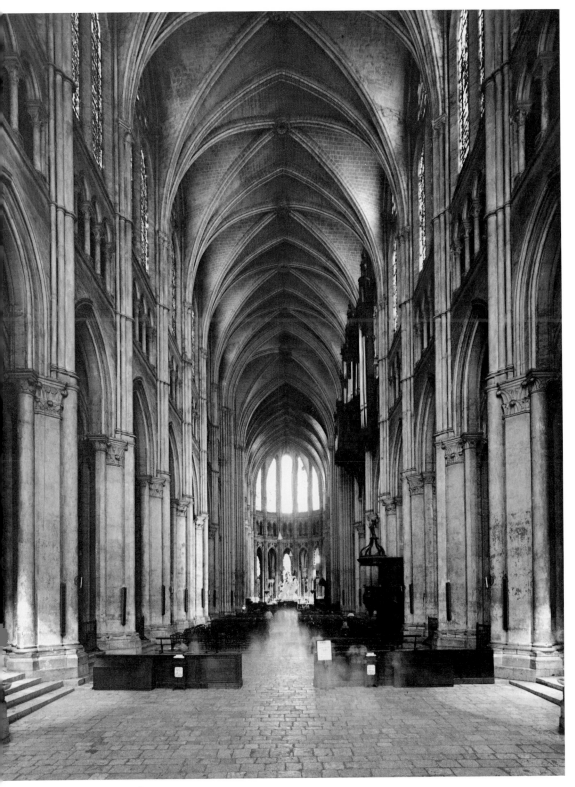

Started
1194

116. Chartres, Notre-Dame, nave interior.

them into a comprehensive design for their building to succeed. More than any individual element, it was this comprehensive approach to design and architectural space, pioneered at Saint-Denis and subsequently diffused throughout the architectural profession, that set twelfth-century architecture apart from that of the eleventh, Gothic apart from Romanesque.

117. Chartres, Notre-Dame, nave exterior.

118. Chartres, Notre-Dame, aerial view from the east.

Conclusion

Cultural history is often written as a succession of cultural products: ideas, doctrines, architectural elements, and the like. In this book, by emphasizing the cognitive processes or working methods of eleventh- and twelfth-century builders and masters, we have traced a transformation every bit as significant as that in the buildings and treatises they produced. In many ways, the crucial period was the eleventh century. During that century, certain builders and masters began to be distinguished from ordinary craftsmen or educated men by a process we can glimpse only dimly, mainly in the ever greater distances over which they were recruited. About the expertise that set them apart, however, we can be more certain: they demonstrated an increasingly thorough mastery of such specialized problems as piers, moldings, capitals, and other architectural details; concepts, *quaestiones* and the knowledge of how to manipulate such elements of knowledge to arrive at new results. Instead of seeing their task as teaching what their predecessors had taught them about specific issues, masters began systematically to move beyond older texts, paying attention to what their contemporaries said about problems and proposing solutions of their own. Builders similarly learned how to combine individual architectural elements to produce original results instead of imitating existing designs, continually renewing regional styles with new variations and often even crossing regional boundaries. Yet the essential point is not so much the originality of the product as the fact that the effort to produce something original led eleventh-century masters and builders into a deeper understanding of their areas of knowledge than the effort to reproduce existing models could ever have done.

The time consumed by this first stage, nearly a century, is a measure of the difficulty of the work involved. We may well suppose that, although each generation of specialists exceeded the expertise of their predecessors, each individual could go only so far independently. (A modern parallel might be found in the origins of quantum theory. Einstein, who had been introduced to the range of late nineteenth-century physics as a part of his schooling, proved able to retrace in a matter of months the path that had taken Planck decades, and within a few more months had seen far deeper into the problems than Planck ever would.)[1] By the twelfth century, however, the expertise into which young masters and builders were initiated had achieved a level that permitted the qualitative jump we saw in Abelard and the master builder of Saint-Denis: the shift to handling entire systems of concepts and design elements. Surprisingly few of Abelard's ideas or the builder of Saint-Denis's design elements were copied directly, at least by their most important successors. But their working methods set a standard of coherence, both intellectual and aesthetic, that the masters and builders of the later twelfth century understood and adopted.

The disciplines formed as a result of the history we have traced did not, of course, cease to exist after the twelfth century; indeed, they persist, with unbroken continuity to our own time. But if in this broader sense the process we have described is ongoing, there is another in which the first decades of the thirteenth century mark the end of the developments that are the subject of this book. From the 1210s and 1220s, inquiries turned in different directions, resulting in new experiments in both architecture and scholarship. The coincidence in timing may not be entirely accidental. By the 1220s, the lines of inquiry begun in the 1150s had been pursued for more than half a century and over several intellectual generations, time enough, perhaps, to have exhausted the patience and interest of builders and masters, if not all of the conceivable buildings and ideas. But the process by which the shift from one direction of investigation to another happened was different in every case, depending upon the circumstances and materials of each discipline.

The history of grammar in the early thirteenth century is still difficult to judge be-

cause little work has been done on the subject,[2] but for logic the coalescence of doctrine can be seen in the appearance of new textbooks. The works of Peter of Spain and William of Sherwood offered little that was new, but by conveniently summarizing the issues of terminist logic, they won places in the logic curriculum that they retained until the end of the Middle Ages.[3] More significant, perhaps, for the later history of philosophy is that different teaching traditions had emerged for Oxford and Paris: the dominance of the studium of Paris had been broken.

A rather different kind of culmination proved decisive for theology. At first glance the Fourth Lateran Council of 1215 had little to do with learning, being a legislative rather than an educational gathering, but many of its decrees dealt with matters that had been intensely debated in the twelfth century. Decrees on penance, the sacraments, and other issues both summarized the conclusions of twelfth-century masters and removed the issues from the arena of dispute: once the council had spoken, although details could legitimately be discussed, the main premises had to be accepted. In the next half-century, theologians moved on to argue questions raised by the translation of Aristotle's works on natural philosophy, ethics, and metaphysics; already in the 1220s, William of Auvergne was tackling the nature of the soul and cognition. But although such issues have generally been more interesting to intellectual historians, they were less central to the daily practice of the faithful than the matters that had been settled in the twelfth century. Far from a thirteenth-century "philosophical revolution," as David Knowles called it, the work of the thirteenth-century schools was simply a natural advance along the path cleared by their predecessors.

In architecture, the close of the twelfth-century period of experimentation was

1. On this, see T. S. Kuhn, *Black Body Theory and the Origins of the Quantum Discontinuity* (Oxford, 1978).
2. G. L. Bursill-Hall, *Speculative Grammars of the Middle Ages* (The Hague and Paris, 1971), 29–30.

3. John Marenbon, *Later Medieval Philosophy* (London and New York, 1987), 42–43. For more detail on later developments, see *The Cambridge History of Later Medieval Philosophy*, ed. Norman Kretzmann, Anthony Kenny, Jan Pinborg (Cambridge, 1982), although early thirteenth-century logic is not (given the book's topical organization) discussed intensively in any one place.

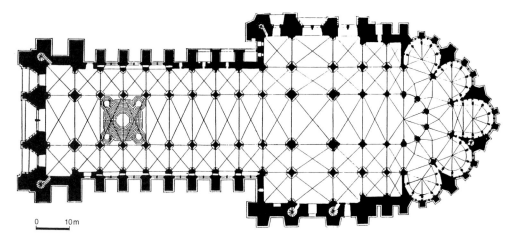

119. Reims, Notre-Dame, plan.

120. Reims, Notre-Dame, nave section.

marked by the cathedral of Reims, the coronation church of the kings of France (Figure
119).[4] Jean d'Orbais, the first master builder
at Reims, had not only absorbed the lessons of
Bourges, Chartres, and other buildings under
construction at the end of the twelfth century
but had also introduced innovations of his
own that opened the possibilities of future
experimentation. The most obvious is the impact of the elevational system of Reims on the
future of Gothic architecture (Figures 120
and 121). The builder borrowed the three
stories and their proportional relationship
from Chartres, but he altered the individual
elements in subtle ways: instead of viewing
the window as a hole punched through the
wall, for example, Jean conceived of it as an
opening to be filled with bar tracery, one of
the single most significant innovations of the
period (Figures 122 and 123). This concep-

4. To the works cited by Bony, add Peter Kurmann, *La
Façade de la cathédrale de Reims*, 2 vols. (Lausanne and Paris,
1987); Barbara Abou-El-Haj, "The Urban Setting for Late
Medieval Church Building," *Art History* 11 (1988): 17–
41; R. Branner, "Die Architektur der Kathedrale von
Reims im dreizehnten Jahrhundert," *Architectura* 1
(1971): 15–37; R. Mark and Huang Yun-Sheng, "High
Gothic Structural Development: The Pinnacles of Reims
Cathedral," *Science and Technology in Medieval Society*, ed. P.
Long, Annals of the New York Academy of Sciences, no.
441 (New York, 1985), 125–39; J.-P. Ravaux, "Les Campagnes de construction de la cathédrale de Reims au XIIIe
siècle," *Bulletin monumental* 137 (1979): 7–66; F. Salet,
"Chronologie de la cathédrale," *Bulletin monumental* 125
(1967): 347–94.

121. Reims, Notre-Dame, chevet interior.

1208

122. Reims, Notre-Dame, ambulatory and chapels.

123. Reims, Notre-Dame, chevet exterior. The elevation of Reims, the coronation church of the kings of France, was one of the most successful schemes devised in medieval architecture, and it was copied in dozens of buildings right to the end of the Middle Ages.

tion of the window as an opening to be composed and patterned with tracery creates the potential for exploring the geometric elements of window design and leads to the great rose windows of the transepts and facades. Another important development is the increased use of sculpture on the building's exterior (Figure 120). Once concentrated primarily in portals, figure sculpture at Reims appears on the exterior of the radiating chapels, as well as on the clerestory. Together with the more lavish use of architectural sculpture, the effect enriches the building's exterior. Even the engineering of the flying buttresses at Reims represents a synthesis of past experiences and simultaneously points in future directions. The heaviness and cumbersome quality of the Chartres buttresses is refined by the experience of the leaner and steeper design of Bourges to produce a well-engineered scheme of two layers of flyers (Figure 123), the upper for the timber roof, the lower for the main vaults, that prevailed as the model for decades.

It remained for Robert de Luzarches, the first master of Amiens Cathedral, begun circa 1220, to begin the process of searching for a new architectural synthesis.[5] He took the structural system of Reims, a much more efficient and lighter system than had been used at Chartres, but he significantly changed the proportions of the elevation and introduced a new complexity to the design (Figure 124). The general elevation at Amiens has the same three stories as at Chartres and Reims, but it has been considerably extended in height. The ratio of height to width is now 3 to 1, with the result that the balance between laterally expanding and vertically rising space is abandoned in favor of an overpowering sense of height. Interestingly, this effect was achieved by narrowing the width and pushing

the height of the side-aisles to unprecedented levels (Figure 125). In fact, the impressively tall piers of Amiens recall the tall piers of Bourges. Their height not only allows the aisle space—now in itself taller than most naves built in the twelfth century—to merge into the nave, but leads to such attenuation of the main piers as to negate the visual sense of their supporting function.

With the structural solution involving exploitation of the flying buttress firmly fixed, the upper stories of the nave at Amiens announce an important new direction in Gothic architecture. The builder's attention turned decisively to design. The front screen of the wall passage at Amiens, for example, is no longer a continuous series of arches. Instead, this wall passage offers a sophisticated attempt to integrate horizontal continuity with the rhythmic grouping of the vertical elements (Figure 126). Visual equilibrium is maintained by introducing trefoils in the tympana beneath the pair of relieving arches in each bay. The double units created by these arches are carried into the clerestory. In fact, the division between the two upper stories, wall passage and clerestory, is intentionally blurred by having the main verticals in the clerestory win-

5. Amiens, Musée de Picardie, *La cathédrale d'Amiens* (Amiens, 1972); S. Bonde, C. Maines, and R. Mark, "Archaeology and Engineering: The Foundations of Amiens Cathedral," *Kunstchronik* 42 (1989): 341–48; G. Durand, *Monographie de l'église Notre-Dame, cathédrale d'Amiens* (Paris, 1901–3); A. Erlande-Brandenburg, "La Façade de la cathédrale d'Amiens," *Bulletin monumental* 135 (1977): 253–93; S. Murray, "Looking for Robert de Luzarches," *Gesta* 29 (1990): 111–31; S. Murray and J. Addiss, "Plan and Space at Amiens Cathedral," *Journal of the Society of Architectural Historians* 49 (1990): 44–67.

124. Amiens, Notre-Dame, plan.

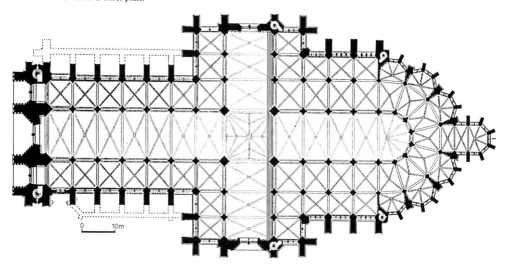

125. Amiens, Notre-Dame, north side-aisle.

126. Amiens, Notre-Dame, nave elevation. The lower story, up to the one interrupted horizontal molding, that distinctive band of carved foliage at the base of the wall passage, makes up half the total height. Above the foliage, the design becomes more complex in vertical ascendency and in the progressive subdivision and layering of the moldings and tracery.

b. 1218-1220

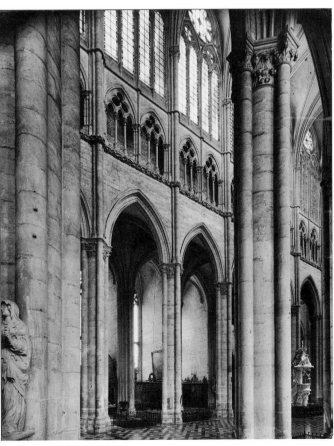

dows actually begin at the base of the wall passage. The window design uses the chartrain pattern of twin lancets surmounted by an oculus but, because of the use of bar tracery from Reims, each lancet at Amiens is treated as a full window on a smaller scale with two lancets and a small oculus. Thus the whole window becomes a screenwork of delicately carved stone tracery in which each element or subdivision of the design is differentiated by separate layers to preserve clarity.

Subsequent builders followed in the direction laid out by Robert de Luzarches, with the linear art of tracing lacelike patterns of great geometric precision in window tracery and, later, on gables and other architectural elements, becoming their chief concern. The new style, Rayonnant, takes its name from the radiating tracery of rose windows. Some of the most sophisticated examples first appeared in Parisian buildings, many associated with royal patronage, like Louis IX's Sainte-Chapelle, or with longstanding royal associations, like Saint-Denis. The rebuilding begun there in the 1230s finally joined the two parts of Abbot Suger's church, the facade and the chevet, with a nave and transept in the Rayonnant style. The Rayonnant style, identified with the chief artistic center of Europe, Paris, or with the patronage of the ideal christian ruler, Louis IX, made the Gothic style internationally popular across Europe from Scandinavia and Bohemia to southern Spain and the northern British isles.

What we see in the thirteenth century, therefore, is a redirection of energies made possible by the consensus arrived at through twelfth-century debate and experimentation. It is hardly conceivable, for example, that speculations about the relationship between theological and philosophical truths could have assumed an important place in scholarly life if doctrinal issues that affected daily practices had remained unsettled; or that builders could have undertaken elaborate decorative programs while still uncertain about the engineering needed to support the vaults. It would not even be correct to suggest that thirteenth-century builders and masters knew everything their predecessors did and more. When, after several generations of borrowing

proven engineering, some late thirteenth-century builders devised elevations that departed from the standard, they made errors in the positioning of flying buttresses that builders a century earlier had known how to avoid: a pointed reminder that knowledge not applied to new problems is often knowledge forgotten.

A final perspective on these developments is provided by Panofsky's notion that Gothic architecture and scholasticism shared a common "mental habit." We have found a sense in which this is true, although the common elements concern mental process—how problems were conceived of and solved—rather than the characteristics Panofsky believed to be expressed in the works themselves. But the idea that this habit "spread" from one discipline to another, or to both from the society as a whole, has proven seriously misleading. The changes in medieval culture between 1000 and 1200 do not mean that everyone in medieval society was equally affected or, indeed, affected at all. It was the degree of specialization, and the number of areas affected by it, that differentiated European culture in the thirteenth century from what it had been in the tenth. Far from expressing some kind of zeitgeist, medieval accomplishments in architecture and learning reveal intellectual abilities that set masters and builders apart both from society as a whole and from each other. The builders and masters did not reflect cultural change; they produced it.

Bibliography

This bibliography is confined principally to the works cited in this book. Valuable additional references can be found in the bibliographies contained in Jean Bony, *French Gothic Architecture*; Peter Dronke, ed., *A History of Twelfth-Century Western Philosophy*; and James J. Murphy, *Medieval Rhetoric*.

Abel, J., Mark, R., and O'Neill, K. "Photoelastic and Finite Element Analysis of a Quadripartite Vault." *Experimental Mechanics* 13 (1973): 322–29.

Abelard, Peter. *Dialectica*. Edited by L. M. de Rijk. 2d ed. Assen, 1970.

Abelard, Peter. *Ethics*. Edited and translated by D. E. Luscombe. Oxford, 1971.

Abelard, Peter. *Historia Calamitatum*. Edited and translated by J. T. Muckle, *Mediaeval Studies* 12 (1950): 163–213.

Abelard, Peter. *Logica "Ingredientibus"* and *Logica "Nostrorum petitioni sociorum."* Edited by Bernhard Geyer. Beiträge zur Geschichte der Philosophie und Theologie des Mittelalters, vol. 21, nos. 1–4 Münster 1919–1921, 1933.

Abou-El-Haj, Barbara. "Ritual, Image, and Subordination in Thirteenth-Century Reims." In *World Art: Themes of Unity in Diversity*, Acts of the 26th International Congress of the History of Art, edited by I. Lavin. University Park, Penn., 1989. 3: 653–64.

Abou-El-Haj, Barbara. "The Urban Setting for Late Medieval Church Building: Reims and Its Cathedral between 1210 and 1240." *Art History* 11 (1988): 17–41.

Abulafia, Anna Sapir. "An Eleventh-Century Exchange of Letters between a Christian and a Jew." *Journal of Medieval History* 7 (1981): 153–74.

Acland, J. *Medieval Structure: The Gothic Vault*. Toronto, 1972.

Adam Balsamiensis Parvipontani. *Ars disserendi*. In *Twelfth Century Logic: Texts and Studies*, vol. 1, edited by L. Minio-Paluello. Rome, 1956.

Addiss, James Morton. "Spatial Organization in Romanesque Church Architecture." Ph.D. diss., State University of New York at Binghampton, 1983.

Adelman of Liège. "Poème rhythmique d'Adelman de Liège." *Notices et documents . . . Soc. Hist. France . . . cinquantième anniversaire*, edited by J. Havet. 71–92. Paris, 1884.

Alexander, K., Mark, R., and Abel, J. "The Structural Behavior of Medieval Ribbed Vaulting." *Journal of the Society of Architectural Historians* 36 (1977): 241–51.

Alpert of Metz. *De diversitate temporum*. Edited by Anna Sapir Abulafia and H. van Rij. Amsterdam, 1980.

Amiens, Musée de Picardie. *La cathédrale d'Amiens*. Amiens, 1972.

Anciaux, Pierre. *La Théologie du sacrement de pénitence au XIIe siècle*. Louvain-Gembloux, 1949.

Anderson, W. *The Rise of the Gothic*. Salem, N.H., 1985.

Andrews, F. *The Mediaeval Builder*. Wakefield, 1974.

Anfray, M. "Les Architectes des cathédrales." *Cahiers techniques de l'art* ½ (1947): 5–16.

Anselm of Besate. *Rhetorimachia*. Edited by Karl Manitius. In *MGH. Quellen zur Geistesgeschichte des Mittelalters*, vol. 2. Weimar, 1958.

Anselm of Canterbury. *Sancti Anselmi opera omnia*. Edited by F. S. Schmitt. Edinburgh, 1946.

Anselm of Canterbury. *Works*. Edited and translated by Jasper Hopkins and Herbert Richardson. Toronto and New York, 1974–76.

Aristoteles Latinus. Edited by George Lacombe et al. Bruges and Paris, 1939–76.

Artistes, artisans et production artistique au moyen âge. Edited by X. Barral i Altet. Vol. 1, *Les Hommes*, Paris, 1986; Vol. 2, *Commande et travail*, Paris, 1987; Vol. 3, *Fabrication et consommation de l'oeuvre*, Paris, 1990.

Aubert, Marcel. "La Construction au moyen âge." *Bulletin monumental* 118 (1960): 241–59 and 119 (2961): 7–42, 81–120, 181–209, 297–323.

Aubert, Marcel. "Eglise Saint-Front." *Congrès archéologique (Périgueux)* 90 (1927): 45–65.

Aubert, Marcel. "Les Enduits dans les constructions du moyen âge." *Bulletin monumental* 115 (1957): 111–17.

Aubert, Marcel. "Les Plus Anciennes Croisées d'ogives." *Bulletin monumental* 93 (1934): 1–67, 137–237 (separately published, Paris, 1934).

Baldwin, John W. "Masters at Paris from 1179 to 1215: A Social Perspective." In *Renaissance/Renewal*, 138–72.

Baldwin, John W. *Masters, Princes and Merchants: The Social Views of Peter the Chanter and His Circle*. Princeton, 1970.

Barnes, Carl F., Jr. "The Gothic Architectural Engravings in the Cathedral of Soissons." *Speculum* 47 (1972): 60–64.

Barnes, Carl F., Jr. *Villard de Honnecourt: The Artist and His Drawings, A Critical Bibliography*. Boston, 1982.

Barrow, Julia. "Education and the Recruitment of Cathedral Canons in England and Germany 1100–1225." *Viator* 20 (1989): 117–38.

Baudri de Bourgueil. *Les Oeuvres poétiques de Baudri*, edited by P. Abrahams, 82. Paris, 1926.

Beaujouan, Guy. *L'Interdépendance entre la science scholastique et les techniques utilitaires (XIIe, XIIIe et XIVe siècles)*. Paris, 1957.

Beaujouan, Guy. "Réflexions sur les rapports entre théorie et pratique au moyen âge." In *The Cultural Context of Medieval Learning*, edited by J. E. Murdoch and E. D. Sylla. Boston Studies in the Philosophy of Science 26; Synthese Library 76. Dordrecht and Boston, 1975. 437–77.

Bechmann, Roland. "L'Architecture gothique: Une expression des conditions du milieu." *Pour la science*, no. 4 (1978): 94–105.

Bechmann, Roland. *Les Racines des cathédrales*. Paris, 1981.

Bégule, L. *La Cathédrale de Sens: Son architecture, son décor* Lyon, 1929.

Benton, John F. "Philology's Search for Abelard in the *Metamorphosis Goliae*." *Speculum* 50 (1975): 199–217.

Berengar of Tours. *Ep. ad Ascetinum*. In *Texts and Manuscripts: Essays Presented to G. I. Lieftinck*, vol. 2, edited by R. B. C. Huygens. Amsterdam, 1972. 18–19.

Berengar of Tours. *Rescriptum contra Lanfrannum*. Edited by R. B. C. Huygens. CCCM 84 Turnholt, 1988.

Besnard, A. *L'Eglise de Saint-Germer de Fly et sa Sainte-Chapelle*. Paris, 1913.

Bideault, Maryse, and Lautier, Claudine. *Ile-de-France gothique*. Vol. 1, *Les Eglises de la vallée de l'Oise et du Beauvaisis*. Paris, 1987.

Bilson, J. "Durham Cathedral: The Chronology of Its Vaults." *Archaeological Journal* 79 (1922): 101–60.

Bismanis, Maija R. "The Necessity of Discovery." *Gesta* 28 (1989): 115–20.

Blanc, Annie, and Lorenz, Claude. "Observations sur la nature des materiaux de la cathédrale Notre-Dame de Paris." *Gesta* 29 (1990): 132–38.

Blanc, A., Lebouteux, P., Lorenz, J., and Debrand-Passard, S. "Les Pierres de la cathédrale de Bourges." *Archéologia* 171 (1982): 22–35.

Blum, Pamela Z. "The Lateral Portals of the West Facade of the Abbey Church of Saint-Denis: Archaeological and Iconographic Considerations." In *Abbot Suger and Saint-Denis*, edited by P. Gerson. New York, 1986.

Blum, Pamela Z. *Saint-Denis, the Central Portal: Restorations and Survivals*. Berkeley, 1992.

Blumenkranz, B. *Les Auteurs chrétiens latins du moyen âge sur les juifs et le judaisme* Paris, 1963.

Bonde, S., Maines, C., and Mark, R. "Archaeology and Engineering: The Foundations of Amiens Cathedral." *Kunstchronik* 42 (1989): 341–48.

Bony, Jean. "La Collégiale de Mantes." *Congrès archéologique (Paris-Mantes)* 104 (1946): 163–220

Bony, Jean. "Diagonality and Centrality in Early Rib-Vaulted Architectures." *Gesta* 15 (1976): 15–25.

Bony, Jean. "L'Edifice comme univers." *Cahiers de médecine de France*, 1949, 21–29.

Bony, Jean. "Essai sur la spiritualité de deux cathédrales: Notre-Dame de Paris et Saint-Etienne de Bourges." *Chercher Dieu*, Rencontres 13 (Paris, 1943): 150–67.

Bony, Jean. *French Gothic Architecture of the 12th and 13th Centuries.* Berkeley, 1983.

Bony, Jean. "French Influences on the Origins of English Gothic Architecture." *Journal of the Warburg and Courtauld Institutes* 12 (1949): 1–15.

Bony, Jean. "The Genesis of Gothic: Accident or Necessity?" *Australian Journal of Art* 2 (1980): 17–31.

Bony, Jean. "La Genèse de l'architecture gothique: 'Accident ou necessité'?" *Revue de l'art* 58/59 (1983): 9–20.

Bony, Jean. *Notre-Dame de Mantes.* Paris, 1947.

Bony, Jean. "Les Premiers Architectes gothiques." In *Les Architectes célèbres,* edited by P. Francastel. Paris, 1959. 2: 28–32.

Bony, Jean. "The Stonework Planning of the First Durham Master." In *Medieval Architecture and Its Intellectual Context: Studies in Honour of Peter Kidson,* edited by E. Fernie and P. Crossley. London, 1990. 19–34.

Bony, Jean. "La Technique normande du 'mur épais' à l'époque romane." *Bulletin monumental* 98 (1939): 153–88.

Bony, Jean. "What Possible Sources for the Chevet of Saint-Denis?" In *Abbot Suger and Saint-Denis,* edited by P. Gerson. New York, 1986. 131–42.

Boussard, Jacques. *Nouvelle Histoire de Paris de la fin du siège de 885–886 à la mort de Philippe Auguste.* Paris, 1976.

Bouttier, M. "La Construction de l'abbatiale de Saint-Denis au XIIIe siècle." *Bulletin monumental* 145 (1987): 357–86.

Branner, Robert. *The Cathedral of Bourges and Its Place in Gothic Architecture.* Edited and annotated by Shirley Prager Branner. Cambridge, 1989.

Branner, Robert. *La Cathédrale de Bourges et sa place dans l'architecture gothique.* Paris and Bourges, 1962.

Branner, Robert. "Encore Bourges." *Journal of the Society of Architectural Historians* 25 (1966): 299–301.

Branner, Robert. *Gothic Architecture.* New York, 1961.

Branner, Robert. "Gothic Architecture." *Journal of the Society of Architectural Historians* 32 (1973): 327–33.

Branner, Robert. "Gothic Architecture 1160–1180 and Its Romanesque Sources." In *Acts of the Twentieth International Congress of the History of Art, New York, 1961. Studies in Western Art.* Princeton, 1963. 1: 92–104.

Branner, Robert. "High Gothic Architecture." *The Year 1200.* Vol. 2, *A Background Survey.* New York, 1970. 7–32.

Brun, Pierre-Marie. "Les fouilles du chanoine Chenesseau sous le choeur de la cathédrale Sainte-Croix d'Orléans." In *Etudes ligériennes d'histoire et d'archéologie médiévales,* edited by R. Louis. Auxerre, 1975. 443–49.

Bruzelius, Caroline. "The Construction of Notre-Dame de Paris." *Art Bulletin* 69 (1987): 540–69.

Bruzelius, Caroline. *The Thirteenth-Century Church at Saint-Denis.* New Haven and London, 1986.

Bursill-Hall, G. L. *Speculative Grammars of the Middle Ages.* The Hague and Paris, 1971.

Cali, François. *L'Ordre ogival: Essai sur l'architecture gothique.* Paris, 1963.

Cambridge History of Later Medieval Philosophy: From the Rediscovery of Aristotle to the Disintegration of Scholasticism, 1100–1600. Edited by Norman Kretzmann, Anthony Kenny, Jan Pinborg. Cambridge, 1982.

Cameron, John. "The Early Gothic Continuous Capital and Its Precursors." *Gesta* 15 (1976): 143–50.

Camus, Marie-Thérèse. "La Reconstruction de Saint-Hilaire-le-Grand de Poitiers à l'époque romane: La Marche des travaux." *Cahiers de civilisation mediévalé* 25 (1982): 101–20, 238–71.

Camus, Marie-Thérèse. "Les Voûtes de la nef de Saint-Hilaire-le-Grand de Poitiers du XIe au XIXe siècle." *Bulletin archéologique,* n.s. 16 (1980): 57–94.

Capitani, O. "Per la storia dei raporti tra Gregorio VII e Berengario di Tours." *Studi gregoriani* 6 (1959–61): 99–145

Carlson, Eric G. "The Abbey Church of Saint-Etienne at Caen in the Eleventh and Early Twelfth Centuries." Ph.D. diss., Yale University, 1968.

Carlson, Eric G. "A Charter for Saint-Etienne, Caen: A Document and Its Implications." *Gesta* 25 (1986): 61–68.

Carty, Carolyn M. "The Role of Gunzo's Dream in the Building of Cluny III." *Gesta* 27 (1988): 113–24.

Caviness, Madeline H. "Images of Divine Order and the Third Mode of Seeing." *Gesta* 22 (1983): 99–120.

Caviness, Madeline H. " 'The Simple Perception of Matter' and the Representation of Narrative, ca. 1180–1280." *Gesta* 30 (1991): 48–64.

Caviness, Madeline H. *Sumptuous Arts at the Royal Abbeys in Reims and Braine.* Princeton, 1990.

Chadefaux, M.-C. "Le Portail royal de Chartres." *Gazette des Beaux-Arts* 6th ser. 76 (1970): 273–84.

Chatillon, F. "Recherches critiques sur les différents personnages nommés Manegold." *Revue du Moyen Age latin* 9 (1953): 153–70.

Chédeville, André. *Chartres et ses campagnes XIe–XIIIe siècles.* Paris, 1973.

Chenesseau, Georges. *Sainte-Croix d'Orléans: Histoire d'une cathédrale gothique réédifiée par les Bourbons (1599–1829),* 3 vols. Paris, 1921.

Chenu, M.-D. *Nature, Man, and Society in the Twelfth Century.* Edited and translated by Jerome Taylor and Lester K. Little. Chicago, 1968.

Chenu, M.-D. *La Théologie au douzième siècle.* 3d ed. Paris, 1976.

Chevallier, M.-A., and Pressouyre, L. "Fragments récemment retrouvées du Portail Royal de Chartres." *Revue de l'art* 57 (1982): 67–72.

Clark, William W. "Capetians in Merovingian Paris: Architecture and Its Audience at the Beginning of the Gothic Period." In *Artistic Integration in Early Gothic Churches,* edited by K. Brush et al. Toronto, 1992.

Clark, William W. "The Early Capitals of Notre-Dame-de-Paris." In *Tribute to Lotte Brand Philip.* New York, 1985. 34–42.

Clark, William W. *Laon Cathedral, Architecture (2). The Aesthetics of Space, Plan and Structure.* Courtauld Institute Illustration Archives, Companion Text 2. London, 1986.

Clark, William W. "Merovingian Revival Acanthus Capitals at Saint-Denis." In *L'Acanthe dans la sculpture monumental de l'antiquité à la Renaissance,* edited by Léon Pressouyre and Maylis Baylé. Paris, 1992.

Clark, William W. *Merovingian Revival in Early Gothic Paris: Architecture and Its Audience in the Reign of Louis VII.* Forthcoming.

Clark, William W. "The Nave of Saint-Pierre at Lisieux: Romanesque Structure in a Gothic Guise." *Gesta* 16, no. 1 (1977): 29–38.

Clark, William W. "Spatial Innovations in the Chevet of Saint-Germain-des-Prés." *Journal of the Society of Architectural Historians* 38 (1979): 348–65.

Clark, William W. "Suger's Church at Saint-Denis: The State of Research." In *Abbot Suger and Saint-Denis,* edited by P. Gerson. New York, 1986. 105–30.

Clark, William W., and King, Richard. *Laon Cathedral, Architecture (1).* Courtauld Institute Illustration Archives, Companion Text 1. London, 1983.

Clark, William W., and Ludden, Franklin M. "Notes on the Archivolts of the Sainte-Anne Portal of Notre-Dame-de-Paris." *Gesta* 25 (1986): 109–18.

Clark, William W., and Mark, Robert. "Le Chevet et la nef de Notre-Dame de Paris: Une comparison entre les premières élévations," *Journal d'histoire de l'Architecture* 2 (1989): 69–88.

Clark, William W., and Mark, Robert. "The First Flying Buttresses: A New Reconstruction of the Nave of Notre-Dame de Paris." *Art Bulletin* 66 (1984): 47–65.

Classen, Peter. "Die Hohen Schulen und die Gesellschaft im 12. Jahrhundert." *Archive für Kulturgeschichte* 48 (1966): 155–80.

Clerval, A. *Les Ecoles de Chartres au moyen âge.* Paris, 1895.

Cobban, A. C. *The Medieval Universities: Their Development and Organization.* London, 1975.

Colchester, L. S. *Wells Cathedral.* London, 1987.

Colchester, L. S., ed. *Wells Cathedral, A History.* Shepton Mallet, 1982.

Colish, Marcia. "Another Look at the School of Laon." *Archives d'histoire doctrinale et littéraire du moyen âge* 64 (1986): 7–22.

Colish, Marcia. "Systematic Theology and Theological Renewal in the Twelfth Century." *Journal of Medieval and Renaissance Studies* 18 (1988): 135–56.

Colombier, Pierre du. *Les Chantiers des cathédrales.* Rev. ed. Paris, 1973.

Conant, Kenneth John. *Carolingian and Romanesque Architecture 800–1200.* 2d ed. Pelican History of Art. Baltimore, 1966.

Conant, Kenneth John. *Cluny: Les Eglises et la maison du chef d'ordre* Mâcon, 1968.

La Construction au moyen âge. Actes du congrès de la Sociétés historiens medievistes de l'enseignement superieur public, Besançon, 1972. Paris, 1973.

Courtenay, Lynn T. "Where Roof Meets Wall: Structural Innovations and Hammer-Bean Antecedents, 1150–1250." *Science and Technology in Medieval Society,* edited by P. Long. Annals of the New York Academy of Sciences, 441. New York, 1985. 89–124.

Crosby, Sumner McKnight. *The Royal Abbey of Saint-Denis from Its Beginning to the Death of Suger, 475–1151.* Edited and completed by Pamela Z. Blum. New Haven and London, 1987.

Crosby, Sumner McKnight, and Blum, P. Z. "Le Portail central de la façade occidentale de Saint-Denis." *Bulletin monumental* 131 (1973): 209–66.

Crossley, Paul. "Medieval Architecture and Meaning: The Limits of Iconography." *Burlington Magazine* 130 (1988): 116–21.

David, M. "La Fabrique et les manoeuvres sur les chantiers des cathédrales en France jusqu'au XIVe siècle." *Etudes d'histoire du droit canonique dédiés à Gabriel Le Bras.* Paris, 1965. 2: 1113–30.

Delhaye, Philippe. "L'Organisation scolaire au XIIe siècle," *Traditio* 5 (1947): 211–68.

Deneux, H. "L'evolution des charpentes du XIe au XVIIIe siècles." *L'Architecte,* n.s. 4 (1927): 49–53, 57–60, 65–68, 73–75, 81–89.

Denifle, H., and Chatelain, E. *Chartularium Universitatis Parisiensis.* 4 vols. Paris, 1889–1897.

Denny, Don. "The Last Judgment Tumpanum at Autun: Its Sources and Meaning." *Speculum* 57 (1982): 532–47.

Desportes, Pierre. *Reims et le rémois au XIIIe et XIVe siècles.* Paris, 1979.

Devisse, Jean. *Hincmar Archeveque de Reims.* 3 vols. Geneva, 1975.

Dictionnaire des églises de France. Edited by J. Brosse. 5 vols. Paris, 1966–69.

Dimier, A. *Les Moines Bâtisseurs.* Paris, 1964.

Draper, Peter. "Recherches récentes sur l'architecture dans les îles Britanniques à la fin de l'époque rommane et au début du gothique." *Bulletin monumental* 144 (1986): 305–28.

Draper, Peter. "William of Sens and the Original Design of the Choir Termination of Canterbury Cathedral 1175–1179." *Journal of the Society of Architectural Historians* 42 (1983): 238–48.

Dronke, Peter. "New Approaches to the School of Chartres." *Anuario de estudios medievales* 6 (1971): 117–40.

Dronke, Peter, ed. *A History of Twelfth-Century Western Philosophy.* Cambridge, 1988.

Droste, Thorsten. *Romanische Kunst in Frankreich.* Cologne, 1989.

Duby, Georges. *The Europe of the Cathedrals, 1140–1280.* Geneva, 1966.

Duby, Georges, Chedéville, André, Le Goff, Jacques, and Rossiaud, Jacques. *Histoire de la France urbaine.* Vol. 2, *La Ville médiévale des Carolingiens à la Renaissance.* Paris, 1980.

Dunlop, I. *The Cathedrals' Crusade.* New York, 1982.

Durand, G. *Monographie de l'église Notre-Dame, cathédrale d'Amiens.* Paris, 1901–3.

Durliat, Marcel. "La Construction de Saint-Sernin de Toulouse: Etude historique et archéologique." In *La Construction au moyen âge. Actes du congrès de la Société des Historiens Médiévistes de l'Enseignement Supérieur Public (Besançon, 2–4 juin 1972).* Paris, 1973. 201–11.

Durliat, Marcel. "La Construction de Saint-Sernin de Toulouse au XIe siècle." *Bulletin monumental* 121 (1963): 151–70.

Dynes, W. "Concept of Gothic." In *Dictionary of the History of Ideas,* edited by P. P. Weiner. New York, 1973. 2: 366–74.

Ebbensen, Stan. "Anonymous Aurelianus II, Aristotle, Alexander, Porphyry and Boethius: Ancient Scholasticism and Twelfth Century Europe." *CIMAGL* 16 (1976): 1–128.

Ebbensen, Stan. *Commentators and Commentaries on Aristotle's Sophistichi elenchi: A Study of Post-Aristotelian Ancient and Medieval Writings on Fallacies.* 3 vols. Corpus Latinorum Commentariorum in Aristotelem Graecorum 7. Leiden, 1981.

Ebbensen, Stan, Fredborg, Karin Margareta, and Nielsen, Lauge Olaf. "Compendium Logicae Porretanum ex Codice Oxoniensi Collegii Corporis Christi 250: A Manual of Porretan Doctrine by a Pupil of Gilbert's." *CIMAGL* 46 (1983).

Ebbensen, Stan, and Iwakuma, Yukio. "Instantiae and 12th Century Schools." *CIMAGL* 44 (1983): 81–85.

Ebbensen, Stan, and Mortensen, Lars Brje. "A Partial Edition of Stephen Langton's Summa and Quaestiones with Parallels from Andrew Sunesen's Hexaemeron." *CIMAGL* 49 (1985): 25–224.

Ehlers, Joachim. "Deutsche Scholaren in Frankreich während des 12. Jahrhunderts." In *Schulen und Studium im sozialen Wandel des hohen und späten Mittelalters,* edited by Johannes Fried. Sigmaringen, 1986. 97–120.

Enlart, C. *Manuel d'archéologie française.* Vol. 1, *Architecture religieuse.* Paris, 1919.

Erdmann C. "Gregor VII. und Berengar von Tours." *Quellen und Forschungen aus italienischen Archiven und Bibliotheken* 28 (1937–38): 48–74.

Erlande-Brandenburg, Alain. *L'Art gothique.* Paris, 1983.

Erlande-Brandenburg, Alain. *La Cathédrale.* Paris, 1989.

Erlande-Brandenburg, Alain. *La Cathédrale gothique.* Paris, 1990.

Erlande-Brandenburg, Alain. "La Façade de la cathédrale d'Amiens," *Bulletin monumental* 135 (1977): 253–93.

Evans, G. R. "Anselm of Canterbury and Anselm of Havelberg: The Controversy with the Greeks." *Analecta Praemonstratensia* 53 (1977): 158–75.

Evans, G. R. *Anselm and a New Generation.* Oxford, 1980.

Evans, G. R. "*Inopes verborum sunt Latini*: Technical Language and Technical Terms in the Writings of St. Anselm and Some Commentators of the Mid-Twelfth Century." *Archives d'histoire doctrinale et littéraire du moyen âge* 54 (1976): 113–34.

Evans, G. R. "A Work of 'Terminist Theology'? Peter the Chanter's *De Tropis Loquendi* and Some Fallacie." *Vivarium* 20 (1982): 40–58.

Evans, Joan, ed. *The Flowering of the Middle Ages.* London, 1967.

Evans, Michael. "The Geometry of the Mind." *Architectural Association Quarterly* 12 (1980): 32–55.

Expositio to the *Liber Papiensis.* MGH. *Leges,* vol. 4.

Fernie, Eric. "La Fonction liturgique des piliers cantonnés dans la nef de la cathédrale de Laon." *Bulletin monumental* 145 (1987): 257–66.

Fernie, Eric. "Historical Metrology and Architectural History." *Art History* 1 (1978): 383–99.

Ferruolo, Stephen. *The Origins of the University.* Stanford, 1985.

Ferruolo, Stephen. "*Parisius-Paradisus:* The City, Its Schools, and the Origins of the University of Paris." In *The University and the City: From Medieval Origins to the Present,* edited by Thomas Bender. Oxford, 1988. 22–43.

Fillitz, H. *Das Mittelalter 1.* Propyläen-Kunstgeschichte, 5. Berlin, 1969.

Fitchen, J. *The Construction of Gothic Cathedrals.* Oxford, 1961.

Flint, Valerie I. "The 'School of Laon': A Reconsideration." *Recherches de théologie ancienne et médiévale* 43 (1976): 89–110.

Focillon, H. *Art d'occident.* Paris, 1938.

Foucaud, O. "La Restauration de Saint-Sernin de Toulouse de 1860 à 1862: 29 nouveaux documents iconographiques signés de Viollet-le-Duc et Esquié." *Bulletin monumental* 147 (1989): 333–44.

Frankl, Paul. *The Gothic.* Princeton, 1960.

Frankl, Paul. *Gothic Architecture.* Pelican History of Art. Baltimore, 1962.

Fredborg, Karin Margareta. "The Commentaries on Cicero's *De Inventione* and *Rhetorica ad Herennium* by William of Champeaux." *Cahiers de l'Institut du moyen âge grec et latin* 17 (1976): 1–39.

Fredborg, Karin Margareta. "The Commentary of Thierry of Chartres on Cicero's *De Inventione.*" *CIMAGL* 7 (1971): 1–36.

Fredborg, Karin Margareta. "The Dependence of Petrus Helias' *Summa super Priscianum* on William of Conches' *Glose super Priscianum.*" *CIMAGL* 11 (1973): 1–57.

Fredborg, Karin Margareta. "Petrus Helias on Rhetoric." *CIMAGL* 13 (1974): 31–41.

Fredborg, Karin Margareta. "Some Notes on the Grammar of William of Conches." *CIMAGL* 46 (1983): 21–41.

Fredborg, Karin Margareta. "Speculative Grammar." In Dronke, *Philosophy,* 177–98.

Fredborg, Karin Margareta. "Tractatus glosarum Prisciani in Ms. Vat. lat. 1486." *CIMAGL* 21 (1977): 21–44.

Fried, Johannes, ed. *Schulen und Studium im Sozialen Wandel des hohen und späten Mittelalters.* Sigmaringen, 1986.

Friedmann, Adrien. *Paris: Ses rues, ses pariosses du Moyen Age à la Révolution* Paris, 1959.

Froidevaux, Y.-M. *Techniques de l'architecture ancienne, construction et restauration.* Liège, 1985.

Fulbert of Chartres. *The Letters and Poems of Fulbert of Chartres.* Edited and translated by Frederick Behrends. Oxford, 1976.

Gall, Ernst. "Les Architectes gothiques." In *Les Architectes célèbres,* edited by P. Francastel. Paris, 1959. 2: 34–42.

Gall, Ernst. *Die gotische Baukunst in Frankreich und Deutschland.* 2d ed. Braunschweig, 1955.

Gardner, Stephen. "The Influence of Castle Building on Ecclesiastical Architecture in the Paris Region, 1130–1150." In *The Medieval Castle, Romance and Reality,* edited by K. Reyerson and F. Powe. Medieval Studies at Minnesota, no. 1. Minneapolis, 1984. 97–123.

Gardner, Stephen. "The Theory of Centripetal Implosion and the Birth of Gothic Architecture." *World Art: Themes of Unity in Diversity,* Acts of the 26th International Congress of the History of Art, edited by I. Lavin. University Park, Penn., 1989. 1: 111–16.

Gardner, Stephen. "Two Campaigns in Suger's Western Block at St.-Denis." *Art Bulletin* 66 (1984): 574–87.

Garlandus Compotista. *Dialectica.* Edited by L. M. de Rijk. Assen, 1959.

Gerald of Wales. *Giraldi Cambrensis Opera.* Edited by John S. Brewer, James F. Dimock, and George F. Warner. 8 vols. *Rerum Britannicarum Medii Aevi Scriptores,* no. 21 1861–91.

Gerson, Paula, ed. *Abbot Suger and Saint-Denis: A Symposium* New York, 1986.

Gervaise of Canterbury. *Opera historica.* Edited by William Stubbs. *Rerum Britannicarum Medii Aevi Scriptores,* vol. 73, no. 1. 1879.

Ghellinck, J. de. *Le Mouvement théologique du xiie siècle.* 2d ed. Bruges, 1948.

Giacone, Roberto. "Masters, Books and Library at Chartres according to the Cartularies of Notre-Dame and Saint-Père." *Vivarium* 12 (1974): 30–51.

Gibson, Margaret. "The Continuity of Learning circa 850-circa 1050." *Viator* 6 (1975): 1–13.

Gibson, Margaret. "The Early Scholastic 'Glosule' to Priscian, 'Institutiones Grammaticae': The Text and Its Influence." *Studi Medievali* 20, no. 1 (1979): 235–54.

Gibson, Margaret. *Lanfranc of Bec.* Oxford, 1978.

Gibson, Margaret. "Lanfranc's Commentary on the Pauline Epistles." *Journal of Theological Studies* 22 (1971): 86–112.

Gibson, Margaret. "Lanfranc's Notes on Patristic Texts." *Journal of Theological Studies,* n.s. 22 (1971): 435–50.

Gimpel, Jean. *The Cathedral Builders.* New ed. Translated by Teresa Waugh. New York, 1985.

Goldthwaite, Richard A. *The Building of Renaissance Florence: An Economic and Social History.* Baltimore, 1980.

Grabmann, Martin. *Die Geschichte der scholastischen Methode.* 2 vols. Freiburg, 1911–13.

Green-Pedersen, N. J. *The Tradition of the Topics in the Middle Ages: The Commentaries on Aristotle's and Beothius' Topics.* Munich and Vienna, 1984.

Green-Pedersen, N. J. "William of Champeaux on Boethius' Topics according to Orleans Bibl. Mun. 266." *CIMAGL* 13 (1974): 13–30.

Grinnell, Robert. "Franciscan Philosophy and Gothic Art." In *Ideological Differences and World Order: Studies in the Philosophy and Science of the World's Cultures,* edited by F. S. C. Northrop. Northford, Conn., 1949.

Grivot, Denis, and Zarnecki, George. *Gislebertus, Sculptor of Autun.* New York, 1961.

Grodecki, Louis. *Gothic Architecture.* New York, 1977.

Grodecki, Louis. "Problèmes de l'espace dans la définition de la sculpture gothique." *A travers l'art français du moyen âge au XXe siècle: Hommage à René Jullian. Archives de l'art français* 25 (1978): 77–85; reprinted in *Le Moyen Age retrouvé,* Paris, 1990, 2: 9–117, 510–11.

Grodecki, Louis. *Saint-Germain-des-Prés.* Paris, 1945.

Grodecki, Louis. "Le Vitrail et l'architecture au XIIe et au XIIIe siècles." *Gazette de Beaux-Arts,* 6th ser. 36 (1949): 5–24.

Grodecki, Louis. *Le Vitrail roman*. Fribourg, 1977.

Grodecki, Louis, and Brisac, C. *Gothic Stained Glass*. Ithaca, N.Y., 1985.

Guillerme, A. *Les Temps de l'eau: La Cité, l'eau et les techniques*. Paris, 1983.

Guisberti, F. "A Twelfth Century Theological Grammar: The *Tractatus de tropis loquendi* by Peter the Chanter." In *Materials for a Study on Twelfth Century Scholasticism*, History of Logic, vol. 2. Naples, 1982.

Gurevich, Aron. *Medieval Popular Culture*. Cambridge Studies in Oral and Literate Culture, no. 14. Translated by János M. Bak and Paul A. Hollingsworth. Cambridge, 1988.

Gurevich, Aron. "The West Portal of the Church of St Lazaire in Autun: The Paradoxes of the Medieval Mind." *Peritia* 4 (1985): 251–60.

Hahnloser, H. R., ed. *Villard de Honnecourt*. 2d ed. Graz, 1935.

Hardy, Chantal. "La Fenêtre circulaire en l'Ile-de-France au XIIe et XIIIe siècles." Ph.D. diss., University of Montreal, 1983.

Hardy, Chantal. "Les Roses dans l'élévation de Notre-Dame de Paris." *Bulletin monumental* 149 (1991): 153–199.

Häring, Nikolaus M. "Chartres and Paris Revisited." In *Essays in Honour of Anton Charles Pegis*, edited by J. Reginald O'Donnell. Toronto, 1974. 268–329.

Häring, Nikolaus M. "Petrus Lombardus und die Sprachlogik in der Trinitätslehre der Porretanerschule." In *Miscellanea Lombardiana*, 113–26. Novara, 1957.

Hartmann, Wilfried. "Manegold von Lautenbach und die Anfänge der Frühscholastik." *Deutsches Archiv für Erforschung des Mittelalters* 26 (1970): 47–149.

Harvey, John. *English Mediaeval Architects: A Biographical Dictionary down to 1550*. 2d ed. Gloucester, 1984.

Harvey, John. *The Gothic World, 1100–1600*. New ed. New York, 1969.

Harvey, John. *The Master Builders*. New York, 1971.

Harvey, John. *The Medieval Architect*. London, 1972.

Harvey, John. *The Medieval Craftsman*. London, 1975.

Haskins, Charles Homer. *The Renaissance of the Twelfth Century*. Cambridge, Mass., 1927.

Hearn, M. F. *Romanesque Sculpture*. Ithaca, 1981.

Héliot, Pierre. *Du carolingien au gothique*. Mémoires présentés par divers savants à l'Académie des inscriptions et belles-lettres, no. 15–2. Paris, 1966.

Héliot, Pierre. "Du roman au gothique: Echecs et réussites." *Wallraf-Richartz Jahrbuch* 35 (1973): 109–48.

Héliot, Pierre. "La Diversité de l'architecture gothique à ses débuts en France." *Gazette des Beaux-Arts*, 6th ser. 69 (1967): 269–306.

Héliot, Pierre. "L'Etude de l'architecture française au moyen âge: Bilan, perspectives et programme." *Gazette des Beaux-Arts*, 6th ser. 66 (1965): 240–45.

Héliot, Pierre. "Les Oeuvres capitales du gothique français primitif et l'influence de l'architecture anglaise." *Wallraf-Richartz Jahrbuch* 20 (1958): 85–114.

Héliot, Pierre. "Remarques sur l'abbatiale de Saint-Germer et sur les blocs de façade du XIIe siècle." *Bulletin monumental* 114 (1956): 81–114.

Héliot, Pierre. "Les Tranformations de l'architecture française au temps de Philippe Auguste." *Bulletin de la commission départementale d'histoire et d'archéologie du Pas-de-Calais* 11, no. 3 (1983): 363–81.

Henriet, Jacques. "La Cathédrale Saint-Etienne de Sens: Le Parti du premier maître et les campagnes du XIIe siècle." *Bulletin monumental* 140 (1982): 81–168.

Henriet, Jacques. "Un édifice de la première génération gothique: L'Abbatial de Saint-Germer-de-Fly." *Bulletin monumental* 143 (1985): 93–142.

Henry, D. P. *The Logic of St. Anselm*. Oxford, 1967.

Henry, D. P. "Why 'Grammaticus'?" *Archivium Latinitatis Medii Aevi* 28 (1958): 165–80.

Heriger of Lobbes. *De corpore et sanguine Domini*. In *Oeuvres de Gerbert*, edited by A. Olleris. Paris, 1867. 279–88.

Heurtevent, R. *Durand de Troarn et les origines de l'hérésie bérengarienne*. Paris, 1912.

Hilberry, Harry H. "The Cathedral at Chartres in 1030." *Speculum* 34 (1959): 561–72.

Hildebert. *Epitaphium Berengarii*. PL 171: 1049–50.

Horn, Walter. "On the Origins of the Mediaeval Bay System." *Journal of the Society of Architectural Historians* 17 (1958): 2–23.

Horn, Walter. "Survival, Revival, Transformation: The Dialectic of Development in Architecture and Other Arts." In *Renaissance/Renewal*, 711–57.

Hugh of St. Victor. *De Sacramentis*. PL 176.

Hugh of St. Victor. *On the Sacraments*. Translated by R. J. Deferrari. Cambridge, Mass., 1951.

Hunt, R. W. "*Absoluta*: The *Summa* of Petrus Hispanus on Priscianus Minor." *Historiographia Linguistica* 2 (1975): 1–22.

Hunt, R. W. *The History of Grammar in the Middle Ages: Collected Papers*. Amsterdam, 1980.

Hunt, R. W. "Hugutio and Petrus Helias." *Medieval and Renaissance Studies* 2 (1950): 174–78.

Hunt, R. W. "Studies on Priscian in the Eleventh and Twelfth Centuries." *Medieval and Renaissance Studies* 1 (1941–43): 194–231; 2 (1950): 1–56.

Hurlimann, M. *French Cathedrals*. Rev. ed. New York, 1967.

Huygens, R. B. C. *Accessus ad Auctores*. Leiden, 1970.

Huygens, R. B. C. "Guillaume de Tyr étudiant." *Latomus* 21 (1962): 811–29.

Huygens, R. B. C. "Mitteilungen aus Handschriften." *Studi medievali*, 3d ser. 3 (1962): 747–72.

Huygens, R. B. C. "Textes latins du XIe au XIIIe siècle." *Studi medievali*, 3d ser. 8 (1967): 451–503.

Ivo of Chartres. *Correspondence*. Edited by J. Leclerc. In *Les Classiques de l'histoire de France au moyen âge*. Paris, 1949.

Ivo of Chartres. Works in *PL* 162.

Iwakuma, Y. "Instantiae: A Study of Twelfth Century Technique of Argumentation with an Edition of MS Paris BN 6674 f. 1–5." *CIMAGL* 38 (1981): 1–91.

Jacobi, Klaus. "Logic (ii): The Later Twelfth Century." In Dronke, *Philosophy*, 227–51.

Jaeger, C. Stephen. "Cathedral Schools and Humanist Learning, 950–1150." *Deutsche Vierteljahrsschrift* 61 (1987): 569–616.

James, John. *Chartres, les constructeurs*. 3 vols. Chartres, 1979–.

James, John. "An Investigation into the Uneven Distribution of Early Gothic Churches in the Paris Basin 1140–1240." *Art Bulletin* 66 (1984): 15–46.

James, John. *The Template-Makers of the Paris Basin*. Leura, Australia, 1989.

James, John. "What Price the Cathedrals?" *Transactions of the Ancient Monuments Society*, 1972, 47–65.

Jantzen, Hans. *Die Gotik des Abendlandes*. Cologne, 1962.

Jantzen, Hans. *High Gothic*. New York, 1962.

Jantzen, Hans. "Über den gotischen Kirchenraum." In *Über den gotischen Kirchenraum und andere Aufsätze*. Berlin, 1951. 7–20.

Jeauneau, E. "Deux Rédactions des gloses de Guillaume de Conches sur Priscien." *RTAM* 27 (1960): 212–47.

John of Salisbury. *Metalogicon*. Edited by C. C. I. Webb. Oxford, 1929.

John of Salisbury. *Metalogicon*. Translated by Daniel D. McGarry. Berkeley, 1962.

Johnson, H. T. "Cathedral Building and the Medieval Economy." *Explorations in Entrepreneurial History*, 2d ser. 4 (1966–67): 191–210.

Joubert, F. "Recent Acquisitions, Musée de Cluny, Paris. Tête de Moïse provenant du portail droite de Saint-Denis." *Gesta* 28 (1989): 107.

Karlinger, H. *Die Kunst der Gotik*. Berlin, 1926.

Kergall, Hervé. *La France gothique*. Paris, 1989.

Kergall, Hervé. "Mieux voir et comprendre l'architecture gothique." *Gazette des Beaux-Arts*, 6th ser. 127 (1985): 129–36.

Kidson, Peter. "Canterbury Cathedral: The Gothic Choir." *Archaeological Journal* 126 (1969): 244–46.

Kidson, Peter. "Panofsky, Suger and St. Denis." *Journal of the Warburg and Courtauld Institutes* 50 (1987): 1–17.

Kimpel, Dieter. "L'Apparition des elements de serie dans les grands ouvrages." *Histoire et archéologie*, no. 47 (Nov. 1980): 40–59.

Kimpel, Dieter. "Le Développement de la taille en série dans l'architecture médiévale et son rôle dans l'histoire économique." *Bulletin monumental* 135 (1977): 195–222.

Kimpel, Dieter. "L'Organisation de la taille des pierres sur les grands chantiers d'églises du XIe au XIIIe siècle." *Pierre et métal dans le bâtiment au moyen âge*, edited by O. Chapelot and P. Benoît. Paris, 1985. 209–17.

Kimpel, Dieter, and Suckale, Robert. *Die gotische Architektur in Frankreich 1130–1270*. Munich, 1985.

Klein, Bruno. "Chartres und Soissons: Überlegungen zur gotischen Architektur um 1200." *Zeitschrift für Kunstgeschichte* 49 (1986): 437–66.

Klein, Bruno. "Die Rezeption von Chartres und Soissons am Anfang des 13. Jahrhunderts." *Kunstchronik* 38 (1985): 203.

Klein, Peter K. "Programmes eschatologiques, fonction et réception historiques des portails du XIIe siècle: Moissac—Beaulieu—Saint-Denis." *Cahiers de civilisation médiévale* 33 (1990): 317–49.

Kneepkens, C. H. *Het Iudicium Constructionis: Het Leerstuk van de Constructio in de 2de Helfte van de 12de Eeuw*. 4 vols. Nijmegen, 1987.

Kneepkens, C. H. "The Quaestiones Grammaticales of the MS Oxford, Corpus Christi College 250: An Edition of the Second Collection." *Vivarium* 23 (1985): 98–123.

Knowles, D. *The Evolution of Medieval Thought*. New York, 1964.

Kostof, Spiro. "The Architect in the Middle Ages, East and West." In *The Architect: Chapters in the History of the Profession*, edited by S. Kostof. New York, 1977. 59–95.

Kraus, H. *Gold Was the Mortar*. London and Boston, 1979.

Kretzmann, Norman. "The Culmination of the Old Logic in Peter Abelard." In *Renaissance/ Renewal*, 488–511.

Kuhn, Thomas S. *Black Body Theory and the Origins of the Quantum Discontinuity*. Oxford, 1978.

Kuhn, Thomas S. *The Essential Tension*. Chicago, 1977.

Kuhn, Thomas S. *The Structure of Scientific Revolutions*. 2d ed. Chicago, 1970.

Kunst, H.-J. "Freiheit und Zitat im der Architektur des 13. Jahrhunderts: Die Kathedrale von Reims." *Bauwerk und Bildwerk in Hochmittelalter*, edited by K. Clausbert et al. Giessen, 1981. 87–102.

Kurmann, Peter. *La Façade de la cathédrale de Reims*. 2 vols. Lausanne and Paris, 1987.

Kusaba, Yoshio. "Some Observations on the Early Flying Buttress and Choir Triforium of Canterbury Cathedral." *Gesta* 28 (1989): 175–89.

Laistner, M. L. W. *Thought and Letters in Western Europe A.D. 500 to 900.* 2d ed. Ithaca, N.Y., 1966.

Lalbat, C., G. Marguerite, and J. Martin. "De la stéréotomie médiévale: La Coupe des pierres chez Villard de Honnecourt." *Bulletin monumental* 145 (1987): 387–406.

Lambert, Elie. "Caen romane et gothique." *Bulletin de la Société des Antiquaires de Normandie* 43 (1935): 5–70.

Lambert, Elie. "La Cathédrale de Laon." *Gazette des Beaux-Arts,* 5th ser. 13 (1926): 361–84.

Lambert, Elie. "Les Origines de la croisée d'ogives." *Bulletin de l'office international des Instituts d'archéologie et d'histoire de l'art, Paris* 3 (1936–37): 131–46.

Landgraf, Artur M. *Einführung in die Geschichte der theologischen Literatur der Frühscholastik, unter dem Gesichtspunkte der Schulenbildung.* Regensburg, 1948.

Lanfranc of Bec. *Liber de corpore et sanguine Domini.* PL 150.

Lapeyre, A. *Des Façades occidentales de Saint-Denis et de Chartres aux portails de Laon.* Mâcon, 1960.

Lasko, P. "The Concept of Regionalism in French Romanesque," *Akten des XXV. Internationalen Kongresses für Kunstgeschichte, Wien, 1983.* Vol. 3, *Probleme und Methoden des Klassifizierung,* edited by J. White, 17–25.

Lasteyrie, Robert de. *L'Architecture religieuse en France à l'époque gothique.* 2 vols. Paris, 1926–27.

Lasteyrie, Robert de. *L'Architecture religieuse en France à l'époque romane.* 2 vols. Paris, 1929.

Lautier, C. "Les Pientres-verriers des bas côtés de la nef de Chartres au début du XIIIe siècle." *Bulletin monumental* 148 (1990): 7–45.

LeClerc, Jean. "The Renewal of Theology." In *Renaissance/Renewal,* 68–87.

Lefèvre-Pontalis, Eugène. *L'Architecture religieuse dans l'ancien diocèse de Soissons.* 3 vols. Paris, 1894–96.

Lefèvre-Pontalis, Eugène. "Etude historique et archéologique sur l'église de Saint-Germain-des-Prés." *Congrès archéologique (Paris)* 82 (1919): 301–66.

Lefèvre-Pontalis, Eugène. *Monographie de l'église Saint-Maclou de Pontoise.* Pontoise, 1888.

Lefèvre-Pontalis, Eugène. "L'Origine des arcs-boutants." *Congrès archéologique (Paris)* 82 (1919): 367–96.

Lefèvre-Pontalis, Eugène. "Pontoise, église Saint-Maclou." *Congrès archéologique (Paris)* 82 (1919): 76–99.

Le Goff, Jacques. "How Did the Medieval University Conceive of Itself?" In *Time, Work, and Culture in the Middle Ages,* translated by Arthur Goldhammer. Chicago, 1980. 122–34.

Le Goff, Jacques. *Les Intellectuels au moyen âge.* Paris, 1955.

Le Goff, Jacques. *La Naissance du Purgatoire.* Paris, 1981.

Le Goff, Jacques, and Rémond, René. *Histoire de la France religieuse.* Vol. 1, *Des Dieux de la Gaule à la papauté d'Avignon.* Paris, 1988.

Lesne, Emile. *Histoire de la propriété ecclésiastique en France.* 6 vols. Lille, 1910–43; vol. 5, *Les Ecoles de la fin du VIIIe siècle à la fin du XIIe.* Mémoires et travaux des Facultés Catholiques de Lille no. 50. 1940.

Levis-Godechot, N. *Chartres.* La-Pierre-Qui-Vire, 1987.

Libera, A. de "Logique et théologie dans la Summa 'Quoniam homines' d'Alain de Lille." *7th Symposium on Medieval Logic and Semantics.* Poitiers, 1985.

Lloyd, G. E. R. *Greek Science after Aristotle.* New York, 1973.

Logica Modernorum. Edited by L. M. de Rijk. 2 vols. in 3. Assen, 1962–67.

Lohr, C. H. "The Medieval Interpretation of Aristotle." In *Cambridge History of Later Medieval Philosophy: From the Rediscovery of Aristotle to the Disintegration of Scholasticism, 1100–1600,* edited by N. Kretzmann, A. Kenny, J. Pinborg. Cambridge, 1982.

Lopez, R. "Economie et architecture médiévale: Cela aurait-il tué ceci?" *Annales, économies, sociétés, civilisations* 7 (1952): 433–38.

Lottin, Odon. *Psychologie et morale aux XIIe et XIIIe siècles.* 6 vols. Louvain and Gembloux, 1942–60.

Luscombe, David E. *The School of Peter Abelard: The Influence of Abelard's Thought in the Early Scholastic Period.* Cambridge, 1969.

Lyman, Thomas. "Format and Style: The Adaptation of Cartoons to Reused Marble at Saint-Sernin." *Artistes, artisans et production artistique au moyen âge,* 3: 223–33.

Lyman, Thomas. "Notes on the Porte Miègeville Capitals, and the Construction of Saint-Sernin in Toulouse." *Art Bulletin* 49 (1967): 25–36.

Lyman, Thomas. "The Politics of Selective Eclecticism: Monastic Architecture, Pilgrimage Churches, and 'Resistance to Cluny.'" *Gesta* 27 (1988): 83–92.

Lyman, Thomas. "Raymond Gairard and Romanesque Building Campaigns at Saint-Sernin in Toulouse." *Journal of the Society of Architectural Historians* 37 (1978): 71–91.

Lyman, Thomas. "The Sculpture Programme of the Porte des Comtes Master at Saint-Sernin in Toulouse." *Journal of the Warburg and Courtauld Institutes* 34 (1971): 12–39.

Lyman, Thomas. "Le Style comme symbole chez les sculpteurs romans: Essai d'interprétation de quelques inventions thématiques à la Porte Miègeville de Saint-Sernin." *Cahiers de Saint-Michel de Cuxa* 12 (1981): 161–79.

Lyman, Thomas. "La Table d'autel de Bernard Gilduin et son ambiance originelle." *Cahiers de Saint-Michel de Cuxa* 13 (1982): 53–73.

Lyman, Thomas. "Terminology, Typology, Taxonomy: An Approach to the Study of Architectural

Sculpture of the Romanesque Period." *Gazette des Beaux Arts*, 6th ser. 88 (1976): 223–27.

Lynch, Kevin. *The Image of a City*. Cambridge, Mass., 1960.

McClendon, Charles B. *The Imperial Abbey of Farfa: Architectural Currents of the Early Middle Ages*. New Haven and London, 1987.

MacKinney, L. C. *Bishop Fulbert and Education at the School of Chartres*. Notre Dame, Ind., 1957.

McKitterick, Rosamund. *The Carolingians and the Written Word*. Cambridge, 1989.

Mâle, Emile. *Religious Art in France: The Thirteenth Century*. Princeton, 1984.

Mâle, Emile. *Religious Art in France: The Twelfth Century*. Princeton, 1978.

Marenbon, John. "Gilbert of Poitiers." In Dronke, *Philosophy*, 328– 57.

Marenbon, John. *Later Medieval Philosophy: An Introduction*. London and New York, 1987.

Mark, Robert. "Gothic Cathedrals and Structural Rationalism." *Transactions of the New York Academy of Sciences*. 2d ser. 33 (1977): 607–24.

Mark, Robert. *Gothic Structural Experimentation*. Cambridge, Mass., 1982.

Mark, Robert. *High Gothic Structure: A Technological Reinterpretation*. Princeton, 1984.

Mark, Robert. *Light, Wind, and Structure*. Cambridge, Mass., 1990.

Mark, Robert. "The Structural Analysis of Gothic Cathedrals." *Scientific American*, Nov. 1972, 90– 99.

Mark, Robert. "Structural Experimentation in Gothic Architecture." *American Scientist* 66 (1978): 542–50.

Mark, Robert, and Clark, William W. "Gothic Structural Experimentation." *Scientific American*, Nov. 1984, 176–85.

Mark, Robert, and Jonash, R. S. "Wind Loading on Gothic Structure." *Journal of the Society of Architectural Historians* 29 (1970): 222–30.

Mark, Robert, and Taylor, W. "The Technology of Transition: Sexpartite to Quadripartite Vaulting in High Gothic Architecture." *Art Bulletin* 64 (1982): 579–87.

Medieval Art and Architecture at Canterbury before 1220. Edited by N. Coldstream and P. Draper. British Archaeological Association Conference Transactions 1979. London, 1982.

Merlet, Lucien. "Lettres d'Ives de Chartres et d'autres personnages de son temps, 1087–1130." *Bibliothèque de l'école des Chartes*. 4th ser. 1 (1855): 443–71.

Merlet, René, and Clerval, A. *Un manuscrit chartrain du XIe siècle*. Chartres, 1893.

Meulen, Jan van der. *Notre-Dame de Chartres: Die vorromanische Ostanlage*. Berlin, 1975.

Meulen, Jan van der, and Hohmeyer, J. *Chartres, Biographie der Kathedrale*. Cologne, 1984.

Meulen, Jan van der and Speer, A. *Die fränkische*

Königsabtei Saint Denis: Ostanlage und Kulturgeschichte. Darmstadt, 1988.

Mews, Constant J. "Orality, Literacy, and Authority in the Twelfth-Century Schools." *Exemplaria* 2 (1990): 476–500.

Michler, Jürgen. "La Cathédral Notre-Dame de Chartres: Resonstitution de la polychromie originale de l'interieur." *Bulletin monumental* 147 (1989): 117–31.

Michler, Jürgen. "Über die Farbfassung hochgotischer Sakralraüme." *Wallraf-Richartz Jahrbuch* 39 (1977): 29–68.

Michler, Jürgen. "Zur Stellung von Bourges in der gothischen Baukunst." *Wallraf-Richartz Jahrbuch* 41 (1980): 27–86.

Mines, carrières et métallugie dans la France médiévale. Edited by P. Benoît and P. Braunstein. Paris, 1983.

Minio-Paluello, L. "The *Ars Disserendi* of Adam of Balsham 'Parvipontanus,'" *Medieval and Renaissance Studies* 3 (1954): 116–69.

Montclos, J. de. *Lanfranc et Bérengar: La Controverse eucharistique du XIe siècle*. Louvain, 1971.

Moore, C. *Development and Character of Gothic Architecture*. 2d ed. New York, 1904.

Morrison, Karl F. *History as a Visual Art in the Twelfth-Century Renaissance*. Princeton, 1990.

Mortet, Victor. "Hugue de Fouilloi, Pierre le Chantre, Alexandre Neckam et les critiques dirigées au douzième siècle contre le luxe des constructions." In *Mélanges d'histoire offerts à M. Charles Bémont*. Paris, 1913. 105–37.

Mortet, Victor. "La Maîtrise d'oeuvre dans les grandes constructions du XIIe siècle et la profession d'appareilleur." *Bulletin monumental* 70 (1906): 263–70.

Mortet, Victor. "Note historique sur l'emploi de procédés matériels et d'instruments usités dans la géometrie pratique au moyen âge." *Congrès international de philosophie, 2 session, Geneva, 1904*. Geneva, 1905. 925–42.

Mortet, Victor. *Recueil de textes relatifs à l'histoire de l'architecture et à la condition des architectes en France au moyen âge, XIe-XIIe siècles*. Paris, 1911.

Mortet, Victor, and Deschamps, Paul. *Recueil de textes relatifs à l'histoire de l'architecture et à la condition des architectes en France, au Moyen Age. Tome II: XIIe-XIIIe siècles*. Paris, 1929.

Murphy, James J. *Medieval Rhetoric: A Select Bibliography*. 2d ed. Toronto, 1989.

Murray, Alexander. *Reason and Society in the Middle Ages*. Oxford, 1978.

Murray, Stephen. "Looking for Robert de Luzarches: The Early Work at Amiens Cathedral." *Gesta* 29 (1990): 111–31

Murray, Stephen, and Addiss, J. "Plan and Space at Amiens Cathedral." *Journal of the Society of Architectural Historians* 49 (1990): 44–67.

Musée d'Angoulême. *Paul Abadie, architecte, 1812–*

1884: Entre archéologie et modernité, edited by Claude Laroche et al. Angoulême, 1984. 87–101.

Mussat, André. "A propos des interprétations de l'architecture gothique." Archive de l'art français 25 (1978): 69–75.

Mussat, André. "Les Cathédrales dans leurs cités." Revue de l'art 55 (1982): 9–22.

Mussat, André. "L'Etude régionale: Identité culturelle et expressions artistiques, mythes et réalitiés," Akten des XXV. Internationalen Kongresses für Kunstgeschichte, Wien, 1983. Vol 3, Probleme und Methoden des Klassifizierung, edited by J. White, 37–44.

New York. Metropolitan Museum of Art. The Royal Abbey of Saint-Denis in the Time of Abbot Suger (1125–1151). Edited by S. Crosby, J. Hayward, C. Little, and W. Wixom. New York, 1981.

New York. Metropolitan Museum of Art. The Year 1200. Edited by K. Hoffman. New York, 1970.

Nielsen, Lauge. "On the Doctrine of Logic and Language of Gilbert Porreta and His Followers." CIMAGL 17 (1976): 40–69.

Nivet, Jean. Sainte-Croix d'Orléans. Orléans, 1984. Esp. 28–39.

Nonfarmale O., and Manaresi, R. R. "Il Restauro del 'Portail Royal' della Cattedrale di Chartres." Arte Medievale, 2d ser. 1 (1987): 259–75.

Panofsky, Erwin. Gothic Architecture and Scholasticism. Latrobe, Pa., 1951, and subsequent reprintings.

Panofsky, Erwin, ed. Abbot Suger on the Abbey Church of St.-Denis and Its Art Treasures. 2d ed. by Gerda Panofsky-Soergel. Princeton, 1979.

Paré, Gérard M., Brunet, A., Tremblay, P. La Renaissance du XIIe siècle: Les Ecoles et l'enseignement. Paris and Ottawa, 1933.

Parkes, M. B. "The Influence of the Concepts of Ordinatio and Compilatio on the Development of the Book." In Medieval Learning and Literature: Essays Presented to Richard William Hunt. Oxford, 1976. 115–41.

Pessin, M. "The Twelfth-Century Abbey Church of Saint-Germer-de-Fly and Its Position in the Development of First Gothic Architecture." Gesta 17 (1978): 71.

Peter the Chanter. Summa de Sacramentis et animae consiliis. Edited by Jean-Albert Dugauquier. Analecta mediaevalia Namurcensia, nos. 4, 7, 16, 21.

Peter Lombard. Libri IV Sententiarum. Grottaferrata, 1971–81.

Peter of Poitiers. Sententiae Petri Pictaviensis. Vol. 1. Edited by Philip S. Moore and Marthe Dulong. Notre Dame, 1943.

Pevsner, Nikolaus. "The Term 'Architect' in the Middle Ages." Speculum 17 (1942): 549–62.

Pevsner, N., and Metcalfe, P. English Cathedrals. 2 vols. London, 1986.

Pierre et métal dans le bâtiment au moyen âge. Edited by O. Chapelot and P. Benoît. Paris, 1985.

Pinborg, J. Die Entwicklung der Sprachtheorie im Mittelalter. Münster and Copenhagen, 1967.

Plagnieux, P. "Le Portail de XIIe siècle de Saint-Germain-des-Prés à Paris: Etat de la question et nouvelles recherches." Gesta 28 (1989): 21–29.

Post, Gaines. "Alexander III, the Licentia docendi and the Rise of the Universities." In Anniversary Essays in Mediaeval History by Students of Charles Homer Haskins. Boston, 1929. 255–77.

Post, Gaines. Studies in Medieval Legal Thought. Princeton, 1964.

Prache, Anne. "Les Arcs-boutants au XIIe siècle." Gesta 15 (1976): 31–42.

Prache, Anne. Saint-Remi de Reims: L'Oeuvre de Pierre de Celle et sa place dans l'architecture gothique. Bibliothèque de la Société française d'archéologie, no. 8. Geneva, 1978.

Radding, Charles M. The Origins of Medieval Jurisprudence: Pavia and Bologna 850–1150. New Haven and London, 1988.

Radding, Charles M. A World Made by Men: Cognition and Society, 400–1200. Chapel Hill, 1985.

Radding, Charles M., and Clark, William W. "Abélard et le bâtisseur des Saint-Denis: Etudes parallèles d'histoire des disciplines." Annales, économies, sociétés, civilisations 43 (1988): 1263–90.

Rashdall, Hastings. The Universities of Europe in the Middle Ages. Edited by Frederick M. Powicke and Alfred B. Emden. 3 vols. Oxford, 1936.

Recherche. Vol. 1, Le Problème de l'ogive, edited by H. Focillon. Paris, 1939.

Régnier, L. Excursions archéologiques dans le Vexin français. 2 vols. Evreux, 1922–27.

Reinhardt, Hans. "Les églises romanes de la Champagne après l'an mil." Cahiers de civilisation médiévale 4 (1961): 149–58.

Reinhardt, Hans. "Die Entwicklung der gotischen Travée." Gedenkschrift Ernst Gall. Berlin, 1965. 123–42.

Renaissance and Renewal in the Twelfth Century. Edited by Robert L. Benson and Giles Constable. Cambridge, Mass., 1982.

Rijk, L. M. de. La Philosophie au moyen âge. Leiden, 1985.

Robert of Melun. Sententiae. Edited by R. Martin. In Spicilegium Sacrum Lovaniense 21 (1947).

Rouse, Richard H. "Florilegia and Latin Classical Authors in Twelfth and Thirteenth-Century Orléans." Viator 10 (1979): 131–60.

Rouse, Richard H., and Rouse, Mary A. "The Florilegium Angelicum: Its Origin, Content, and Influence." In Medieval Learning and Literature: Essays Presented to Richard William Hunt. Oxford, 1976. 66–114.

Rouse, Richard H., and Rouse, Mary A. "Statim Invenire: Schools, Preachers and New Attitudes to the Page." In Renaissance/Renewal, 201–25.

Roux, Canon J. La Basilique Saint-Front de Périgueux. Périgueux, 1920.

Rudolph, C. *Artistic Change at St.-Denis: Abbot Suger's Program and the Early Twelfth-Century Controversy over Art.* Princeton, 1990.

Rupprecht, Berhard. *Romanische Skulptur in Frankreich.* Munich, 1975.

Salet, Francis. *La Madeleine de Vézelay.* Melun, 1948.

Salet, Francis. "Notre-Dame de Paris, état présent de la recherche." *La sauvegarde de l'art français* 2 (1982): 89–113.

Samaran, C. "La Vie estudiantine à Paris au moyen âge." In *Aspects de l'Université de Paris,* edited by L. Halphen et al. Paris, 1949. 103–32.

Sauerländer, Willibald. "Abwegige Gedanken über frühgotische Architektur und 'The Renaissance of the Twelfth Century.'" In *Etudes d'art médiévale offerté à Louis Grodecki.* Paris, 1981. 167–83.

Sauerländer, Willibald. "Architecture and the Figurative Arts: The North." In *Renaissance/Renewal,* 671–710.

Sauerländer, Willibald. "Die Geographie des Stile," *Akten des XXV. Internationalen Kongresses für Kunstgeschichte, Wien, 1983.* Vol. 3, *Probleme und Methoden des Klassifizierung,* edited by J. White. 27–35.

Sauerländer, Willibald. "Gislebertus von Autun: Eines Beitrag zur Entstehung seines künstlerischen Stils," *Festschrift Theodor Müller: Studien zur Geschichte der europäischen Plastik.* Munich, 1965. 17–29.

Sauerländer, Willibald. *Gothic Sculpture in France 1140–1270.* London and New York, 1972.

Sauerländer, Willibald. *Das Königsportal in Chartres.* Frankfurt, 1984.

Sauerländer, Willibald. "'Premiere architecture gothique' or 'Renaissance of the Twelfth Century'? Changing Perspectives in the Evaluation of Architectural History." *Sewanee Mediaeval Colloquium Occasional Papers,* no. 2 (1985): 25–43.

Sauerländer, Willibald. *Le Siècle des cathédrales 1140–1260.* Paris, 1989.

Sauerländer, Willibald. "Style or Transition? The Fallacies of Classification Discussed in the Light of German Architecture 1190–1260." *Architectural History* 30 (1987): 1–29.

Sauerländer, Willibald. "Uber die Komposition des Weltgerichts-Tympanons in Autun." *Zeitschrift für Kunstgeschichte* 29 (1966): 261–94.

Secret, Jean. *Saint-Front.* La Pierre-qui-Vire, 1970.

Sellier, Charles. "Notes présentées par M. Charles Sellier sur la chapelle Saint-Aignan." *Proces-verbaux de la Commission municipale du vieux Paris.* 1908. 3–6.

Severens, Kenneth W. "The Cathedral at Sens and Its Influence in the Twelfth Century." Ph.D. diss., Johns Hopkins University, 1968.

Severens, Kenneth W. "The Continuous Plan of Sens Cathedral." *Journal of the Society of Architectural Historians* 34 (1975): 198–207.

Severens, Kenneth W. "The Early Campaign at

Sens, 1140–1145." *Journal of the Society of Architectural Historians* 29 (1970): 97–107.

Severens, Kenneth W. "William of Sens and the Double Columns at Sens and Canterbury." *Journal of the Warburg and Courtauld Institutes* 33 (1970): 307–13.

Shelby, Lon R. "The Contractors of Chartres." *Gesta* 20 (1980): 173–78.

Shelby, Lon R. "The Education of Medieval Master Masons." *Medieval Studies* 32 (1970): 1–26.

Shelby, Lon R. "The Geometrical Knowledge of Mediaeval Master Masons." *Speculum* 47 (1972): 395–421.

Shelby, Lon R. "Medieval Masons' Templates." *Journal of the Society of Architectural Historians* 30 (1971): 140–54.

Shelby, Lon R. "Medieval Masons' Tools: The Level and the Plumb Rule." *Technology and Culture* 2 (1961): 127–30.

Shelby, Lon R. "Medieval Masons' Tools: II. Compass and Square." *Technology and Culture* 6 (1965): 236–48.

Shelby, Lon R. "The Practical Geometry of Medieval Masons." *Studies in Medieval Culture* 5 (1975): 133–44.

Shelby, Lon R. "The Role of the Master Mason in Medieval English Building." *Speculum* 39 (1964): 387–403.

Shelby, Lon R. "The 'Secret' of the Medieval Masons." In *On Pre-Modern Technology and Science: Studies in Honor of Lynn White, Jr.,* edited by B. Hall and D. West. Human Civilitas, no. 1. Malibu, 1976. 201–19.

Silvestre, H. "Notice sur Adelman de Liège, évêque de Brescia (d. 1061)." *Revue d'histoire ecclésiastique* 56 (1961): 866–71.

Simson, Otto von. *The Gothic Cathedral.* 2d ed. New York, 1967.

Simson, Otto von. *Das Mittelalter II.* Propyläen-Kunstgeschichte, 7. Berlin, 1972.

Smalley, Beryl. "La Glossa ordinaria: Quelques prédécesseurs d'Anselme de Laon." *RTAM* 9 (1937): 365–400.

Smalley, Beryl. *The Study of the Bible in the Middle Ages.* 2d ed. Oxford and New York, 1952.

Somerville, R. "The Case against Berengar of Tours: A New Text." *Studi gregoriani* 9 (1972): 55–75.

Southern, R. W. "Lanfranc of Bec and Berengar of Tours." In *Studies in Medieval History Presented to Frederick Maurice Powicke,* edited by R. W. Hunt et al. Oxford, 1948. 27–48.

Southern, R. W. *The Making of the Middle Ages.* New Haven and London, 1953.

Southern, R. W. *Medieval Humanism and Other Essays.* Oxford, 1970.

Southern, R. W. *Platonism, Scholastic Method and the School of Chartres.* Reading, 1979.

Southern, R. W. "St. Anselm and Gilbert Crispin,

Abbot of Westminster." *Medieval and Renaissance Studies* 3 (1954): 78–115.

Southern, R. W. *Saint Anselm and His Biographer: A Study of Monastic Life and Thought 1059–c. 1130.* Cambridge, 1963.

Southern, R. W. "The Schools of Paris and the School of Chartres." In *Renaissance/Renewal*, 113–37.

Sprandel, R. *Ivo von Chartres und seine Stellung in der Kirchengeschichte.* Stuttgart, 1962.

Stein, H. *Les Architectes des cathédrales gothiques.* Paris, 1911, 1930.

Stock, Brian. *The Implications of Literacy.* Princeton, 1983.

Stoddard, Whitney. *Monastery and Cathedral in France.* Middletown, 1966.

Stoddard, Whitney. *Sculptors of the West Portals of Chartres Cathedral.* New York, 1987.

Stoddard, Whitney. *The West Portals of Saint-Denis and Chartres.* Cambridge, Mass., 1954.

Strasbourg, Les Musées de la Ville. *Les Bâtisseurs des cathédrales gothiques.* Edited by R. Recht. Strasbourg, 1989.

Stratford, Neil. "Romanesque Sculpture in Burgundy, Reflections on Its Geography, on Patronage, on the Status of Sculpture and on the Working Methods of Sculptors." *Artistes, artisans et production artistique au moyen âge,* 3: 235–63.

Suckale, R. "Neue Literatur über die Abteikirche von Saint-Denis." *Kunstchronik* 43 (1990): 62–80.

Sullivan, Richard. "The Medieval Church and the Patronage of Art." *The Centennial Review* 33 (1989): 108–30.

Swaan, W. *The Gothic Cathedral.* New York, 1969.

Thiébaut, Jacques. *L'Architecture médiévale du Nord, Pas-de-Calais: Les Eglises.* Lille, 1983.

Thiébaut, Jacques. *Les Cathédrales gothiques en Picardie.* Amiens, 1987.

Thierry of Chartres. *Commentary on Cicero's De Inventione.* Edited by K. M. Fredborg. Toronto, 1987.

Thomas, Bernice L. "The Christ of Autun and a Bishop's Seal." Ph.D. diss., Boston University, 1984.

Thorndyke, Lynn. *University Records and Life in the Middle Ages.* New York, 1944.

Toulouse, Musée Saint-Raymond. *Saint-Sernin de Toulouse; Trésors et métamorphoses; Deux siècles de restaurations 1802–1989,* edited by Marie Anne Sire, Daniel Cazes et al. Toulouse, 1989.

Tweedale, Martin M. *Abailard on Universals.* Amsterdam, 1976.

Verdier, Philippe. "La politique financière de Suger dans la reconstruction de Saint-Denis et l'enrichissem,ent du trésor." *Artistes, artisans et production artistique au moyen âge,* 2: 167–82.

Verger, Jacques. "A propos de la naissance de l'uni-versité de Paris: Contexte social, enjeu politique, portée intellectuelle." In *Schulen und Studium im sozialen Wandel des hohen und späten Mittelalters,* edited by Johannes Fried. Sigmaringen, 1986. 69–96.

Verger, Jacques. *Les Universités au moyen âge.* Paris, 1973.

Villette, Jean. "Le portail royal de Chartres a-t-il été modifié depuis sa construction?" *Bulletin de la Société archéologique d'Eure-et-Loir* 115 (1971): 255–64.

Viollet-le-Duc, E. E. *Dictionnaire raisonné de l'architecture française du XIe au XVIe siècle.* 10 vols. Paris 1854–68.

Vroom, Wilhelmus Hermanus. *De financiering van de kathedraalbouw in de middeleeuwen.* Maarssen, 1981.

Waldman, Thomas G. "Art for the Literate: The Example of Suger's Rebuilding of the Abbey Church of Saint-Denis." Paper presented at the Medieval Academy of America Annual Meeting, 1991.

Wallace-Hadrill, J. H. *The Frankish Church.* Oxford, 1983.

Ward, John O. "The Date of the Commentary on Cicero's *De Inventione* by Thierry of Chartres (*ca.* 1095–1160?) and the Cornifician Attack on the Liberal Arts." *Viator* 3 (1972): 219–73.

Ward, John O. "Gothic Architecture, Universities and the Decline of the Humanities in Twelfth-Century Europe." In *Principalities Powers and Estates: Studies in Medieval and Early Modern Government and Society,* edited by L. O. Frappell. Adelaide, 1979. 65–75.

Werckmeister, Otto Karl. "Die Auferstehung der Toten am Westportal von St. Lazare in Autun," *Frühmittelalterliche Studien* 4 (1982): 208–36.

Werner, Karl Ferdinand. "Les Origines." In *Histoire de la France,* edited by Jean Favier. Paris, 1984. 1: 19–46.

Werner, Karl Ferdinand. *Structures politiques du monde franc (VIe– XIIe) siècles).* London, 1979.

Whitehill, Walter Muir. *Spanish Romanesque Architecture of the Eleventh Century.* Oxford, 1941; repr. 1968.

Williams, J. R. "The Cathedral School of Rheims in the Eleventh Century." *Speculum* 29 (1954): 661–77.

Williams, J. R. "Godfrey of Rheims, A Humanist of the Eleventh Century," *Speculum* 22 (1947): 22–45.

Williams, Jane W. "The Windows of the Trades at Chartres Cathedral." Ph.D. diss., University of California at Los Angeles, 1987.

Willis, Robert. *The Architectural History of Canterbury Cathedral.* London, 1845. Reprinted in *Architectural History of Some English Cathedrals,* vol. 1. Chicheley, 1972.

Wilson, C. *The Gothic Cathedral*. London, 1990.

Wolfe, M., and Mark, Robert. "Gothic Cathedral Buttressing: The Experiment at Bourges and Its Influence." *Journal of the Society of Architectural Historians* 33 (1974): 17–27.

Wolff, P. *The Cultural Awakening*. Translated by Anne Carter. New York, 1968.

Woodman, F. *The Architectural History of Canterbury Cathedral*. London, 1981.

Wright, Craig. *Music and Ceremony at Notre Dame of Paris 500–1550*. Cambridge Studies in Music. Cambridge, 1989.

Zink, Jochen. "Das Lazarusportal der Kathedrale Saint-Lazare in Autun." In *Kunst in Hauptwerken: Von der Akropolis zu Goya*, edited by Jörg Traeger. Schriftenreihe der Universität Regensburg, no. 15 (1988): 83–177.

Index